God, People and Power in Malawi

Copyright 2018 Kenneth R. Ross

All rights reserved. No part of this publication may be reproduced, stored in a retrieval system, or transmitted in any from or by any means, electronic, mechanical, photocopying, recording or otherwise without prior permission from the publishers.

First Published by Kachere Series in 1996.

Published by
Luviri Press
P/Bag 201 Luwinga
Mzuzu 2

ISBN   978-99960-66-04-7
eISBN   978-99960-66-05-4

Luviri Reprints no. 4

Luviri Press is represented outside Malawi by:
African Books Collective Oxford (order@africanbookscollective.com)

www.mzunipress.blogspot.com
www.africanbookscollective.com

God, People and Power in Malawi

Democratization in Theological Perspective

Edited by
Kenneth R. Ross

Luviri Press

Luviri Reprints no. 4
Mzuzu
2018

Luviri Reprints

Many books have been published on or in Malawi that are no longer available. While some of these books simply have run their course, others are still of interest for scholars and the general public. Some of the classics have been reprinted outside Malawi over the decades, and during the last two decades, first the Kachere Series and then other publishers have achieved "never out of stock status" by joining the African Books Collective's Print on Demand approach, but there are still a good number of books that would be of interest but are no longer in print.

The Luviri Reprint Series has taken up the task to make those books on or from Malawi, which are out of print but not out of interest, available again, through Print on Demand and therefore worldwide.

While the Luviri Reprint Series concentrates on Malawi, it is also interested in the neighbouring countries and even in those further afield.

Luviri Reprints publish the books as they originally were. Usually a new Foreword is added, and where appropriate, new information has been added. All such additions, mostly in footnotes, are marked by an asterisk (*).

The Editors

Foreword

Of all the research and publication that emerged from a fertile and productive period in the life of the Department of Theology and Religious Studies at Chancellor College, University of Malawi, in the mid-1990s, arguably the project that retains most relevance in relation to national life is the one that led to the publication of *God, People and Power: Democratisation in Theological Perspective* in 1996. While democratic systems were introduced to Malawi at that time and have proved their durability in the years since, it was already apparent that there were many obstacles to be overcome if Malawi were to becoming a truly democratic nation, with government "of the people by the people for the people." Hindrances to democratization that were identified by this book have proved remarkably intractable and hence the analysis it offers retains much relevance.

Over the past two decades I have been closely involved in the collaboration between Scotland and Malawi that aims to address issues of social and economic development. This effort found expression in a Cooperation Agreement signed between the Scottish and Malawian Governments in 2005. This had four strands: health, education, economic development and governance. In the outworking of the Agreement many successful initiatives have been taken in regard to its first three strands. As is widely acknowledged, the one on which least progress has been made is governance. Yet for development in any other sphere to be sustained and effective there is need for sound governance to be in place at all levels of society. Malawians are all too aware that they have too often been let down by failures of governance. Hence this book's identification of factors that tend to undermine good governance remains of critical relevance today.

The original project on which the book is based focussed on Malawi's attempts to build a democratic society after the fall of the one-party system but it formed one part of a much bigger and more international framework. This was the World Council of Churches "Theology of Life" process conducted by its Justice, Peace and Creation unit. This proved to be a highly influential initiative of the WCC. When it adopted its new mission affirmation – *Together Towards Life* – in 2012 it had the concept of "life" at its heart. It begins with the statement that: "We believe in the Triune God who is the creator, redeemer, and sustainer of all life.... A denial of life Is a rejection of the God of life. God invites us into the life-giving mission of the Triune God and empowers us to bear witness to the vision of abundant life for all in the new heaven and earth. How and where do we discern God's life-giving work that enables us to participate in God's mission today?" (§1) This theological framework was already anticipated by *God, People and Power* and it bears continuing study as one component part in the formation of an emerging ecumenical consensus that has informed and energised commitment to the mission of God in our time.

It is, however, its continuing relevance and applicability in the Malawi context that is likely to its main selling point in the years to come. The book pays particular attention to those who have been excluded or disempowered and who now seek to play their full part in the democratic era: women, youth, prisoners, Muslims and minority groups such as Jehovah's Witnesses. With the prevailing system apparently working in favour of the more elite members of society, perspectives that come from the margins raise sharp questions. Perhaps it is these that helped to shape the challenges to democratisation that are identified in the book's conclusion. Many of these remain matters of concern today. Full democratic participation is haunted by the spectre of regionalism, ruthlessly exploited by politicians anxious to secure their own position. Power continues to be concentrated in the Presidency with only limited progress in the separation of powers. Civil society activism tends to be seen by those in power as a threat and is therefore either co-opted or crushed rather than being seen as a welcome contributor to vibrant democratic debate. Participation often seems to be a mission element in Malawi's democracy as people conclude, with Jean-Jacques Rousseau that democracy is no more than their freedom to choose every few years who is going to oppress them! The sense of exclusion and alienation is compounded by the failure of the new dispensation to effectively address economic inequalities in society. If anything, these have widened during the democratic era, fuelling public anger at such egregious abuses of power as the Cashgate corruption scandal. Finally, it remains the case that the life of the churches in Malawi too often mirrors unhealthy aspects of the political system rather than challenging them. Few, if any, organisations are as well-placed as the churches to model and foster democratic participation. Yet the exercise of power within the churches remains very much in need of evangelical critique.

At the end of the day, this is a book that aims to move beyond social analysis, even as it is much indebted to the critiques of social scientists. It aims to make a theological contribution, mindful of C.S. Song's dictum that: "God's politics does not consist of attempts to seize power. What it aims at is the transformation of power." Partial and time-limited as it is, might this reprint provoke and inform attempts to so transform Malawian political life that it will be moving in the direction of the kingdom of God. I am grateful to Luviri Press for the effort they are making to keep the book available and thus make it possible for it to fulfil this calling.

Kenneth R. Ross

Netherlorn, Argyll

June 2018

Contents

Acknowledgments		6
Series Editors' Preface		7
Abbreviations		8
	Introduction	9
1.	The Transformation of Power in Malawi 1992-94: the Role of the Christian Churches *Kenneth R. Ross*	15
2.	The Use of the Bible in Social Transformation *F.L. Chingota*	41
3.	Marching, Suspended and Stoned: Christian Women in Malawi 1995 *Isabel Apawo Phiri*	63
4.	Young People: Participation or Alienation? An Anglican Case *James Tengatenga*	107
5.	Muslim Perspectives on Power *J.C. Chakanza and Hilary Mijoga*	125
6.	Power at the Receiving End: the Jehovah's Witnesses' Experience in One-Party Malawi *Klaus Fiedler*	149
7.	Christian Experience in Malawi Prisons *Hilary Mijoga*	177
8.	Even in the Church the Exercise of Power is Accountable to God *Klaus Fiedler*	187
9.	A Practical Theology of Power for the New Malawi *Kenneth R. Ross*	225
	Bibliography	269

Acknowledgments

The University of Malawi Department of Theology and Religious Studies is grateful for the invitation to participate in the Theology of Life Project of the World Council of Churches Unit III - Justice, Peace and Creation; and for the grant which funded the research on which this book is based.

The editors of the Kachere Series gratefully acknowledge the permission given by *The Nation* newspaper to reproduce some cartoons from "Town Rat and Country Rat" (Oráma and Vunde) and "Zabweka" (Brian Hara).

Series Editors' Preface

The Kachere Series is an initiative of the Department of Theology and Religious Studies at the University of Malawi. It aims to promote the emergence of a body of literature which will enable students and others to engage critically with religion in Malawi, its social impact and the theological questions which it raises. An important starting point lies with the publication of essays and theses which until now have been inaccessible to all but the most dedicated specialist. It is also hoped, however, that the development of theological scholarship in Malawi will stimulate the writing of many new books. General works with popular appeal can be published as *Kachere Books*, with Mambo Press in Gweru. Smaller documents and essays, which are of value as sources for the study of religion in Malawi, can be published as *Kachere Texts*, with CLAIM in Blantyre. It is in the third branch of the series, known as *Kachere Monographs*, that full-length academic treatises are published. Only the fruits of sound primary research which meet rigorous academic standards will be accepted for publication in this prestigious branch of the Series. The Editors intend the Monographs to contribute substantially to the growth of a body of knowledge in the area of theology and religious studies in Malawi. As important resources for study related to this field, we are confident that they will come to be prized not only within Malawi but in every academic centre concerned with religion and society in Africa.

This third Kachere Monograph is a religious and theological study of the dynamics of the exercise of power in church, state and society in Malawi. It originated as a case study in the World Council of Churches "Theology of Life" project, within which it had the specific remit to consider the affirmation that "all exercise of power is accountable to God." It is now issued as a monograph not because it has a single author but because it has a single theme. Moreover, the book is by no means composed of a loosely connected assortment of essays gathered from different times and places. Rather, it is the product of a team which worked closely together over a two-year period in a well-defined field of inquiry. This kind of collaborative research will be encouraged by the Kachere Series. This particular volume is all the more welcome because it addresses an urgently relevant contemporary issue. We are confident that the book will have an immediate application in Malawi at the advent of a new political dispensation and will also be an important resource for all those concerned with the construction of a viable theology of power for today's world.

Kachere Series Editors
Zomba, July 1996

Abbreviations

AFORD	Alliance for Democracy
CCAP	Church of Central Africa Presbyterian
MCP	Malawi Congress Party
NEC	National Executive Committee
NCC	National Consultative Council
PAC	Public Affairs Committee
PCD	Presidential Committee on Dialogue
SDA	Seventh Day Adventist Church
UDF	United Democratic Front
WARC	World Alliance of Reformed Churches
WCC	World Council of Churches

Introduction

This book is offered as a contribution to the construction of a theology of power for today's Africa. Twenty years ago Desmond Tutu threw down the challenge: "I fear that African Theology has failed to produce a sufficiently sharp cutting edge. It has indeed performed a good job by addressing the split in the African soul, and yet it has by and large failed to speak meaningfully in the face of a plethora of contemporary problems which assail the modern African. It has seemed to advocate disengagement from the hectic business of life, because very little has been offered that is pertinent, say, about *the theology of power* in the face of the epidemic of coups and military rule, about development, about poverty and disease and other equally urgent present-day issues."[1] Our theological engagement with issues of power in one contemporary African context aims to be one contribution to addressing the agenda sketched with such deep insight by Archbishop Tutu. The seriousness and the urgency of the issue was once well expressed by another South African theologian, Allan Boesak: "Africa knows too many iron-fisted rulers who have no respect for human rights. The colonial governor's mansion is now occupied by the representatives of new power elites that have as little concern for the people as did the colonialists. All too often "independence" has not meant a new, meaningful life for the people, or a return to the values of African life that would have revitalized society. Values such as the wholeness of life, the meaning of human-beingness, and the relationship between human beings and nature have not been resuscitated in African life, because these values tend to subvert the economic interests of the new elites and their neocolonialist masters."[2] Addressing a situation where people had come through the "second independence" of democratization we found that the suspicions and the questions raised by Boesak were still very much to the point. To consider the meaning of the Christian faith in relation to the socio-political power structures prevailing in Malawi is certainly an exercise which is long overdue. It is the hope of the authors that this study will prove to be a positive contribution towards the completion of that exercise.

The book originated as part of a world-wide process of reflection initiated by the World Council of Churches Unit III - Justice, Peace and Creation under the title "Theology of Life". One of the affirmations around which this process revolved is

---

[1] D.M. Tutu, "Black Theology and African Theology - Soulmates or Antagonists?", in J. Parratt ed., *A Reader in African Christian Theology*, London: SPCK, 1987, p. 54; first published in *Journal of Religious Thought*, 1975; my italics.
[2] A. Boesak, *Black and Reformed: Apartheid, Liberation and the Calvinist Tradition*, Maryknoll: Orbis, 1984, pp. 70-71; an address delivered at the All Africa Conference of Churches' General Assembly held in Nairobi, Kenya, 2-12 August, 1981.

that "All Exercise of Power is Accountable to God."[3] Malawi commended itself as a site for study on that theme not only because it has known much of the abuse of power, both under colonial government and under the one-party regime of Kamuzu Banda, but also because in the 1992-96 period it has been going through a remarkable period of democratization in which attempts have been made to restructure and reorganise the exercise of power. On the invitation of the World Council of Churches, a case study was therefore conducted by members of the Department of Theology and Religious Studies at the University of Malawi between June 1994 and June 1996. We worked together in a context of constant interaction but each member had specific remits which will become apparent in the pages which follow.

The methodology used in the study process was a consultative one. Initial plans were thoroughly discussed in two one-day consultations, held in Blantyre and Lilongwe in November 1994, with a carefully chosen spectrum of people who had worked for positive change in Malawi. Then detailed studies were undertaken in selected areas. The role of religion, and the churches in particular, in the democratic transformation of Malawi was studied by documentary research and also by field research designed to tune in to popular perspectives. In-depth interviews were conducted with 22 prominent persons whom we considered to be playing a key role in seeking a transformation of power in Malawi. We were mindful, at the same time, that a balanced assessment of the exercise of power would require careful listening not only to those who hold power but also to those who are subject to power. Hence we took care to make fruitful contact with those "on the underside" so far as power relations are concerned: women, young people, Muslims, prisoners, Jehovah's Witnesses. The results of interaction with these sectors of the population, in which we used the techniques of questionnaire, interview and participant-observation, are found among the chapters which follow. When we had produced preliminary research results we convened a residential consultative meeting in Zomba from 3 to 5 August 1995. Here we presented our findings for intensive consideration by a carefully chosen panel of seven people who had been deeply engaged in the struggle for justice in Malawi.

One of the recommendations of the panel was that we should issue a preliminary publication of our findings with a view to promoting discussion and response from a broad sample of the Malawi public. We therefore prepared a ten-page pamphlet, entitled "All Exercise of Power is Accountable to God: Reflecting on Government and Politics in the New Malawi." Since we were aiming to communicate with

---

[3] *Now is the Time*, Final Document and Other Texts from the World Convocation on Justice, Peace and the Integrity of Creation, Seoul, Republic of Korea, 5-12 March 1990, Geneva: WCC, 1990, p. 12.

"ordinary" people we published in the two main vernacular languages of Malawi - 5,000 copies in Chichewa/Chinyanja and 2,000 in Chitumbuka.[4] The pamphlet invited people to respond - giving their assessment of what we had written, raising any important points which they thought we had missed, and telling us their stories. Cash prizes were offered to the three most original and stimulating responses. Many people wrote, mostly encouraging us that our analysis of the exercise of power on Malawi was "scratching where they itched!" The winner of the competition was Mr Sebastiano Kupizira, a prisoner in Zomba Central Prison where he has been held on a murder charge for almost 6 years while he waits for his case to come to court.[5] Responses came from all parts of the country, from people of both sexes and all ages so we gained the confidence that we had tested our findings against quite a broad sample of the Malawi population. The issue of the pamphlet also involved us in a public engagement with the political process and attracted comment in the press and from those in high office. A pro-active approach was also taken by Dr Isabel Apawo Phiri whose work on women and the exercise of power led her into highly conflictual situations in both Church and University. Hence her contribution to the study, found in Chapter 3, is based on personal experience in solidarity with other women during 1995. Our study, then, has employed a diversity of research methods which we believe have enabled us to offer some original and critical theological perspectives on the exercise of power in Malawi.

We are grateful to those who freely gave of their time in order to participate in the study: Jande Banda (Department of Public Administration, University of Malawi), Maxwell Banda (Acting Deputy General Secretary, CCAP Synod of Livingstonia), Harry Bwanausi (Chairman, Council of the University of Malawi), Joseph Bvumbwe (Vice-Chairman, Public Affairs Committee), Emmanuel Chimkwita (Malawi High Commissioner to Mozambique), Allan Chiphiko (Minister, CCAP Synod of Nkhoma), Vera Chirwa (Director, Malawi Carer), Edda Chitalo (United Democratic Front Cabinet Minister), Kanyama Chiume (President, Congress for the Second Republic), Chipiliro Daza (former Vice-President, Malawi Democratic Party), Mabvuto Hara (practising lawyer, Blantyre), Cecilia Kadzamira (former Official Hostess, Malawi Government), Peter Kaleso (Malawi High Commissioner to South Africa), Kate Kainja (Malawi Congress Party Spokesperson on Women's

---

[4] K.R. Ross & F.L. Moyo, *Mazaza Ghose Gha Ulongozgi Ghakufuma kwa Chiuta: Kughanaghanira Vya Boma na Ndyale m'Malawi Wasono*, Zomba: University of Malawi Dept of Theology and Religious Studies, 1995; also published in Chichewa/Chinyanja translation as *Udindo Wonse Wolamulira ndi Wa Mulungu: Kulingalira ndi Kuganizira za Boma ndi Ndale za Malawi Watsopano*.

[5] The judicial system is currently unable to accommodate the number of cases which are awaiting trial so it is common for people charged with murder to be held in prison for several years while waiting for their cases to come to court.

Affairs), Kamlepo Kalua (President, Malawi Democratic Party), Janet Karim (Editor, *The Independent*), Brighton Kawamba (World Vision), Misanjo Kansilanga (General Secretary, CCAP Synod of Blantyre), Aaron Longwe (former Director, Foundation for Justice, Peace and the Integrity of Creation), Dixie Maluwa (Lecturer in Education, University of Malawi), Wenson Masoka (General Secretary, Seventh Day Adventist Church), Wambali Mkandawire (musician, Blantyre), Joest Mnemba (Roman Catholic parish priest, Dedza), Anastasia Msosa (Chairperson, Electoral Commission), Jake Muwamba (Malawi High Commissioner to the United Kingdom), Silas Ncozana (former General Secretary, CCAP Synod of Blantyre), Joyce Ng'oma (broadcaster, Malawi Broadcasting Corporation), Matiya Nkhoma (former Deputy General Secretary, CCAP Synod of Livingstonia), Peter Nyanja (Anglican Bishop of Lake Malawi), Matembo Nzunda (AFORD MP and Minister of Local Government and Rural Development), Lymon Phesele (Department of Civil Aviation, Lilongwe), Enoch Phiri (World Vision), John Roche (former Apostolic Administrator, Roman Catholic Diocese of Mzuzu). We are grateful also to many undergraduates in the Department of Theology and Religious Studies who worked in vacations as research assistants and to Fulata Moyo, a doctoral candidate who worked part-time as project administrator. We must express our thanks to the World Council of Churches Unit III which funded the research; and especially to Dr Martin Robra who was our contact person in Geneva. Books, reports, letters, visits and prayers from other branches of the Theology of Life process provided valuable stimulus to our study. Most of all, we are endebted to the members of the public who completed questionnaires, gave interviews or wrote to us in response to the pamphlets. We hope we can repay them in a small way in this book by providing some reflection of the views of the marginalized and excluded whose voices are rarely heard. For as well as seeking out some of those who are most creative and original in their engagement with Malawi society, we did consciously try to listen to voices from the underside of the power structures. We hope that, as a result, we may be able to offer some critical perspectives which can be of service to church and society at a time of profound change and challenge.

Between 1992 and 1994 Malawi underwent a remarkable transition from dictatorship to democracy. Truly a transformation of power! This process is examined in the first chapter by Kenneth Ross who pays particular attention to the role of the Christian churches in the peaceful revolution. Yet, while the political change brought a certain liberation to Malawi, there were many who still felt excluded from the exercise of power. Isabel Phiri gives a vivid personal account of the experience of women seeking to confront injustice and oppression during 1995. James Tengatenga seeks to articulate the perspective of young people, based on his work amongst Anglican youth. Joe Chakanza and Hilary Mijoga offer the results of their attempts to listen to the views of Muslims who, in Malawi history, have always tended to be on the underside when it comes to the exercise of power. No group, however, has been more brutally victimized by those in power than the Jehovah's Witnesses. Their story is told by Klaus Fiedler on the basis of extensive interviews, conducted by students, and documentary research. To be in prison is to be entirely subject to the power of others. Hilary Mijoga offers a study of the views of both criminal and political prisoners in Malawi, examining their experience of Christian faith in a situation of powerlessness. The relation between religious belief and the exercise of power is the major focus in this study. Felix Chingota, in the second chapter, analyzes the use of the Bible in promoting social transformation in Malawi. Klaus Fiedler, in the penultimate chapter, focuses on power relations within and among the churches. Finally, in the last chapter, Kenneth Ross attempts a theological analysis of key points which emerge from consideration of the exercise of power in Malawi today. Democratization in Malawi has been a great sign of hope for many people. Yet today many fear that their hopes were illusory as so much oppression still remains. The theological perspectives offered in this book may help to supply the critique, the renewal and the deepening which democracy needs if it is to prove viable in Malawi. The hope of all the contributors is that it will lead to a deeper awareness, and a more faithful praxis, of the reality that "all exercise of power is accountable to God."

Kenneth R. Ross
Zomba, July 1996

1. The Transformation of Power in Malawi 1992-94: the Role of the Christian Churches

Kenneth R. Ross

The Historical Background

Known in colonial times as Nyasaland, Malawi is a land-locked country bordering Tanzania in the north, Zambia in the west and Mozambique to the east and south. Its fertile soils and abundant water supply have attracted successive waves of migration leading to a current population approaching 11,000,000. The lack of mineral resources and the absence of any substantial industrial base has led to a dependence on agriculture which has become ever more precarious as an expanding population has taken its ecological toll. A British Protectorate was established in 1891 and the Malawian understanding of power was conditioned by 70 years of alien colonial rule. Chiefs who resisted the imposition of British authority were subdued by overwhelming military superiority. Soon European settlers established estates on much of the best land, producing tea, tobacco and cotton which yielded healthy profits to their owners but scant rewards to the Africans on whose labour they depended. Under the *thangata* system Africans were permitted to work plots of land on European estates in return for a considerable amount of labour. The tax demands of the new government were designed to force Africans to work for Europeans for at least part of the year. Both politically and economically, once-proud and independent African communities found themselves subject to a power which seemed to them quite unaccountable.[1] The Christian churches had played a major part in this historical development. It was the Scottish missionary David Livingstone who had first identified the Shire Highlands, in the south of Malawi, as an area suitable for European settlement which he hoped might become the gateway to Africa for "Christianity and commerce."[2] Inspired by this vision Scottish Presbyterian missions had been established in the 1870s and these were highly influential in bringing Malawi under British jurisdiction in 1889-91.[3] However, while the Christian missions functioned as an ideological prop and social support of colonial rule, it also became clear that the new faith provided a basis on which the exercise of power might be challenged. From the early 1900s there emerged a movement to form

---

[1] See B. Pachai, *Malawi: The History of the Nation*, London: Longman, 1973, pp. 81-127.
[2] See B. Pachai, "The Zambezi Expedition 1858-1864: New Highways for Old", in B. Pachai ed., *Livingstone: Man of Africa*, London: Longman, 1973, pp. 29-60.
[3] See A.C. Ross, *Blantyre Mission and the Making of Modern Malawi*, Blantyre: CLAIM, 1996; also Pachai, *Malawi: The History of the Nation*, pp. 70-80.

"African Independent" churches, often provoked by what was perceived to be an ecclesiastical abuse of power within the European missions.[4] This could easily be translated into directly political action as was demonstrated most dramatically in the major insurrection led by the Baptist pastor John Chilembwe in 1915 which seems to have aimed to overthrow the colonial system and establish a free and independent Malawi.[5] Many other Christian converts formed, from 1912, "native associations" where issues of power and accountability were actively discussed.[6]

By the 1940s this movement was being consolidated into the Nyasaland African Congress, a nationwide movement which finally succeeded in securing independence for Malawi in 1964. It was the educational institutions established by the Christian Missions which had trained the leaders of this movement and an appeal to Christian values was an important part of their challenge to the colonial state. This became especially apparent from 1953 when the British government, in face of the practically unanimous opposition of the African population of Nyasaland, allowed the territory to become part of the Federation of Rhodesia and Nyasaland, governed from Salisbury (now Harare). Malawians bitterly resented being incorporated into what they regarded as a racist political union which would lead to the underdevelopment of their country.[7] The battle to achieve greater independence now intensified and the support offered by some of the churches, especially the Church of Scotland, lent legitimacy to the struggle. The conviction that the Federation stood for fundamentally unchristian values invested the political campaign with a powerful moral force.[8] Soon it became clear that the days of colonial rule were numbered and that power was shifting to the Congress movement which commanded overwhelming support in the country. Since the focus of attention was concentrated on the paramount need to secede from the Federation and achieve self-government, there were few who considered critically the nature of the structures of power being established within the now dominant Malawi Congress Party. The young and highly capable leaders such as Orton Chirwa, Henry Chipembere and Kanyama Chiume who had revitalized the Congress movement in the mid-1950s judged that in Malawian society it was necessary to have a leader with the seniority and experience to command the

---

[4] See J.C. Chakanza, "The Independency Alternative: A Historical Survey", *Religion in Malawi*, No. 4 (1994), pp. 32-42.

[5] See G. Shepperson & T. Price, *Independent African*, Edinburgh: University Press, 1958.

[6] See J. McCracken, *Politics and Christianity in Malawi 1875-1940: The Impact of the Livingstonia Mission in the Northern Province*, Cambridge: CUP, 1977, pp. 261-292.

[7] See Pachai, *Malawi: The History of the Nation*, pp. 256-266.

[8] See, e.g., Blantyre Synod Statement on the Present State of Unrest, in the Report of the Committee Anent Central Africa to the Church of Scotland General Assembly, 1958, Appendix I, pp. 16-19.

respect of a largely rural and conservative population. Hence the fateful decision was taken to invite the 60-year old Hastings Kamuzu Banda, an exiled Malawian medical doctor who had maintained a keen interest in his native land, to return home and become the leader of the struggle for independence. From the moment of his arrival the Congress propaganda, as a political tactic, portrayed him in messianic terms as the great leader who would break the hated Federation of Rhodesia and Nyasaland. The younger leaders hoped that "the old man" would act as a figurehead while they retained the real political power. They were not prepared for the way in which he quickly reorganized the Congress party machinery so that it revolved around his personal authority. They were dismayed by his increasingly autocratic style of leadership, but laid aside their reservations until the great goal of independence had been attained. When Dunduzu Chisiza, a young economist of international standing and potentially Banda's main rival for the leadership, was mysteriously killed in a car accident in 1962, they maintained a united front even when Banda refused to allow an inquest into his death. Another straw in the wind concerning the unaccountability of the exercise of power in the new dispensation was Banda's comment, after the violent death of a political opponent, "To those who oppose us, accidents will happen."[9]

It was only a matter of weeks after independence when the majority of the Cabinet broke with Banda. Central to their disagreement was the question of the exercise of power. The "rebel" ministers believed in government based on open debate and collective responsibility. Banda favoured a presidential style of government where all executive authority would be concentrated in his office. He once described the Malawi system of government in these terms: "The Malawi system, the Malawi style is that Kamuzu says it's that and then it's finished. Whether anyone likes it or not, that is how its going to be here. No nonsense, no nonsense. You can't have everybody deciding what to do."[10] Following the "Cabinet crisis", which resulted in the exile of all the ministers who had opposed Banda, the Prime Minister moved quickly to develop a political system based on his own personal authority. He totally dominated the Cabinet. Parliament was turned into a rubber-stamp, subservient to the MCP. Membership of the party came to be understood in terms of personal loyalty to Banda. The judiciary was sidelined through the creation of "traditional courts" which operated without trained lawyers and were notoriously open to political manipulation. Banda formalised his dictatorship by first becoming president when Malawi became a Republic in 1966, and then Life President in 1971. After the 1964 Cabinet Crisis Banda had declared concerning his opponents that, "These people are wild animals now. They must be destroyed. No beating

---

[9] Int. M.W. Kanyama Chiume, 18 January 1995.
[10] Cit. P Short, *Banda*, London & Boston: Routledge & Kegan Paul, 1974, p. 201.

about the bush. Arrest them. But if they resist arrest, anything you do is alright so far as I am concerned. So remember that."[11] Such was the unaccountability of Banda's power that thousands upon thousands of innocent people were detained, tortured and killed on this basis without any question being raised.[12] Everyone in the country fell captive to this systemic terror. As broadcaster Joyce Ng'oma has put it: "I think we all felt detained, though we didn't go into detention."[13] This political climate also allowed Banda to develop a personal business empire which soon dominated the modest Malawi economy.[14] By using the methods of a police state to eliminate every suspicion of dissent, by lavishing patronage on loyal supporters, and by developing a formidable propaganda machine which controlled all the national media, the dictator reached a position of absolute power. The personal aggrandisement of the leader became the all-consuming goal of Malawian political life. Banda himself seemed to become the victim of his own personality cult. Enraptured by power, he largely lost hold of the high purpose which had made him once highly committed to the welfare of his people. As old age advanced upon him he grew ever more out of touch with the people. Yet the system ensured that there was no correction or challenge to his egotistical and despotic style of leadership.[15] The effect of all this on the Malawi people has been vividly evoked by Paul Zeleza:

> Banda's Malawi, a thirty-year contraption of totalitarian power, was a land of pervasive fear where words were constantly monitored, manipulated and mutilated, a country stalked by silence and suspicion, a nation where the monotonous story of the Ngwazi's achievements could be told and retold, a state of dull uniformity that criminalized difference, ambiguity, creativity, an omniscient regime with a divine right to nationalize time and thought, history and the popular will. And so it censored memories, stories, and words that contested and mocked its singular authority, banishing and imprisoning numerous opponents, real and imaginary, hunting and

---

[11] *Ibid*, p. 256.
[12] Some documentation of this sad history can be found in *Malawi: Human Rights Violations 25 Years After Independence*, London: Amnesty International, 1989; *Where Silence Rules: The Suppression of Dissent in Malawi*, Washington and London: Africa Watch, 1990; and *Malawi: Prison Conditions, Cruel Punishment and Detention Without Trial*, London: Amnesty International, 1992.
[13] Joyce Ng'oma, interview by Isabel Apawo Phiri, 9 January 1995.
[14] For recent studies of the Malawi economy see G. Mhone, *Malawi at the Crossroads*, Harare: Sapes Books, 1992; F Pryor, *The Political Economy of Poverty, Equity and Growth: A World Bank Comparative Study of Malawi and Madagascar*, Oxford: OUP, 1991.
[15] For studies of the one-party system in Malawi see Short, *Banda*; T.D. Williams, *Malawi: The Politics of Despair*, Ithaca and London: Cornell University Press, 1978; J.L. Lwanda, *Kamuzu Banda of Malawi: A Study in Promise, Power and Paralysis*, Glasgow: Dudu Nsomba Publications, 1993.

murdering exiled 'rebels', and appropriated and dissolved the boundaries between private and public spheres, individual and collective lives, so that no one was sure of anyone, not of friends or colleagues, or relatives, not even of partners and spouses, and even one's careless dreams could be dangerous. *All was contaminated by this naked, arbitrary power.*[16]

The Christian churches had, to some extent, contributed to the creation of what critics have called the "Frankenstein monster" of the Banda dictatorship.[17] Being deeply involved in the struggle of the people for self-government, they were too close to the Congress movement to be able to develop the critical distance necessary to offer a prophetic critique. From independence in 1964 the church leaders felt their role was to offer all possible support to the government in the task of building the nation. The tenor of the church's message on socio-political issues can be illustrated by a Joint Message from the Catholic and Presbyterian Churches issued on the 10th Anniversary of Independence:

> What has been achieved during this period in all fields is so unbelievable that it confounds even the most optimistic expectations of most of us and there is no doubt that all this achievement is due to the untiring efforts, dedicated, selfless, and responsible leadership of His Excellency the Life President Ngwazi Dr H. Kamuzu Banda. If this country has grown from the ranks of the poor nations into a nation with a viable booming economy, with a healthy educated people, it is due to His Excellency's own dynamic leadership and the stable and peaceful conditions that leadership has created.[18]

It was only with the wisdom of hindsight that the Blantyre Synod of the Church of Central Africa Presbyterian was able to recognise the trap into which it had fallen. In January 1993 it issued a statement to confess that:

> If we look at our own history as the CCAP during the time of the struggle for Independence, we will see that Blantyre Synod was very much in support of the Nyasaland African Congress (later called the MCP). Because of this very verbal stance on the side of the MCP, after Independence, the CCAP was aligned closely with the government and became so assimilated with the government's activities that the Synod was often invited to pray and participate as a Church at various government functions. However, because of this assimilation and alignment with the MCP, the Church gradually lost

---

[16] P.T. Zeleza, "Totalitarian Power and Censorship in Malawi", *Southern Africa Political and Economic Monthly*, Vol. 8 No. 11 (August 1995), p. 33; my italics.

[17] Int. H.W. Bwanausi, 8 December 1994; and M.W. Kanyama Chiume, 18 January 1995.

[18] Joint Message from the Churches of Malawi on the 10th Anniversary of Independence, signed by Most Rev James Chiona, Catholic Archbishop of Blantyre, and Very Rev J.D. Sangaya, General Secretary, CCAP Synod of Blantyre, 1974, p. 2.

its ability to admonish or speak pastorally to the government. We do not want to make the same mistake at this time in order to ensure that the Church retains its prophetic voice throughout the coming years of our country's history.[19]

The fact that most of the Congress, including Banda, were products of the Presbyterian missions and that many remained active members, made it very difficult for the Presbyterian Church to develop an independent position. When many of its lay leaders became victims of the purge which followed the "Cabinet crisis" of 1964, the CCAP was gripped by the climate of fear which dominated the country for the next thirty years. As current Blantyre Synod General Secretary Misanjo Kansilanga has confessed: "The silence of the church was costly to thousands of Malawians who lost their lives and spent their time in prisons."[20] Like all other national institutions the churches were co-opted to support the Banda dictatorship and, to the casual observer, they appeared to be offering unquestioning legitimation to the one-party system.

Yet the churches were perhaps the least amenable of all institutions and even during the most repressive times the danger remained that the church would raise questions about the exercise of power. It is significant that among the first to publicly raise questions about Banda's autocratic style was the Roman Catholic John Chester Katsonga, who founded the Christian Democratic Party in 1960. Katsonga predicted that if the MCP came to power, the people would just move from one form of oppression by the whites to another by Dr Banda![21] After the Cabinet crisis it was very difficult for church leaders to offer any correction or critique to the political leadership. However, attempts were made. Jonathan Sangaya, the General Secretary of Blantyre Synod from 1963 to 1979, never publicly criticised the government but used to seek to counsel the President in private audiences at Sanjika palace. So forthright was his approach that he often incurred Banda's wrath and was repeatedly detained and tortured, though the government never dared to hold him in detention for more than a few days at a time. It is widely believed that his death was caused, directly or indirectly, by government agents acting on the orders of Dr Banda.[22] In later years no church

---

[19] "A Statement on the Role of the Church in the Transformation of Malawi in the Context of Justice and Peace," Produced by the Administrators Conference, Blantyre Synod CCAP, 22-23 January 1994, p. 4.
[20] Rev M.E. Kansilanga, Address on "Church and Politics in Malawi Today", CCAP General Synod Human Rights Workshop, Chongoni, 8 November 1995.
[21] "Mau a Mtsogoleri wa Christian Democratic Party: Kuyankha Mtsogoleri wa Malawi Congress Party;" Mimeo, 1960; cit. J.C. Chakanza, "The Pro-democracy Movement in Malawi: The Catholic Church's Contribution 1960-1992," *Religion in Malawi*, No. 4 (1994), p. 9.
[22] Int. Mrs Christian Sangaya and Mrs Eleanor Kanyuka (nee Sangaya), 20 February 1995.

leader had such direct access to the President but even at the height of Banda's power the latent challenge to the abuse of power found in the church's message occasionally rose to the surface. Saindi Chiphangwi, who succeeded Sangaya as General Secretary of Blantyre Synod, preached sermons on national occasions in the early 1980s which did have this effect. Since these were broadcast on national radio, a thrill could run through the whole country when he spoke such words as:

> Our choices and decisions either as private individuals or as public figures matter *immensely*. If we choose aright we help to build Malawi into "the warm heart of Africa", but if we decide wrongly we make hell for ourselves and for future generations. For this matter, let us not let things drift. Do not leave the future shape and image of Malawi to chance. Assume responsibility now for we are all answerable to God for the future character and image of Malawi.[23]

Chiphangwi reports that many expected him to "disappear" after uttering such words but many others were tremendously encouraged that the authentic voice of the church was being heard. Jack Mapanje, the poet who was one of Malawi's most famous political detainees in the late 1980s, reported that the prisoners used to recall Chiphangwi's sermons and take courage from the knowledge that the church was on their side![24] Roman Catholic Archbishop James Chiona also preached some forthright sermons during this period. On one occasion he commented that it was dehumanising when people were forced to sing praises to the President for the supposed benefits he had brought when, in fact, they were poor and struggling to make ends meet. When he was asked by party officials to apologize, the Archbishop refused flatly, offering instead to take them to the poor of his parish.[25]

At the same time, it has to be acknowledged that the critical witness of the churches was occasional and muted. Moreover, the years of repressive dictatorial rule took their toll on the life of the churches. Not only was their social witness largely silenced but their own institutional life came to reflect the one-party system. When the churches became prominent in the struggle for democratization in Malawi, it was not long before members began to point out how an oppressive "one-party" system of government prevailed *within* the life of the church. At a joint Anglican-Presbyterian Seminar on Civic Education prior to the General Election of 1994, e.g., the point which aroused by far the most interest and support among younger clergy was the need for accountability and democracy in

---

[23] Rev Dr S.D. Chiphangwi, Sermon at Martyr's Day Service, St Michael and All Angels Church, 3 March 1985.

[24] Int. Rev Dr S.D. Chiphangwi, Gaborone, 18 December 1994.

[25] *Moto Magazine*, May/June 1992; cit. J.C. Chakanza, "The Pro-Democracy Movement", p. 12.

the structures of the church!²⁶ A similar point was made by women of Blantyre Synod early in 1995 when they marched to an administrators' meeting to present a petition airing their grievances and calling for "Justice and Peace *in the Church*."²⁷ The need for this was dramatically demonstrated when the administrators not only refused to receive the petition but resolved to suspend all women workers of the Synod!²⁸ Within the same month the same Synod leadership issued a circular which indicated that all "born-again" (i.e. charismatic) members were to be excommunicated from their congregations.²⁹ This attracted comment in the leader column of the main national newspaper: "It is not a fitting epithet that a body which played so pivotal a role in such a noble enterprise as the liberation of a people from the yoke of a seemingly invincible servitude should go down as just another male-dominated institution of social oppression with antiquated ideals."³⁰ As we shall see, the churches, with Blantyre Synod prominent among them, did finally emerge as a powerful force for democratization in Malawi. Yet they did not take account of how far the "one-party" mentality had infiltrated their own ranks. As it championed the cause of political reform, the church was little aware that its call for freedom, justice, accountability and democracy would rebound upon its own structures as radical questions came to be asked about the ecclesiastical use of power.

The Pastoral Letter of 1992

Despite the latent challenge which the churches posed to the excesses of the one-party system, its expression was so rare and so muted that many observers assumed that the churches could be written off as a potential force for political reform and renewal. Every Sunday in churches of all denominations the leaders prayed for the long life and prosperity of the dictator who was ruthlessly exploiting and brutally oppressing the people. At every national occasion the church leaders were there to provide religious legitimation for the political status quo. With the end of the cold war in 1989, the subsequent wave of democratization sweeping across Africa and the increasingly apparent political bankruptcy of the Banda regime, by the early 1990s hopes rose for positive change

---

[26] CCAP Synod of Blantyre, Department of Church and Society, Ecumenical Seminar for Clergy, Chilema, 9-11 February 1994, address by Dr K.R. Ross on "The Theology of Political Action."

[27] "Justice and Peace in the Church", A Statement by Women Representatives Meeting at Chigodi Women's Centre from 30th November to [date omitted] December 1994.

[28] See *The Monitor*, 18 January 1995.

[29] "Za Kubadwa kwa Tsopano/Fellowship", Letter from the Synod Office to all congregations, CCAP Synod of Blantyre, 11 January 1995. "Born-again" in the Malawi context refers to those who adopt "charismatic" practices, notably speaking in tongues.

[30] *The Nation*, 10 February 1995.

in Malawi. Still, few expected that the church would be the source of such change. Indeed the system of political control was so complete that, for most people, it was difficult even to imagine anything different. When a delegation of British lawyers visited Malawi as late as September 1992 they reported that: "We wish to emphasize that the emotion we encountered, among citizens at every level, from villages to Government officials, was fear."[31] In the land "where silence ruled"[32] who could break the spell of fear?

In March 1992 the Roman Catholic Bishops issued their Pastoral Letter, entitled *Living our Faith*.[33] Rarely in modern times can a church document have had such an immediately explosive effect in the life of a nation. Within four days the ruling Malawi Congress Party was convened in emergency session to pass an unreserved condemnation of the bishops. Possession of the letter was declared to be an act of sedition, punishable by severe penalties. There were unrestrained calls at the party convention for the bishops to be killed.[34] When this was followed by a leader entitled "No Mercy" in the government-controlled newspaper, experienced observers feared that the bishops were being set up for assassination.[35] Yet even as the one-party system mustered its forces to stamp out the dissent, it became evident that there had been a dramatic shift in power. Politely but bluntly the Bishops had pointed out the shortcomings of the prevailing political order and their statements had such a ring of truth that the MCP regime was suddenly exposed. It was like the moment in the fairy tale when the little boy pointed out that the Emperor had no clothes! Things could never be the same again. Practically overnight the mode of discourse in everyday conversation began to change. One moment the MCP was all-powerful; the next it was becoming a laughing stock. The sense of liberation was palpable. So decisive was this moment that, in common parlance, modern Malawian history is divided into "before the Pastoral Letter" and "after the Pastoral Letter!"[36] Finally even the leaders of the Malawi

---

[31] "Human Rights in Malawi: Report of a Joint Delegation of the Scottish Faculty of Advocates, the Law Society of England and Wales and the General Council of the Bar to Malawi", 17-27 September 1992, p. 8.

[32] See *Where Silence Rules*.

[33] *Living our Faith*, Pastoral Letter of the Catholic Bishops of Malawi to be Read in Every Catholic Church on 8th March 1992; later published under the title *The Truth Will Set You Free*, Church in the World 28, London: CIIR, 1992.

[34] Tapes of this convention were later widely circulated and transcripts published in order to discredit the MCP Government. See, e.g., *The Nation*, Vol. 1 Nos. 12-21 (2 Sept.-4 Oct. 1993).

[35] See *Malawi News* 14-20 March 1992.

[36] Research conducted at Ntaja, Mwanza, Dowa and Nkhata Bay in November and December 1994 revealed that recognition of the Pastoral Letter as *the* turning-point in recent Malawian political life is practically universal at the popular level. See G. Chigona, Research Notes on Political Transition in Malawi, November-December 1994.

Congress Party had no alternative but to recognise the Pastoral Letter as a blessing![37]

The critically important function of the Pastoral Letter was to introduce, quite suddenly and dramatically, accountability to Malawian public life. First of all, it made the regime accountable to *reality*. Whereas government propaganda ceaselessly promoted the myth that all Malawians had prospered under the beneficent reign of Kamuzu Banda, the Bishops bluntly observed that: "Many people still live in circumstances which are hardly compatible with their dignity as sons and daughters of God. Their life is a struggle for survival. At the same time a minority enjoys the fruits of development and can afford to live in luxury and wealth."[38] Shortcomings in the national education system were noted: widespread illiteracy, falling standards, overcrowding, shortage of teachers and materials, unequal access to education and indiscipline. Regarding the health service, concern was expressed about shortage of health centres, overcrowding and lack of personnel, the poor quality of medical care, and inequality in medical treatment.[39] These were all matters of common knowledge[40] but no one had dared to mention them publicly for fear that this would be regarded as tantamount to sedition. Now the myth of the prosperous Malawi was exploded and people began to address the serious problems of poverty faced by the country.[41] Much of the power of the Pastoral Letter lay in the fact that it voiced what everyone knew but no one had ever dared to say. It thus broke the culture of deceit which had been allowed to develop. The introduction of accountability to reality was an important contribution to national politics.

The Bishops, however, went further to question the entire nature and structure of Malawian political life. They struck to the heart of the problem with the Banda regime when they stated that: "Accountability is a quality of any good government. People are entitled to know how their representatives fulfil their duties. No disrespect is shown when citizens ask questions in matters which

---

[37] The Vice-President of the MCP Gwanda Chakuamba, e.g., declared that "the issuing of the Pastoral Letter by the country's Catholic Bishops in March 1992, was a blessing in disguise for the MCP " *Daily Times*, 29 April 1994.

[38] *Living our Faith*, p. 2.

[39] *Ibid*, pp. 4-7.

[40] The Bishops noted that: "People will not be scandalized to hear these things; they know them. They will only be grateful that their true needs are recognised and that efforts are made to answer them. Feeding them with slogans and half-truths - or untruths - only increases their cynicism and their mistrust of government representatives." (!) *Ibid*, p. 10.

[41] "Poverty alleviation" was the central policy of the new United Democratic Front government which took office in May 1994.

concern them."⁴² This call for accountability to the people marked the beginning of a process of democratization which was to transform Malawian political life during the coming two years. Perhaps the most powerful part of the Letter was found in a section entitled "The Participation of all in public life. The Bishops drew on both biblical texts (Ephesians 4:7-16 and I Peter 4:10-11) and traditional African proverbs to argue that society can be strong only when it enjoys the participation of all its members. What this meant for Malawi was explained as follows:

> Human persons are honoured and this honour is due to them whenever they are allowed to search freely for truth, to voice their opinions and to be heard, to engage in creative service of the community in all liberty within associations of their own choice. Nobody should ever have to suffer reprisals for honestly expressing and living up to their convictions: intellectual, religious or political. We can only regret that this is not always the case in our country.... Academic freedom is seriously restricted; exposing injustices can be considered a betrayal; revealing some evils of our society is seen as slandering the country; monopoly of the mass media and censorship prevent the expression of dissenting views; some people have paid dearly for their political opinions; access to public places like markets, hospitals, bus depots etc, is frequently denied to those who cannot produce a party card; forced donations have become a way of life.⁴³

The Bishops went on to sketch the effects of all this on national life and consciousness, the dark tragedy which had overcome Malawi in the years since independence: "It creates an atmosphere of resentment among citizens. It breeds a climate of mistrust and fear. This fear of harassment and mutual suspicion generates a society in which the talents of many lie unused and in which there is little room for initiative."⁴⁴ First steps towards the restoration of a climate of trust and openness were proposed and these became Malawi's political agenda for the next two years: the establishment of an independent press, open forums of discussion, free association of citizens for social and political purposes, Government accountability, the establishment of independent, accessible and impartial courts of justice.⁴⁵ These were all measures designed to recover the accountability of government to the people and to increase popular participation in political life.

---

⁴² *Living our Faith*, p. 10.
⁴³ *Ibid*, p. 9.
⁴⁴ *Ibid*.
⁴⁵ *Ibid*, pp. 9-11.

For these goals to be achieved, however, there was another level of accountability which played an important role. Johan-Baptist Metz has written of the "dangerous memory" or "subversive memory" of Jesus Christ which the church carries through history. Time and again "this definite memory breaks through the magic circle of the prevailing consciousness."[46] The Malawi Congress Party succeeded by force of propaganda in creating in the country such a culture of deceit that people began to lose their bearings and even their thinking was "colonized" by the "system." The Pastoral Letter, at a stroke, broke through that false consciousness by making the system accountable to the norms and values of the kingdom of God. Thereafter the MCP government could no longer be "a law unto itself" for the church was measuring its policies and actions against the norm or criterion of the biblical message of the kingdom of God. By weighing the existing order against the demands of God's impending kingdom the church supplied a gauge which freed people to make their own assessment of the prevailing system and to take action accordingly. In a predominantly Christian country like Malawi where the biblical message has tremendous resonance, to make the exercise of power accountable to God in this way was a formidable political challenge. When the MCP government made the mistake of asking people to choose between their loyalty to the church and their loyalty to the regime, it soon became clear that its legitimacy was crumbling. The church's memory certainly proved to be "dangerous" and "subversive" so far as the one-party system in Malawi was concerned! By establishing these various levels of accountability the Catholic Bishops ensured that Malawi would never be the same again. What remained was to see whether a peaceful process of political reform could be developed to put into effect the vision which had been expressed in the Pastoral Letter.

The Public Affairs Committee

Despite intense government intimidation, support for the Pastoral Letter was soon made apparent. The following Sunday students of the University of Malawi marched in support of the Bishops, an action which resulted in the closure of the main University campus for the first time in its history.[47] A month later Chakufwa

---

[46] J.B. Metz, *Faith in History and Society: Toward a Practical Fundamental Theology*, London. Burns & Oates, 1980, pp. 89-90.

[47] On 15 March 1992 Catholic students issued a letter entitled "We Support our Bishops" which included the following statements: "We praise and congratulate you for your courage in bringing out the lenten pastoral letter *Living our Faith*. Undoubtedly, this pastoral letter will go down in our history as the most soul-searching document on current realities that has ever come out... As your daughters and sons, we have been deeply distressed by the horrible insults and open abuses against you and the whole Malawian Catholic church The "we support our bishops walk" held on Sunday 15th March 1992 from Chancellor College to Zomba Cathedral for Mass.

Chihana, the Malawian Secretary-General of the Southern African Trade Union Coordinating Council, returned to Malawi to begin a campaign for democratic change. In the speech which he attempted to make, before being arrested on the airport tarmac, Chihana appealed to the Pastoral Letter as an indication of the need for political reform.[48] Later in April an unprecedented wave of strikes swept both the public and private sectors, forcing the government to implement massive wage rises. The strikes were accompanied by rioting and looting directed particularly at properties identified with the Malawi Congress Party it was clear that the government faced a serious crisis. However, for some months it was unclear how the initiative of the Pastoral Letter could be taken up in a positive and constructive way. The Bishops themselves found it advisable to take a low profile for a time. It fell to the Presbyterians to begin to chart a way forward. Silas Ncozana recalls that, at the end of a meeting of the executives of the ecumenical Christian Service Committee, "it was agreed that a delegation be sent to meet with President Banda urging him to protect the lives of the bishops and also to make the necessary political reforms. I was asked to draft a memo which would be presented to Banda by the group. As fear enveloped some of the church leaders chosen to go to the palace, the action agreed at that meeting failed."[49] It now proved to be of significance that the Church of Central Africa Presbyterian belonged to an international fellowship of mutual accountability, namely the World Alliance of Reformed Churches. Bas de Gaay Fortman has noted that "in international presbyterian and reformed circles there was discontent with the neutral attitude which the Church of Central Africa Presbyterian (CCAP) in Malawi had adopted in the tense situation in the country."[50] Meeting in Lusaka early in May, leaders of the WARC Southern African region issued a strong letter supporting the Catholic bishops and calling the CCAP "to be prophetic."[51]

In early June WARC sent a delegation to meet with the leaders of the Presbyterian churches in Malawi and together they presented an open letter to the Life President entitled "The Nation of Malawi in Crisis: the Church's Concern."[52] They made

---

followed by a visit to the bishop's house, bears testimony to our unflinching solidarity for you and what you stand for."
[48] *Independent* (British newspaper), 8 April 1992.
[49] S.S. Ncozana, "Beginning of the End of a Monolithic Government" unpublished paper
[50] B. de G. Fortman, "No Nobodies" unpublished paper, 1995, p. 2. Professor Fortman was a member of the WARC delegation which came to Malawi in June 1992.
[51] "Statement on the Current Situation in Malawi" issued by The Southern Africa Alliance of Reformed Churches, meeting in Lusaka, 29 April to 5 May 1992.
[52] "The Nation of Malawi in Crisis: the Church's Concern" Geneva: World Alliance of Reformed Churches, 2 June 1992. An endorsement of this letter was signed by 55 ministers of the Synod of Livingstonia who agreed to read it out in their congregations. CCAP Synod of Livingstonia, "Statement to CCAP General Synod" 9 June 1992.

direct reference to the Catholic Pastoral Letter, still technically a seditious document, and insisted that the government must address the issues which it raised.[53] At this stage, however, what was required was more than a Presbyterian echo of the Catholic social critique. Practical proposals were needed. The church leaders accordingly called for the appointment of a broadly based Commission with the mandate "to make specific proposals for structural reform towards a political system with sufficient checks and balances on the use of power, and guarantees of accountability at all levels of government; to review the judicial system, in line with the rule of law; to look into the distribution of income and wealth required by the demands of social justice."[54] Meanwhile the letter called for immediate steps to be taken to remove injustices: "end the practice of detention without trial; release or bring to early and fair trial all political detainees; reform conditions of imprisonment, in accordance with human dignity; allow freedom of expression and association, so as to encourage open discussion of the nation's future."[55] These demands were powerfully reinforced by the decision in May of the Western donor community to suspend all development aid to Malawi until there was evidence of greater respect for human rights and "good governance." A process of reform was immediately undertaken by the government. Many political detainees were released. The International Committee of the Red Cross was invited to inspect the prisons. The practice of forced donations and the harassment of people who did not possess party cards was stopped. Painfully slowly, and with many obstructions along the way, the door began to be opened to freedom of expression and freedom of association. However, it was apparent that the government was hoping to placate its critics with relatively superficial reforms while maintaining the underlying structures of repression. Though the President had given a favourable reply to the Presbyterian open letter and had invited church leaders to meet with his ministers, the government stalled and was clearly reluctant to accede to the formation of a forum where fundamental political issues would be addressed.[56]

The resultant delay proved to be a blessing in disguise to the forces of reform. For it provided the opportunity and the constraint to work towards a more broadly representative Commission including not only church leaders but also

---

[53] *Ibid*, p. 2.
[54] *Ibid*.
[55] *Ibid*.
[56] The Hon W.B. Deleza, Minister without Portfolio, told the church leaders on 15 July 1992 that it was no longer necessary for them to meet with government ministers since the Life President had touched on all the issues in his address to the nation on 5 July 1992. See letter of Rt Rev Dr Silas Nyirenda and Rev Misanjo E. Kansilanga to the Hon Minister of State, Mr J.Z.U. Tembo M.P., 28 August 1992, Public Affairs Committee file 1992.

representatives of the Muslim Association, the Malawi Law Society and the Associated Chambers of Commerce and Industry.[57] At this point it was significant that the church leaders included not only clergy but also (lay) elders with a wealth of experience in national affairs.[58] Throughout July and August the Presbyterian church leaders worked hard behind the scenes to bring together a truly national and representative Commission. When the Christian Council, on 26 August 1992, called upon the government to hold a referendum on the system of government, their letter was signed by representatives of the Anglican Church, all three Synods of the CCAP (though one later withdrew), the African Methodist Episcopal Church, the Seventh Day Baptist Church, the Churches of Christ, the Zambezi Evangelical Church, Providence Industrial Mission, the Baptist Church and a number of para-church organizations.[59] Two days later, when the church leaders wrote to the government again, their letter was signed by representatives not only of the Protestant churches but also the Roman Catholic Church, the Muslim Community, the Business Community and the Malawi Law Society.[60] It is worth noting that this was the first time in Malawian history that Christian and Muslim leaders had publicly united to take a strategic socio-political initiative. Silas Ncozana has commented that: "in the process of (PAC's) work, Muslims and Christians grew to know each other as they had never done before."[61] Despite the fact that the Muslim participants were later disowned by the more conservative leadership within their own community, the formation of the PAC was a significant event in the history of Christian-Muslim relations in Malawi.[62]

The significance of this united front was not lost on the government which immediately responded by insisting that the committee should be composed of church leaders only and must exclude the business community and the Law Society.[63] In a series of exchanges the government maintained this position but the church leaders were not to be moved: "The initiative of the Church should not be interpreted in a narrow sense, as if the issues for discussion are exclusively religious. The issues which moved the Church to call for a national dialogue were and remain national issues affecting all aspects of the lives of the citizens of this

---

"It was the lack of response of the MCP government which forced us to invite other people who were interested." Int. Rev Misanjo Kansilanga, 16 November 1994.

[58] Int. T.J. Muwamba, 4 January 1995.

[59] Christian Council of Malawi, Open Letter to the Government of Malawi, 26 August 1992.

[60] Letter of Rt Rev Dr Silas Nyirenda and Rev Misanjo E. Kansilanga to the Hon Minister of State, Mr J.Z.U. Tembo M.P. 28 August 1992, Public Affairs Committee file 1992.

[61] S.S. Ncozana, "Do Not Fear the Muslim President" *The Lamp*, Vol. 1 No. 2 (Oct-Dec 1995), p. 16.

[62] Interviews conducted within the Muslim community by Dr J.C. Chakanza, February 1995.

[63] Letter of Hon J.Z.U. Tembo, Minister of State, to Rt Rev Dr Silas Nyirenda and Rev Misanjo E. Kansilanga, 7 September 1992, Public Affairs Committee file, 1992.

country."[64] When the "Public Affairs Committee" finally sat down with the "Presidential Committee on Dialogue" it did so as the representative organ of a truly national constituency. It was the first time that a non-party organisation had been recognised as having a role to play in national political life. The PAC planned to press for a national referendum on the question of one-party or multi-party system of government when they met the PCD for the first time on 19 October 1992. In order to forestall this initiative the President himself, on 18 October, announced the government's intention to hold such a referendum.[65] This announcement prompted a second "pressure group", the United Democratic Front (UDF), to join Chakufwa Chihana's Alliance for Democracy (Aford) in the public arena. Chihana himself was by this time on trial for sedition. His two year sentence was reduced on appeal to six months (which, suspiciously, kept him in prison until just after the referendum campaign was completed.) It is worth noting that his Mitigation Statement during the appeal case began with the following statement: "I come from a family which has strong Christian traditions, i.e. the fear and adoration of God, respect for human beings and the readiness to assist others in need of help. Throughout my life these Christian values have had considerable influence and have become the bedrock of my present social and political behaviour."[66] While giving attention to the institutional role of the churches, analysis of this period should not neglect the witness of lay Christians in the political arena. At the same time it must be observed that at this early stage the budding political parties worked to a considerable extent under the umbrella of the PAC which remained the engine of political reform during the referendum period. It was the Public Affairs Committee, e.g, which forced the government to address the issue of violence and even to sign a Joint Statement indicating their resolve to "prosecute all persons who engage in incitement to political violence and violence itself and ... to protect the fundamental right of persons to hold political views."[67]

Despite this paper agreement, the MCP government continued to use its familiar tactics of intimidation and violence in a vain attempt to stop the tidal wave of support which was gathering behind the multi-party movement. In the aftermath of the Pastoral Letter it had been immensely important that there were individuals who were prepared to defy such intimidation and to suffer for their convictions. The Bishops themselves had stood by their Letter and had defied all attempts to

---

[64] Letter of Rev M.E. Kansilanga to Hon Bester Bisani M.P Chairman of the Presidential Committee on Dialogue, 12 October 1992, Public Affairs Committee file, 1992.
[65] *Daily Times*, 19 October 1992.
[66] Chakufwa Chihana, "The Bumpy Road to Freedom: Mitigation Statement on Sedition Trial 1992", undated photocopy, p. 1.
[67] Joint Statement by the President's Committee on Dialogue and the Public Affairs Committee, Kwacha Conference Centre, Blantyre, 13 November 1992.

force an apology and retraction. Their firm stand encouraged others to speak out. Prominent among them was Rev Aaron Longwe, a Presbyterian minister in the northern town of Mzuzu, who was detained and interrogated after delivering a sermon on Micah 7:1-7 on 26 April 1992.[68] Soon the message in many pulpits included a biblically based critique of the prevailing one-party system and it was not unusual to hear of ministers being arrested.[69] Many ordinary people also suffered at this time. A woman office-worker arrested in May 1992 as a suspected multi-party sympathiser described her treatment while in detention: "They said 'You are in the hands of the government. We can do anything we like with your life.' Then they ripped the clothes off me. They left me naked. They made me lie down. One pulled my legs. One man had pliers. They forced my knees and my legs apart. They started putting the pliers into my anus. I was crying at the top of my voice."[70] Even after the PAC-PCD dialogue had begun the intimidation continued. A series of assassination attempts on the Acting PAC Chairman Rev Emmanuel Chimkwita has been documented by Amnesty International.[71]

Another target was the PAC Secretary, Rev Misanjo Kansilanga, who on one occasion was denounced as a dissident at a public meeting by an MCP district chairman who remarked to the Life President: "*Bwana kuli chiswe chanu ku MCP Headquarters ndipo tithana nawo anthu oterewa*" which was taken to mean that the President had death squads at the MCP Headquarters who would deal with such people.[72] Kansilanga himself has described his experience during this period: "MCP top brass went to our home areas and informed our relatives that we were not good people. We had become rebels. They were inciting people in our home areas to bash our cars, to burn our property and all sorts of things. I lost a whole granary in my home area and my two houses were burnt down during the referendum campaign period.... My car was stoned and I was followed on several occasions a car following me wherever I went. So we knew that we were in danger."[73] The fact that there were people willing to defy such intimidation meant that the long-established system of political control by means of violence was now

---

[68] On his release he was told not to preach again from the book of Micah! See J.L. Wilkie, "The First Detention (in Mzuzu, Malawi) of the Rev Aaron Longwe and Mr Chenda Mkandawire 27-30 April 1992", Confidential Church of Scotland Report, 7 May 1992.
[69] E.g. when the Church, Peace, Justice and Politics Committee of Livingstonia Synod met on 1 September 1992 its business included the arrest and detention of three of its ministers. Committee Minutes, Livingstonia Synod office.
[70] *Malawi: Preserving the One-Party State Human Rights Violations and the Referendum*, London: Amnesty International, 18 May 1993, p. 2.
[71] *Ibid*, pp. 10-11.
[72] See Letter from the CCAP Synod of Blantyre to the Hon J.Z.U. Tembo, Minister of State, on "Public Denunciation of the Rev Misanjo E. Kansilanga" 6 November 1992.
[73] Int. Rev Misanjo E. Kansilanga, 16 November 1994

breaking down. When relatives and friends of Misanjo Kansilanga advised him to withdraw from his involvement with PAC he told them: "I am not doing my own thing. I did not choose this. But I believe that this is God's work. If it is God's work then it is God himself who has life in his hands, so if I am killed praises will go to God and you shouldn't cry."[74] The fact that there were individuals who were moved by this level of faith and commitment was a highly significant factor in introducing accountability to Malawian political life. Another significant factor in PAC's effectiveness was found in the international links which it made through its member churches. Emmanuel Chimkwita has drawn attention to one particular meeting: "The meeting of the Public Affairs Committee with the Council of Churches in Britain and Ireland (CCBI) in March 1993 was a very important meeting in the history of Malawi. The Pastoral Letter was really a catalyst but the pivotal event in the process of change was the Swanick meeting when the strategy was formed which guided the PAC in the National Referendum and the General Election."[75] The MCP government seems to have recognised the importance of this meeting at the time since it sent two (uninvited) ministers to present its case and suffered considerable loss of face when the ministerial delegation was turned away from the conference which condemned the resistance of the Malawi Government to democratic change.[76]

As the national referendum of 16 June 1993 approached, it became ever more apparent that the government was fighting a losing battle. Huge crowds flocked to the multi-party rallies while MCP campaign meetings in much of the country were subject to a virtual boycott. Only in its heartlands in the Central Region were traditional MCP tactics successful in retaining substantial support.[77] It was no surprise when the electorate voted for a multi-party system by a two-thirds majority. Significant for the future was the fact that the one third which supported the maintenance of the one-party system was concentrated very largely in the Central Region. In the conscientization process necessary to the achievement of such a result, the churches were prominent. The PAC set up an organisation called PACREM Public Affairs Committee Referendum Monitoring which quickly drew attention to any abuses and gave people the confidence that they could vote

---

[74] *Ibid*.

[75] Rev Emmanuel Chimkwita, interview by Klaus Fiedler, 4 December 1994.

[76] See *Daily Times*, 4 March 1993.

[77] These tactics included the use of poison to eliminate opponents, intimidation by Nyau dancers and the threat that all multi-party supporters would be exterminated after the MCP had won the referendum. G. Chigona, Research Notes on interviews conducted at Madisi, 29-30 November 1994.

freely.[78] When interviewed many people have indicated that it was at church that they learned of the possibility of political reform and began to give their support to the multi-party cause.[79] Particularly influential was a further Pastoral Letter from the Roman Catholic Bishops entitled "Choosing our Future." The Bishops' assessment was that "what people are seeking is genuine democracy in which the leaders are servants of the people who elected them and not their masters, in which leaders are answerable and accountable for their actions to those they lead, a true government of the people; not a government by or for the privileged few."[80] The Letter aimed to be educational, explaining the issue to be decided by the referendum and listing the advantages and disadvantages of both single-party and multi-party systems. While genuinely attempting to be balanced, the Letter was read as a stinging indictment of the injustices of the one-party system. This point was not lost on the government whose newspaper carried this response: "The contents of this letter are clearly advocating a multi-party system of government without considering the dangers that this system can bring to this country.... The Church is instilling FEAR and HATRED in the people. This is done every time people congregate at various churches."[81] With such statements the government itself testified to the telling effect which the churches' witness had in mobilising public opinion and bringing the regime to account. The Catholic Press at Balaka was particularly effective as a publisher of material suitable for education in democracy. It was able to produce small pamphlets which sold for 10 tambala (=US$0.025) and were therefore affordable by ordinary people. These were often composed of short extracts from papal encyclicals or UN declarations but also included some locally written statements.[82]

Officially, the churches restricted themselves to spelling out the principles which should guide people in voting. The gap between Christian principles and MCP rule was so obvious, however, that the church was clearly perceived to be on the side of political reform. With few exceptions the "mainstream churches" had effectively

---

[78] See document entitled "PAC Referendum/Election Monitoring Unit", Public Affairs Committee file, 1992.
[79] See G. Chigona, Research Notes on Political Transition in Malawi, conducted at Ntaja, Mwanza, Dowa and Nkhata Bay, November-December 1994.
[80] "Choosing our Future: Pastoral Letter to the Catholic Faithful on the occasion of the National Referendum 1993", Episcopal Conference of Malawi, 2 February 1993.
[81] *Malawi News*, 6-12 March 1993.
[82] Amongst the pamphlets are the Universal Declaration of Human Rights, the Human and People's Rights Adopted by the Organization of African Unity, extracts from *Centesimus Annus*, quotations from Jon Sobrino on "Political Holiness" a Pastoral Letter by the Diocese of Lilongwe, and anonymous statements on such topics as "What is Democracy?" Balaka: Montfort Press, 1992.

"taken sides" with the multi-party movement.[83] The fact that the MCP government actively provoked confrontation with the churches and with Christian values made such a polarisation inevitable. The surprise pro-multi-party vote in southern Dedza, thought to be an MCP stronghold, has been attributed by Harri Englund to the people's primary loyalty to Christianity and the perception that the MCP was now in conflict with the church and the Christian faith.[84] On the basis of intensive fieldwork in a number of villages Englund notes the points in the MCP pre-referendum rhetoric which most offended the Dedza villagers and drove them into the multi-party camp: "Banda's vassals - party leaders at district, regional and national levels - insisted that people were in the first place Malawians and only secondarily Christians. Therefore, the word of Kamuzu was to be obeyed, if it was contradicted by the clergy's views. The cadres themselves appealed increasingly to Christian imagery: Banda was now referred to as *Mpulumutsi*, the Saviour, and his political mission assumed divine qualities. 'God chose Kamuzu' (*Mulungu anasankha Kamuzu*) was the maxim that outraged southern Dedza villagers the most."[85] In retrospect it is easy to see what a major tactical blunder it was for the MCP to provoke such a confrontation with the Christian beliefs and values of much of the population. To a large extent it was the self-absorption and intransigence of the Banda regime which aroused the latent political protest lying within the Christian faith of the Malawian people so that they rallied around the church in their rejection of the one-party system. In the Dedza context, while a wide range of grievances were noted and discussed, Englund notes that: "Christian idioms and practices were the most pronounced preoccupation on the eve of the referendum."[86]

---

[83] For studies of the 1992-93 period see *Kirche und Gesellschaft in Malawi: Die Krise von 1992 in historischer Perspektive*, Hamburg: EMW Informationen No. 98, February 1993; *Malawi: A Moment of Truth*, London: CIIR, July 1993; T. Cullen, *Malawi: A Turning Point*, Edinburgh: The Pentland Press, 1994; J. Newell, "'A Moment of Truth?' The Church and Political Change in Malawi, 1992" *Journal of Modern African Studies*, Vol. 33 No. 2 (1995), pp. 243-262; J. Newell, "'A Difficult Year for us in Many Respects' Pressure for Change and Government Reaction in Malawi in 1992: An Exercise in Contemporary African History" in J. Hyslop ed., *Democratic Movements in Africa*, forthcoming; J. Newell, "An African Army Under Pressure: The Politicization of the Malawi Army and 'Operation Bwezani', 1992-93", *Small Wars and Insurgencies*, Vol. 6 No.2 (Autumn 1995), pp. 159-182; M.S. Nzunda & K.R. Ross ed., *Church, Law and Political Transition in Malawi 1992-94*, Gweru: Mambo, 1995; K.R. Ross, "Not Catalyst but Ferment: The Distinctive Contribution of the Churches to Political Reform in Malawi 1992-93", in P Gifford ed., *The Christian Churches and Africa's Democratisation*, Leiden: E.J. Brill, 1995, pp. 98-107; J.K. van Donge, "Kamuzu's Legacy: the Democratisation of Malawi. Or Searching for the Rules of the Game in African Politics", *African Affairs*, Vol. 94 (1995), pp. 227-257

[84] H. Englund, "Between God and Kamuzu: The Transition to Multi-Party Politics in Central Malawi" unpublished paper, 1995, pp. 23-37.

[85] *Ibid*, p. 26.

[86] *Ibid*, p 28

The Church as Power-Broker

The victory of the multi-party advocates in the National Referendum of June 1993 led to the legalising of opposition political parties and the promise of a General Election which was finally held on 17 May 1994. In the struggle for legitimacy between government and opposition during this period the churches played an important role as power brokers. By virtue of the fact that they were not seeking political office for themselves church leaders came to exercise a distinctive influence on the unfolding political drama. The MCP government had long been aware of the ideological power of religion in the political realm. Systematically and successfully over many years it had pressed the churches into service to supply it with religious legitimation. Much was made in the party propaganda of the fact that Banda was an elder of the Church of Scotland. Indeed the issue of the *Daily Times* which reviewed the year 1991 singled out as the highlight of the year the "TRIUMPHANT MOMENT" in which Dr Banda had been presented with a scroll to mark the 50th anniversary of his ordination to the eldership.[87] It was a major blow, in the aftermath of the Pastoral Letter, when the Church of Scotland made it clear it no longer regarded Banda as an active elder.[88] The extent to which the government was stung into serious over-reaction at that time is a measure of how much it depended on the unquestioning support of the church. This was further indicated, after almost all churches had rallied behind the work of PAC, by the importance which the government attached to the continuing support of the Nkhoma Synod the Central Region section of the CCAP which had strong historical links with the MCP leadership.[89] As it struggled to retain an air of legitimacy it turned to ministers of the Nkhoma Synod to officiate at government functions and to generally show solidarity with the MCP. This they were willing to do especially during the early referendum period.[90] Belatedly the Nkhoma Synod did seek to draw back from its unqualified support of the MCP government with a statement in April 1993 that "the Synod believes that genuine Christians can support either side of the referendum question without violating the genuine ideals

---

[87] *Daily Times*, 30 December 1991 - most of the front page of this issue is taken up with a colour photograph of Banda receiving the commemorative scroll.

[88] Rev Dr Chris Wigglesworth, General Secretary of the Church of Scotland Board of World Mission and Unity, BBC broadcast, 13 March 1992. Confirmation that there was something phoney about Banda's claims to be a church elder had a very powerful effect among Malawians in undermining his legitimacy at that time.

[89] For the history of the Nkhoma Synod see C.M. Pauw, "Mission and Church in Malawi: The History of the Nkhoma Synod of the Church of Central Africa Presbyterian 1889-1962" D.Th. University of Stellenbosch, 1980.

[90] See, e.g., *Daily Times*, 6 November 1992.

and principles of Christianity."[91] This attempt at "neutrality" did not convince the other churches which saw it simply as an evasion of the demands of the gospel. It did, however, leave the government even more bereft of the church endorsement on which it had depended in the past. In desperation the MCP attempted to supply its own religious legitimation. When it launched its campaign newspaper, the *Guardian Today*, it was striking to note how many articles were devoted to portraying the MCP as having a divine mandate. This was epitomized by a cartoon series on the theme "MCP Points to God!; Multi-Party - Horns of the Devil!"[92] Such desperate propaganda revealed how much the MCP government had depended on the legitimation which it had received from the churches in the preceding years. Once the churches had broken out of that ideological captivity, the MCP government faced a crisis of legitimacy which it was unable to surmount.

On the other hand, the emergent opposition was able constantly to appeal to the prophetic critique of the churches as justification for its political initiative. Indeed, the manifesto of the United Democratic Front, the first to be issued by an opposition party after the referendum, began with a quotation from the Lenten Pastoral Letter and stated that the movement for political reform had been initiated in response to the call from the Catholic Bishops.[93] Occasions such as the Requiem Mass held in May 1993 for four politicians who were widely believed to have been assassinated by government agents ten years earlier, were highly charged politically and very damaging to the credibility of the government.[94] It was no surprise that, when UDF leader Bakili Muluzi made his victory speech after the National Referendum, he went out of his way to thank the churches: "In particular, I would like to single out the seven Catholic Bishops and the [Presbyterian] Blantyre Synod."[95] In a country where the Christian faith is highly esteemed by a large proportion of the population, the legitimacy which the churches bestowed on the opposition movement, in face of government attempts to brand its leaders "dissidents" and "confusionists", was a considerable factor in enabling the forces of change to succeed. At the popular level a significant factor was that many church songs were adapted to give expression to the movement for political liberation. Church choirs are very popular among young people and they took their church music as a medium for expressing a particular political message.

---

[91] *Daily Times*, 30 April 1993.
[92] See, e.g., *Guardian Today*, 19-25 May 1993.
[93] *UDF Manifesto*, July 1993, p. 1.
[94] See *The Monitor*, 18 May 1993. One of the first actions of the newly elected UDF government in June 1994 was to appoint a Commission to investigate the "Mwanza accident." The release of its report, which confirmed suspicions of foul play, in January 1995 led to the immediate arrest of former President Kamuzu Banda and his right hand man John Tembo.
[95] *UDF News*, 17-24 June 1993.

So *Ndiri ndi Bwenzi Langa Yesu* (I have my beloved friend Jesus) became *Ndiri ndi Bwenzi Langa Muluzi* (I have my beloved friend Muluzi - the leader of the UDF).[96] In this way there occurred at the popular level a conflation of Christian belief with the call for political reform. Particularly influential were the songs of Paul Banda and the Alleluya Band, a well-known Malawian pop group. In a powerful song like *Tiyamike Chauta* (Let us praise God) they played on the symbols of the opposing sides in the referendum - the hurricane lamp of the multi-party side and the black cock of the one-party side - to suggest an identification of multi-party with the light of Jesus Christ and of one-party with the darkness of Satan.[97] A notable feature of the ideological struggle was that the opposition began to argue that Rev John Chilembwe, a Baptist pastor, not *Ngwazi* Kamuzu Banda, was the father of Malawian politics.[98] There were good historical grounds for doing so since Chilembwe led an armed rising against British colonial rule in 1915.[99] A popular song during the campaign period, entitled *Kuno Kwathu ku Malawi*, suggested that just as Chilembwe fought against the oppression of the colonialists so Muluzi would fight against the oppression of Dr Banda and the MCP.[100] It was notable that when the new government announced the public holidays for the 1995 calendar, Kamuzu Day was missing and Chilembwe Day had been introduced![101]

For the churches there was a struggle involved in adapting to the new role as power-broker. On the one hand, some church leaders became so involved in the political arena that they eventually left the church ministry in order to devote themselves to politics. From Blantyre Synod Rev Peter Kaleso became Aford Vice-President before later joining the UDF and becoming Ambassador to South Africa.[102] From Livingstonia Synod Aaron Longwe embarked on full-time human rights work with the newly established Foundation for Justice, Peace and the Integrity of Creation.[103] From the Baptist Church Emmanuel Chimkwita became first a shadow cabinet minister and parliamentary candidate then later Ambassador to Mozambique.[104] In each case it had to be made clear that they were acting as politicians in their own right and no longer as representatives of their churches. On

---

[96] G. Chigona, Research conducted at Ntaja, 23 November 1994.
[97] Paul Banda, *Chikondi*, (cassette tape), Andiamo Productions 1993.
[98] See, e.g., *The Monitor*, 28 April to 4 May 1993.
[99] A full account of the rising is found in Shepperson & Price, *Independent African*.
[100] G. Chigona, Research conducted at Ntaja, 24 November 1994.
[101] For discussion of the political importance of the "Chilembwe myth" see K. Fiedler, "Joseph Booth and the Writing of Malawian History", *Religion in Malawi*, No. 6 (1996).
[102] See, e.g., *The New Voice*, 15 March 1994.
[103] See, e.g., *The Democrat*, 29 November-2 December 1993.
[104] See, e.g., *Daily Times*, 19 November 1993.

the other hand, there were those who believed that the churches became too detached from the political process, especially in the post-referendum period. When legislation was being passed in Parliament to establish the National Consultative Council and the National Executive Committee as the bodies which would oversee the transition to a multi-party political system, the Public Affairs Committee declined to be represented and thus left the process of reform entirely in the hands of the political parties.[105] This allowed the government later to claim that PAC was a body which had a role only in the pre-referendum period and which was now obsolete.[106] However, the Christian Council responded by affirming very clearly that "PAC is a relevant body and there is need for its continuity now and after the General Elections. The Church being the Conscience of Society shall continue to play this noble and prophetic role.... The formation of NCC and NEC does not mean the non-existence of PAC. PAC is here to stay for ever in Malawi."[107] In the run-up to the General Election PAC was particularly active in working to avoid the "Kenyan scenario" of a divided opposition allowing the old regime to remain in power.[108] In civic education and election monitoring the churches remained by far the most effective organisation and contributed significantly to the General Election being a very peaceful and highly efficient exercise.[109]

On 17 May 1994 Bakili Muluzi, leader of the UDF, won Malawi's first democratic Presidential election while in the new multi-party Parliament UDF won 85 seats, MCP 56 and AFORD 36. Anastasia Msosa, the Chairperson of the Electoral Commission, commented that: "When you use the church, usually it is very effective. During the elections, if you appealed through the church it produced quick and effective results. The political change was positive in a short time because it came through the church."[110] To many Christians the peaceful transition to democracy was testimony to the power of prayer since, above all, the churches had engaged with the political process by turning to God and calling for divine help and guidance. In terms of the political process, the Public Affairs Committee made the church a significant force as a power broker. Integral to this development was the unity of the various groupings which allowed the PAC

---

[105] Int. T.J. Muwamba, 4 January 1995.
[106] *Daily Times*, 9 November 1993.
[107] Christian Council of Malawi, Press Release, 12 November 1993.
[108] See PAC meetings with Leaders of Different Political Parties, 14 December 1993 and 6 January 1994, Public Affairs Committee files, 1993, 1994.
[109] PACREM was replaced by PACGEM - Public Affairs Committee General Election Monitoring. See Public Affairs Committee file, November 1993.
[110] Anastasia Msosa, Chairperson of the Electoral Commission for 1994 General Election, interview by Isabel Apawo Phiri, 29 December 1994.

Secretary to sign himself in communications with government: "On behalf of the country's Religious Communities I beg to remain, Yours very sincerely, Misanjo E. Kansilanga."

A new kind of power would now be exercised in Malawi. It would be accountable - to the opposition in Parliament, to the free press, to the freedom of expression and freedom of association now enjoyed by the people at large. Would it also be accountable to God? When Bakili Muluzi accepted the office of President he immediately invited the churches to offer correction to his government whenever it might stray from the path.[111] This gave the churches the opportunity to subject the exercise of power in Malawi to the Gospel of Jesus Christ. How would they respond? History suggests that the church's social witness is strongest when there is some great evil to be confronted. Where the church often falters is when the great evil has been defeated and it is time for social and political reconstruction. What role would the churches play in shaping the exercise of power in the new Malawi? Answers to such questions may be sought by examining the prevailing understanding of power within the life of the churches and, especially, by attending to those who have been most excluded from power - the poor, the women, the young people, the prisoners, the Muslims, the Jehovah's Witnesses. To their voices we shall attempt to listen in the pages which follow.

---

[111] *The Nation*, 23 May 1994.

2. The Use of the Bible in Social Transformation

F.L. Chingota

Introduction

Keen observers of the advent of multi-party politics in Malawi could not fail to notice that an appeal to the Bible was central to the argument of proponents of change. The 1992 Lenten Pastoral Letter of the Roman Catholic Bishops, which set ablaze the fire of democratization, was explicitly based on biblical exposition. The key passage which determined the bishops' understanding of the meaning of human life and society is Genesis 1:26f: "Then God said, 'Let us make man in our image' ... in the image of God he created him; male and female he created them."[1] This passage affirms that because men and women carry in themselves the breath of the divine life they are "sacred" and enjoy the personal protection of God. Human life is thus inviolable. Armed with such an interpretation of the biblical passage, the bishops went on to look critically at the economic and political life of Malawian society, pointing out what they thought was against the Word of God. Engagement with the biblical text was therefore, from the beginning, a central feature in the struggle for social and political change in Malawi from 1992. When the CCAP leaders together with the WARC delegation carried forward the movement for change with their open letter to Dr Banda, they based their argument on Proverbs 13:34: "Righteousness exalts a nation but sin is a reproach to any people".[2] In this way the Bible came to be a central text in public discourse concerning the transformation of Malawi. In the ensuing struggle between the advocates of multiparty politics and the defenders of one-party system both sides sought legitimation for their positions from the Bible. Therefore the question which needs to be answered is: What were the predominant biblical power traditions which were used during the transition period?

Definition of Terms

In the Bible, God's power is viewed from six different perspectives: as God's liberating acts; as God's royal rule; as God's empowering wisdom; as God's holy presence; as God's vindication of the poor; and as God's renewing judgement.[3] In the first tradition God is viewed as a man of war who comes to fight with a strong hand against the oppressors of his people. A good example of this is the liberation

---

[1] *Living our Faith*, p. 2.
[2] "The Nation of Malawi in Crisis: The Churches' Concern", 2 June, 1992, p. 2.
[3] I have adopted Hans-Ruedi Weber's classification of biblical power traditions. See H. Weber, *Power: Focus for a Biblical Theology*, Geneva: WCC, 1989, pp. 22f.

of the Israelites from Egypt. Moreover, because the exodus was connected to the making of the covenant at Mt Sinai, the second aspect of God's liberating acts is the power of his steadfast covenant love. There is a third aspect to God's liberating acts and that is the power of his elusive presence.[4] God retains his freedom to come or to go, to speak or to be silent, to intervene or not to intervene. He cannot be controlled by any human being.

In the second royal tradition, God is recognised as a King. However, here on earth he delegates his power to earthly kings who rule on his behalf. Thus earthly rulers are stewards of God's power. However, God remains the ultimate ruler and can overrule the decisions of earthly rulers. In this context there is a reflection on the nature of human authority under God's rule as simply provisional. Jesus was the expected Messiah, the king and yet he died on the cross. The crucifixion of the king underlines a transformation of power.[5]

The wisdom tradition recognises human freedom. People are given the power of choice and that power must be exercised in relation to creation. At the same time it recognises the limitation of human freedom.[6] In the fourth tradition there is a recognition that there is power when God's holiness, sacrifice and forgiveness are made to bear upon human affairs. Moreover the power of prayer and praise of believers is recognized in this tradition.[7] In the fifth tradition God's power is seen through his vindication of the poor who are prepared to suffer passively, and whose laments and praise come before the heavenly Judge.[8] In the sixth tradition God's power shall be seen when this dark period shall be replaced by a brighter one.[9]

Methodology

I used a questionnaire, interviews, newspapers and preached sermons to gather information for this chapter. In the case of the questionnaire, I was assisted by six research assistants, two for each of the three regions. There were 23 questions and some of them required information on: home district, date of birth, gender, type of employment and denomination. Moreover the interviewees were asked to indicate by a tick out of four options how they felt about the situation in Malawi before the referendum and then give reasons for their choice. They were also asked to describe by ticking one of the given options the situation in Malawi before the

---

See Weber, *Power*, pp. 39-42.
Ibid, pp. 57-65.
Ibid, pp. 78-80.
Ibid, pp. 102-107
Ibid, pp. 125-129.
Ibid, pp. 148-156.

referendum and resultant situation after the referendum. The interviewees were asked to indicate whether or not they voted during the referendum and the general election, and whether any biblical passage influenced their decision. They were asked to briefly explain the message contained in the passages.

The Department of Theology and Religious Studies conducted interviews with a number of people who were thought to have played significant roles during the transition. Reports from these interviews were also used. Local newspapers which appeared from 1992 to 1994 were surveyed for references to the Bible. The preached sermons were mostly those delivered at Zomba CCAP congregation during this transition period. A number of secondary sources like books and reports from human rights organizations were used.

The Malawian Situation before the Referendum

The Pastoral Letter of the Roman Catholic bishops was very critical of the socio-economic and political situation in Malawi before the referendum. On the social level, for example, the bishops found fault with the educational and health services in the country. They were particularly critical of the government's policy of requiring that all teachers remain in their own regions. The implementation of this policy meant that a number of teachers from the northern region who were working in southern and central regions had to be 'repatriated' back home, creating thereby a shortage of teachers in many schools. They also expressed their displeasure at the criteria used in selection of pupils for secondary school and third-level institutions. They called for a government-church partnership in education. The health services were also found lacking in many ways: overcrowding and lack of personnel, and particularly inequality in medical treatment. Regarding the economic situation the bishops pointed out the inequality in the distribution of resources resulting in a growing gap between the rich and the poor. The wages of workers were noted to be very inadequate and there was injustice in the prices paid to producers. On the political level the bishops noted that there was little participation of people in the decision making process in the country. There was no freedom of expression and association. Furthermore, the judicial system left a lot to be desired. Cases were not justly tried resulting in imprisonments of many Malawians without proper trial.

The foregoing is a description of the Malawian situation as the bishops saw it. The question is: Did every Malawian see the situation in the same way the bishops did? A questionnaire was given to 351 people representing the following denominations: Presbyterian, Roman Catholic, Anglican, Assemblies of God, Seventh Day Adventist, Church of Christ, Church of the Nazarene, Jehovah's Witnesses, Bible

Believers, Living Waters, Christadelphian, Last Church of God and His Christ, Good News Revival, Apostles of John, Oasis of Life, Blackman's Church, Apostolic Faith, New Apostolic Faith, United Apostolic Faith, United Pentecostal Church, Baptist Church, Zambezi Evangelical Church, Lutheran Church, Way of the Truth, Ethiopian Church, and Zionist Church. Most of the respondents were Presbyterians and Roman Catholics who represent more than half of the Christians in Malawi. They were asked to tell how they felt about the situation in Malawi before the referendum. 183 respondents said they were 'concerned' with the situation, 35 said they were 'not concerned', 67 said they were 'indifferent', and 66 said they were 'satisfied' with the situation.

The majority of the respondents expressed concern with the situation in Malawi before the referendum. The causes of concern included detention without trial, harassment by MYP, lack of freedom of expression, being forced to buy party membership cards (even for unborn child), lack of freedom of worship, abuse of human rights, the government was dictatorial, inequality in the distribution of wealth, people fed to crocodiles, people forced to attend party functions (even when sick), farm produce by small farmers were bought at low prices, university selection was unfair, forced to pay taxes, women forced to dance for the leadership, women were forced to join CCAM, forced to pay school fees, killings by political leaders of those who opposed them, development was regionalistic, forced to contribute money as gifts.

If ten areas of concern can be picked up and arranged according to the number of respondents then the list will be as follows: lack of freedom of expression (70), people forced to buy party membership cards (38), people forced to attend political functions (25), harassment by members of Malawi Young Pioneers and members of Youth league (22), detention without trial (17), lack of freedom of worship (12), abuse of human rights (11), government being dictatorial (11), people forced to pay taxes (9), and people forced to give gifts for the president (9). The people's greatest area of concern regarding the situation in Malawi before the referendum was political.

It is significant to note at this point that Dr Banda touched at almost all the areas of concern in his July 5, 1992 address to the nation of Malawi and in each case he tried to defend himself.[10] For example on the question of freedom of expression he maintained that there was freedom of expression in Malawi citing the existence of some small publications.[11] Dr Banda acknowledged that there had been harassment

---

[10] "An Address to the Nation by His Excellency The Life President, Dr H Kamuzu Banda of the Republic of Malawi" 5 July, 1992, published by the Ministry of Information and Tourism.
[11] There were in circulation publications such as *Moni* magazine and the *Financial Post*.

of people by members of Youth League for Party membership cards. He also conceded the fact that gifts were forcibly collected for him. However, he argued that these unacceptable acts were done by thieves, hooligans and dissidents who disguised themselves as members of Youth League. Detention without trial was explained as being due to local political realities and national security consideration. He argued that in a situation of political strife, tribal violence and civil unrest consideration and specific precautions for national security were unavoidable. On the question of human rights Dr Banda argued that the fact that refugees from Mozambique were well looked after in Malawi was an indication of Malawi's observation of human rights. He maintained that the government was not dictatorial. This was evidenced by the way the 1992 Parliamentary elections were conducted.[12] The question of freedom of worship was argued for in the *Guardian Today* of 12-18 May 1993. It was argued in the paper that Dr Banda, being a God-fearing man who fought for the country's freedom and independence, allowed freedom of worship. However, according to the writer of that article, freedom of worship should not mean preaching politics in the pulpits.[13]

In spite of attempts to clarify the situation, the fact remains that the people's greatest area of concern regarding the situation in Malawi before the referendum was political. This is in fact borne out by those who indicated that they were satisfied with the situation. The reasons given were the following:

there was security	47
commodities were cheap	22
commodities like sugar were available	10
people lived in harmony	10
there was enough money	8
freedom of worship	5
there was price control	3
commercial business was booming	2
there was medicine in the hospitals	1
education was at its peak with trained teachers	1

---

[12] In the Parliamentary election 78 out of 136 MPs were new and amongst those who lost their parliamentary seats were a cabinet minister, four deputy ministers, one Deputy Speaker, and a chairman of Public Accounts Committee.

[13] In fact, in the *Malawi News* of 14-20 March 1992 there was an article in Chichewa entitled "Refutation of Bishops Pastoral Letter" The article gave a summary of the decision of the MCP meeting in Lilongwe which discussed the Pastoral Letter, saying "delegates to the meeting condemned in the strongest terms the practice by the Bishops to introduce politics into the Roman Catholic Church. They have turned the pulpit which was set apart for the proclamation of the Word of God into a place where seeds of confusion are sown"

The high number of respondents on the item of security can be seen as a reflection of the problems which accompany any transition. Moreover, heavy security can also be seen as a factor which contributed to the lack of freedom of expression. Thus if that item can be put aside then our table clearly indicates that the economic situation in Malawi before the referendum was seen by most Malawians as better than it is today. However the respondents to the questionnaire described the situation in Malawi before the referendum as:

a period when there was peace and calm	105
a period of darkness	72
slavery	70
a period when people felt totally powerless	38
a period of open abuse of power by political leaders	38
a period of political manipulation of religion	10
a period when God was blessing this country	7
a period when God appeared distant from man	4

The experience of many people before the referendum was not satisfactory. They experienced it as a period of darkness. Others regarded it as a period of slavery, a period during which there was an open abuse of power by political leaders and the people felt completely powerless. It was a period when there was political manipulation of religion such that some felt that God was far away from them.

The Bible and the Movement for Change

In the light of the fact that 67.4% of the respondents indicated that they were not satisfied with the situation in Malawi before the referendum, it is proper to ask whether everyone wanted change. When asked whether there was any need to change the system of government from the one party system to multi-party system of government, 280 answered positively, 49 answered negatively while 12 were undecided.

Those who wanted a change of the system of government gave the following biblical passages which can be grouped together under the following themes: a) human beings are made in God's image (Gen 1:27) therefore human life must be protected. b) The then rulers were disobedient to God (1 Kings 11:11; Prov 28:21; Dan 3:1-10; Matt 27:21; Lk 4:7-8; 18:19; 19:43f; 1 Pet 3:10-11). c) There was a need for people to be delivered from oppressive rulers (Exod 3:8; 12:37-42; 18:4-8; 20:3-13; 23:15; Deut 16:1-6; 1 Kings 12:1-11; 2 Kings 9; 2 Chron 32:15; Ezra 3; Job 36:15; Ps 119:153; Prov 17:1; 18:5,21; Eccl 8:9; Is 1:17; 46:11-17; 51; 56:1; Jer 34:8-22; Ezek 13:10; Zech 8:16-18; Lk 1:46-55; Eph 6:9; 1 Thess 5:3; Titus 2:11). d) There was need to change leadership (1 Sam 8:1-16:12; 1 Kings 2;

Dan 2:37-47). e) The people have the right of choice (Jos 24:15; Job 34:4; Matt 7:7). f) Multiparty form of government is good (Eccl 4:7-10). g) There is time for change (Eccl 3:1-18). h) There were already signs of a new age (Matt. 24:3-8).

Messages calling for a change of the political system were delivered even during church worship services. At Zomba CCAP Church, for example a message based on Gen 9:1-7 was delivered on 8 November 1992 by the Rev Dr Felix Chingota. In his address he argued that the responsibility for the preservation of the world is a shared responsibility. In this light he called for referendum, arguing that it would allow a shared responsibility. Dr Chingota touched also on the trial of Chakufwa Chihana and argued it was a trial of Malawian laws to see whether they were meant to preserve life or not rather than a trial of Chihana. Referendum would allow a shared responsibility because, according to Gen 2:15-3:13, human beings were created free and responsible.[14] Therefore Malawians should use their God-given freedom to extract themselves from the bondage of one party system and choose a political system that would guarantee freedom of choice, participation in decision-making by the majority of the population, and accountability. Further criticism of MCP's economic administration of the country especially with regard to labour relationship on tobacco estates was made by the Rev Mezuwa Banda in a sermon which was delivered in Zomba CCAP congregation on 13 December 1992. Basing his message on Isaiah 8:21-9:7 and John 1:1-18, Rev Banda argued that tenants on tobacco estates lived in abject poverty (darkness) contrary to the MCP political slogan of *kwacha* meaning 'dawn.'[15]

Mention must perhaps be made here of those people who though desirous of political change did not see it coming through political involvement. Good examples of these are Pastor Masoka of the Seventh Day Adventist Church and C.B. Phiri of the Church of Christ. Pastor Masoka's attitude to politics was

---

[14] This passage formed the basis of a sermon which was preached by Rev Dr F.L. Chingota in Zomba CCAP congregation on 21 January, 1993.

[15] Because of this sermon the Rev Mezuwa Banda was called for questioning at the Police Eastern Division. Summoned also for questioning were elders of the congregation and Rev Dr Chingota who was at the time the care-taker minister for the congregation because the then minister-in-charge, the Rev G.C. Kazembe had just retired and the new minister for the congregation, Rev R.G. Chimowa had not yet arrived. In fact on the day Rev R.G. Chimowa was inducted into the Zomba congregation a message was delivered by Dr Chingota (Lecturer at Chancellor College and Moderator of Zomba Presbytery) based on Mark 1:1-13 on the theme of "The Ministry of the Church" He said that as Jesus Christ identified himself with sinners in his baptism so it is the duty of the Church to speak on behalf of the oppressed. Such ministry can lead the church, guided by the Spirit, into conflict with forces of evil as Jesus Christ was led into the wilderness to be tried by Satan.

expressed in the *New Express* of 11-17 June 1993. In an interview with Felix Mponda, Pastor Masoka said that the SDA Church follows the counsel of Jesus Christ who said that his Kingdom was not of this world. However, the SDA Church recognises that liberty is a gift to human beings from the Creator. The Church emphasises that foremost amongst blessings granted to all mankind is the right to religious liberty, that is, the right to worship God according to the dictates of each individual's conscience as long as he does not infringe upon the rights of others. Political changes, according to Pastor Masoka, fall within the fulfilment of prophecy.[16] According to Pastor Masoka the spheres of Government and the Church are separate. If the government trespasses upon the sphere of the Church then the latter must respond by waiting upon the Lord in prayer who will intervene in his own good time rather than by direct political involvement.

Similar sentiments were expressed by C.B. Phiri of Church of Christ.[17] He maintained that, according to Rom 13:1, citizens of a country are enjoined to be submissive to earthly rulers for even Jesus recognised the power of a judge (John 19:11). The Church has its own particular role to play in society and that is to preach the Gospel (Matt 28:18f; Mk 16:15f), to make people repent of their sins and to direct them to Jesus Christ and not to direct their attention to the forthcoming national referendum because even God did not like his people to have earthly kings (1 Sam 8:4-7, 10-19). However, argued Phiri, if the rule of the earthly kingdom conflicts with worship of the Church in such a way that Christians are prevented from attending Sunday service, then Christians are taught by the Bible to obey God rather than men (1 Pet 4:12-16), to resist any temptation to worship man (Acts 5:28f.) and to passively endure persecution. It is up to God to judge and God will reward and punish accordingly. It must be noted that for Phiri the MCP government had not infringed upon the rights of the Church. There was no persecution of the faithful. Therefore there was no need for a change of system of government.[18] However, to the extent that Phiri's ideas could lead to a point where one may wish a change of government then the article can be regarded

---

[16] This is perhaps with reference to the book of Daniel, an apocalyptic book which teaches that the Kingdom of God shall be established by the intervention of God alone. This view was clearly spelt out by Pastor Masoka in a statement which appeared in the *New Voice* newspaper of 29 November-5 December 1993, in which he said that the SDA Church believes that all nations and the inhabitants therein are a creation of God. Therefore God rules over all nations as the only sovereign Lord. He is the only source of all authority, be it dominions or authorities (Colossians 1:16-17). God sets up kings and dethrones them at his appointed times. Therefore all authority exercised by government is derived from God.

[17] The title of his article which appeared in the *Guardian Today* of 21-27 April 1993 is "True Servants of God should not be involved in politics"

[18] One wonders whether Mr C.B. Phiri knew about the persecution of Jehovah's Witnesses? See chapter 6.

as falling between the camp which advocated change of political system and the other which did not see any need for that.

Those who did not see any need for a change of system of government gave the following passages which can again be grouped under the following themes: a) the then leadership of the country was anointed and therefore to seek change was really to conspire and rebel against God (Ps 2:1-3). b) During this period there was harmony (Ps 133:1; Prov 16:7; Matt 5:9). c) People should therefore be submissive to the anointed leadership (Prov 1:1; Eccl 4:5; Rom 13:1; Titus 3:1-2). d) The advocates of change were motivated by hate which was without justifiable reason (John 15:25). Similarly there were messages which were delivered by pastors during Sunday worship urging Christians not to change the system of government. For example it was noted during an interview conducted by G. Chigona that pastors from Nkhoma Synod of the Church of Central Africa Presbyterian would very often admonish people to vote against any sort of political change.[19] On the basis of Mark 9:7 the pastors would pronounce the Banda regime to be ordained of God. In the Central Region district of Dowa suspected multiparty sympathisers were excommunicated from church membership. One way of ensuring the continuation of the political system was by arguing that religious leaders have nothing to do with political matters, the two are incompatible. This was made clear in the *Malawi News* of 5-11 December 1992 in which a clergyman was made to say 'I am not a politician, I am a man of God and the two are rarely mixed' Moreover the Pastoral Letter was dubbed as work of the devil who scatters and turns peaceful atmosphere into pandemonium. Furthermore, it was argued in the *Malawi News* of 23-29 May 1992, that the Christian religion supports the one-party system. It was claimed that just as in the 1961 general election the opposition parties were effectively defeated so too in heaven in a collective vote Satan was thrown out of the heavenly council.[20]

Faith and Voting

When the time came for voting in the referendum, 268 people did exercise their right to vote but 71 failed to do so. The important question is whether the decision

---

[19] G. Chigona, Research Notes on Interviews conducted at Madisi, 29-30 November 1994. It is significant to note that Nkhoma Synod was not a signatory to the letter of 2 June 1992 written to the then Life President, Dr Banda, by the delegation from WARC and leaders of the Presbyterian Church, a letter which called for a change of the political system. Moreover, Rev Maseko of Nkhoma Synod was forced to withdraw his name from a letter written by the Christian Council of Malawi, a letter which he co-signed, and in which the Council called for a change of political system.

[20] This was perhaps in reference to the passage in Isaiah 14:12-15.

to vote or not to vote was based on religious conviction. On this issue, 133 said they were not influenced by the Bible and 226 said they were; and, of these, 207 gave specific passages which influenced their decision. Amongst those who voted because of religion there were those who wanted the *status quo* to remain and there were those who voted because they wanted change. The latter gave the following as their reasons for wanting change: a) human beings are created in God's image (Gen 1:26-27; Col 1:16). b) The situation was oppressive (Exod 20; Num 11:16-20; Dt 5:6f; 1 Sam 15:35; Prov 13:3; 18:5; Eccl 5:8; Is 1:7; 61:1-3; Jer 34:8-22; Ezek 13:10; Lk 4:7f; Eph 6:9; 1 Thess 5:3). c) They hungered for righteousness (Matt 5:6; 7:7-8; John 8:32), deliverance from oppression (Is 41:1-4, 8-10; 43:1-5; 61:1-3; Matt 24:1-14), and change of leadership (1 Sam 15:35; Dan 2:44; Acts 1:1-26). There were also those who voted because they wanted to exercise their democratic right (Jos 24:15; 1 Sam 8:4-9; Job 34:4; Matt 27; Lk 2:1-7; 20:25). Amongst those who did not vote some acknowledged the need for a change of leadership but said that such change can be done by God alone (1 Sam 16:11-12; Is 47:1-15; Dan 2:1-44; 1 Thess 5:3; 2 Tim 3:1-9). Others did not vote because they believed that politics and church are not mates (1 Tim 4:1; James 4:4; 1 John 2:15-17). The results of this referendum was that those who wanted the introduction of multiparty system of government won.

During the transitional period the people of Malawi were asked to vote twice, in a referendum and in a general election. In the first vote the people were asked to choose between two forms of government and in the second vote they were asked to choose rulers. The second can surely be regarded as party politics. In this light it is possible for one to vote in the referendum and to refrain from voting in the general election. On this issue respondents can be divided into groups: the first group is of those who voted in the referendum and in the general election; the second group consist of those who voted in the referendum but did not vote in the general election; the third group comprises those who did not vote in the referendum but voted in the general election; and the fourth group consists of those who voted neither in the referendum nor in the general election. The following are reasons which those who voted on both occasions gave: 1) to exercise the right to vote 2) in order to change government and leadership 3) in order to have good chances of employment 4) in order to have freedom of expression 5) in order to have real democracy 6) in order that those who were mistreating others should also experience pain, 7) in order to retain the one party system of government.

There are two reasons on which I wish to make a few comments. The first one is reason number (6). This was the reason which was given by a member of Jehovah's Witnesses. The Jehovah's Witnesses suffered a lot during the MCP rule. In reason number (6) we have a spirit of vengeance. However, let it be pointed out that not all members of Jehovah's Witnesses feel the same. Another member of the Jehovah's Witnesses said that they are not interested in vengeance because they know that those who persecuted them did so in ignorance, they did not know what they were doing. They should be forgiven. Another reason which I wish to comment on is reason number (7). It was impossible to retain the one party system after the results of the referendum indicated victory for the advocates of multiparty system of government. Perhaps those who gave this reason (and they were three) wanted to say that they wanted MCP to remain in power in a multiparty government.

Those who voted in the referendum but failed to vote in the general election gave the following reasons: 1) immaturity of the opposition leaders, 2) wanted one party system of government, 3) wasn't decided, 4) was not interested, 5) had nobody in mind, 6) was not partisan. Those who failed to vote in both the referendum and the general elections gave the following reasons: 1) was not concerned, 2) obey the government in power, 3) confused by promises, 4) had no problems with MCP, 5) was afraid of MCP harassment, 6) non-partisan 7) church does not allow, 8) was undecided. Those who voted in the general elections only gave the following reasons: 1) wanted the MCP to remain in power, 2) to exercise the right to vote, 3) wanted change, 4) wanted a good leader, 5) wanted bright future. A number of members of Jehovah's Witnessess and an SDA Pastor did not vote because their denominations are non-partisan.

Perspectives on Power

Hans-Ruedi Weber has noted six traditions of power in the Bible: i) God's liberating acts, ii) God's royal rule, iii) God's empowering wisdom, iv) God's holy presence, v) God's vindication of the poor, and vi) God's renewing judgement. In the questionnaire I gave the following alternatives regarding the factors which were determinative in the political change: a) the power of God, b) the determination of leaders of multi-party advocates, c) people's determination, d) prayers of religious men and women, e) cunningness of leaders of multi-party advocates, e) power of Satan, f) evil deeds of leaders of single-party advocates.

The answers of the respondents can be tabulated as follows:

power of God	101
of leaders of multiparty advocates	72
people's determination	59
evil deeds of leaders of single-party advocates	53
prayers of religious men and women	27
cunningness of leaders of multiparty advocates	15
power of Satan	11

If we take the first five factors and relate them to Weber's classification of traditions of power in the Bible then we can say that Weber's (i) corresponds to 'power of God' in the table. In this respect, it is worth noting how pervasive is liberation theology even at grassroot level. Weber's (ii) corresponds to 'the determination of the leaders of multiparty advocates' and to 'the evil deeds of leaders of single-party advocates' This reflects the view that God works through chosen leaders and that the welfare of society is dependent upon the extent to which leaders regard themselves as stewards of God's authority and therefore as accountable to him. 'People's determination' corresponds to Weber's (iii), that is, God's empowering wisdom. R.E. Murphy has defined wisdom thinking as 'an approach to life which is shared by all Israelites in varying degrees.'[21] The important point here is that wisdom is not necessarily a prerogative of an elite group, but is essentially a popular endeavour. Wisdom tradition was also aware of human limitations, that there are areas in which man cannot tread. Hence the slogan 'The fear of the Lord is the beginning of wisdom' It is only in the recognition of human limitation that one gets wisdom. Lastly Weber's (iv) and (v) correspond to 'prayers of religious men and women' Power is here seen as effected through worship or through men and women who passively endured the suffering caused by ruthless rulers.

This analysis of power can also be looked at from the point of view of the texts which influenced the respondents to vote and the texts which were used in sermons. Those who wanted a change of the system of government and voted in the referendum cited texts from the Pentateuch,[22] the history books,[23] the prophetic books,[24] and from the writings section.[25] 31 respondents cited texts from the Pentateuch, 22 cited texts from the history books, 15 cited texts from the prophetic literature, and 58 respondents cited texts from the writings section. From sermons it was found out that texts were used from the Pentateuch (Gen 2:15-3:19; 9:1-7; Exod 32:1-35; Num 9:15-23; Dt 4:1-14; 17:14-20 - all were cited by one preacher; Dt 30:11-20 - was used as a text on a Sunday a week before the referendum in all Blantyre Synod congregations), from the prophetic books (Is 9:1-7 - was used by one preacher) and from the writings (Prov 14:34; Neh 1:1-11; Dan 5:1-31 used by one preacher respectively). From newspapers and other documents one finds that texts from the Pentateuch (Gen 1:26f; Exod 3:3-7; 14:1-

---

[21] R.E. Murphy, *Wisdom Literature*, Grand Rapids: Eerdmans, 1981, p. 3.
[22] Gen 1:26-7; Exod 3:8; 12:37-42; 18:4-8; 20:3-13; 23:15; Num 11:16-20; Deut 5:6f. 16:1-6.
[23] Jos 24:15; 1 Sam 8:1-16:12; 1 Kings 2; 11:11; 12:1-11; 2 Kings 9.
[24] Is 1:7, 17; 41:1-4, 8-10; 43:1-5; 46:11-17; 47:1-15; 51; 56:1; 61:1-3; Jer 34:8-22; Ezek 13:10; Zech 8:16-18.
[25] Job 34:4; 36:15; Ps 119:153; Prov 13:3; 17:1; 18:5,21 28:21;, Eccl 3:1-18; 4:7-10; 5:8; 8:9; Dan 2:1-47; 3:1-10, Ezra 3; 2 Chr 32:15.

14) were cited by ten writers, from history books (1 Sam 13) was cited by one person, from the prophetic books (Is 1:15-17; Amos 5:24) were cited in two documents, and from the writings (Prov 14:34 and Ps 127:1) were cited in two documents. If we add up the figures it will be noticed that 43 people used texts from the Pentateuch, 23 used texts from the history books, 18 used texts from the prophetic books, and 63 used texts from the writings section of the Old Testament. The breakdown of books in the writings section according to users is as follows: Dan 2:37-47 (6 respondents); 3:1-10 (1); 5:1-31 (1); Ezra (1); Neh 1:1-11 (1); Ps 119:153 (1); 127:1 (1); Eccl 3:1-18 (1); 4:7f (2); 5:8 (1); 8:9 (4); Job 34:4 (16); 36:1 (1); Prov 14:34 (2); 17:1 (1); 18:5 (1); 28:21 (2), 2 Chr 32:15 (1). Clearly the section of the Old Testament which was used the most is the Writings section and two points might be noted here. First, in this section Job 34:4 was cited by most people. Job is part of the wisdom literature of the Old Testament. The number of people who cited texts from the wisdom literature is 56. This is more than the users of the Pentateuch.

The text of Job 34:4 which was used the most reads: "Let us discern for ourselves what is right; let us learn together what is good." This text was mostly used to support an individual's right to vote. This underlines the importance of popular power in determining the results of the elections. Second, texts from the book of Daniel are the ones which were favourites. Daniel is part of the apocalyptic literature. In the book of Daniel one of the most important themes is God's intervention on behalf of the poor faithful people who passively endured the persecution of the Seleucid king Antiochus Epiphanes.

The second section of the Old Testament which was cited most is the Pentateuch section. D.J.A. Clines has described the main theme of the Pentateuch as a partial fulfilment of God's threefold promise of progeny, relationship between God and Israel, and land which was given to Abraham.[26] It is a movement forward or eschatology. Abraham is called by God to leave his native land and go to a place which God would show him. Later on his descendants were called to leave the oppressive land of Egypt to go to a land of promise. This is Exodus and thus Exodus or liberation can be said to be the main theme of the Pentateuch.

The third most important section of the Old Testament which was used is the history section. Gerhard von Rad has argued that the history of the Israelites covered in Judges to 2 Kings especially in the books of kings is the history of kings.[27] The welfare or the curse of the nation was dependent upon whether or not the king was obedient to the Mosaic law. From this analysis of the texts which

---

[26] D.J.A. Clines, *The Theme of the Pentateuch*, Sheffield: JSOT, 1978, p. 29.

[27] G. von Rad, *Old Testament Theology*, Vol. 1, ET, London: SCM, 1975, p. 344.

were used in the transition period it can be seen that the power traditions can be arranged in terms of priority as follows: first God's empowering wisdom tradition, second, God's liberating acts, third, God's royal rule, fourth, God's holy presence.

The results of the textual analysis differ somewhat from those gathered from answers to the question regarding the factors which determined the result of the elections. Whereas in the latter case the power tradition of God's liberating acts was rated as first, in the former analysis it is the power tradition of God's empowering wisdom which is rated as first. Perhaps there is no need here to choose between the two, rather we should see both as significant. This observation is supported by the answers given to the question 'How would you describe the results of the referendum?' The answers to this question can be tabulated as follows:

liberation from slavery	81
disastrous for the country	81
empowerment of ordinary people	73
dawning of a new age	39
victory for religion	32
judgment on those who abuse power	21
victory for Satan	13

Those who regarded the results of the referendum positively singled out 'liberation from slavery' and 'empowerment of ordinary people' as the two main results of the referendum. On the face of it this description of the results of the referendum may appear to be inappropriate given the fact that the majority of the people who were dissatisfied with the situation in Malawi before the referendum described the situation as a period of darkness. If the period before the referendum could be described as a period of darkness then the results of the referendum ought to be described as dawning of a new age. However, only 37 respondents saw the results of the referendum in this way. The difficulty can perhaps be resolved by interpreting 'darkness' symbolically. Darkness can be used to describe a state of anxiety and hopelessness. The state of the Israelites in the Babylonian captivity is described in this way (Dt 28:65-67). Moreover in the creation story found in the book of Genesis which was written in the exilic period the words 'without form and void', and 'darkness' (Gen 1:2) should be taken as descriptive of the life and faith of the Israelites during the Babylonian captivity. If the 'period of darkness' can be interpreted in this way then the phrase has the same sense as 'period of slavery' or 'period when people were powerless.' One is reminded here of the way the Rev M. Banda used the text of Is 9:1-7 where darkness is contrasted with light. Rev Banda applied the theme of darkness to describe the status of tenants on tobacco estates. For him the life of the tenants was one of misery and servitude which could only be described as 'darkness'

The question which now needs to be answered is: How relevant are the two power traditions of 'God's liberating acts' and 'God's empowering wisdom' to the Malawi's transition period (1992-1994) or even before and after? Let me look at each one of them in turns.

God's Liberating Acts

According to Weber, this power tradition has three main aspects: the power of Yahweh's holy war; the power of the steadfast covenant love; the power of God's elusive presence. The first aspect emphasises the point that victory is due to God only. There is a recognition here that there are hurdles which can be overcome by God alone. Kamlepo Kalua, president of Malawi Democratic Party (MDP) would agree to this. Answering a question from Klaus Fiedler in an interview[28] he said that the road to transition was not an easy one. It was possible only through the power of God and the Holy Spirit. Chipiliro Daza[29] and Nyokase Madise[30] echoed the same sentiments when said that the people were very fearful during the transition because they were not certain whether the multiparty advocates would win. What was needed in the transition according to Peter Kaleso[31] was 'to loosen the grip which Dr Banda had on the people.' The political muscle of the MCP was exercised through the Malawi Young Pioneers, a para-military wing of the Malawi Congress Party. It was a big hurdle to break that muscle.[32] The hurdle was broken by the Malawi Army through an action commonly known as 'Operation Bwezani.'[33] The military action can rightly be described as divine intervention to

---

[28] Int. by K. Fiedler, 1995.
[29] Int. by I.A. Phiri, 3 February 1995.
[30] Int. by I.A. Phiri, 4 January 1995.
[31] Int. by K.R. Ross, 10 April 1995.
[32] It must be noted that the members of the MYP were protected by a presidential decree to the effect that no member of the MYP could be arrested by the police without the consent of the president. In fact, on 10 November 1965, speaking in the Legislative Assembly, Dr Banda said: "The Young Pioneers cannot be arrested without my consent. If a Young Pioneer arrests anybody and brings them to the police station, the police officer in charge of that station must not release them. If he does release them, he is committing a crime. *Where Silence Rules: The Suppression of Dissent in Malawi*, An Africa Watch Report, Oct 1990, p. 15. Thus the members of MYP enjoyed a form of immunity from prosecution if ever they committed any act of lawlessness. During the transition period they committed many crimes and any call from the public and the Public Affairs Committee to the government to disarm them fell on deaf ears.
[33] For a theological reflection upon "Operation Bwezani" see J. Tengatenga, "Operation Bwezani: a Theological Response" in M.S. Nzunda & K.R. Ross ed., *Church, Law and Political Transition*

liberate a powerless people from the grip of a dictatorial leadership. It was a miracle for the whole affair was ignited by such a small matter as a brawl between a soldier and a member of MYP at a beer hall. No one expected that such an incident would take on national proportions.

The second aspect of God's liberating acts which is worth pondering about is 'the power of God's elusive presence.' This aspect emphasises that God cannot be domesticated. The Malawian churches have been accused of keeping silent in the face of gross abuses of human rights by politicians. Giving a summary of the church relationship with the state Rev Aaron Longwe[34] noted that in the early years of Malawian church history the church was controlling the political life of the country. During the colonial period the church played a very important role preparing the local leadership such as Levi Mumba. Leaders of the Nyasaland African Congress which was started in 1944 were people who had been to mission schools. In fact it can be said that from 1874 to 1964 when Malawi gained its independence, the churches were in the forefront fighting for justice. From 1964 the church became more and more politicised, it compromised its prophetic ministry.

The point Longwe was making was also echoed by Simeza in an article 'The Church and State in Malawi.'[35] He has noted some of the subtle ways through which the church was politicised. He notes firstly that the holders of high offices in the MCP were prominent members of the church and the president even presided over major ecumenical functions. Secondly the president insisted on saying that the role of the church was in the spiritual realm whereas it was the duty of the state to look to the physical well being of the nation. The aim was to give the MCP a free hand in its daily abuse of people's God-given rights, oppression, exploitation of the voiceless poor, mismanagement of the country's resources, corruption, thuggery, victimization, nepotism, tribalism and other corrupt practices. Thirdly, the government tried to divide the church. It supported the big orthodox churches while grudgingly tolerating the smaller and more fundamentalist ones. One consequence of this marginalization was the setting on fire of the doors of Christian churches by a Muslim zealot. The other consequence of this discrimination was that when the members of the Jehovah's Witnesses were being persecuted by the state for not buying MCP membership cards, the churches stayed mute.

---

in Malawi 1992-94, Gweru: Mambo, 1995, pp. 101-109. *Bwezani* means "return", thus the purpose of the military operation was to disarm the MYP
[34] Int. by K. Fiedler, 3 December 1994.
[35] *The Monitor*, 20 May 1993.

The accusation has been accepted by Blantyre Synod of the CCAP. In a statement issued by a conference of church administrators which was held on 22-23 January 1993 it was said:

> If we look at our own history as the CCAP during the time of the struggle, we will see that Blantyre Synod was very much in support of the Nyasaland African Congress (later called MCP).... Because of this verbal stance on the side of MCP, after independence, the CCAP was aligned closely with the government and became so assimilated that the Synod gradually lost its ability to admonish or speak pastorally to the government.[36]

It is certainly correct to say that the church as an organisation stayed mute during the one party period. However there were people who raised lonely voices of criticism. K.R. Ross has cited the example of Blantyre Synod ministers such as Jonathan Sangaya, Saindi Chiphangwi, Peter Kaleso, and Silas Ncozana.[37] Except for Kaleso the other three were at different times General Secretaries of Blantyre Synod. Prophetic voice was also heard from Pastor Masoka of the Seventh Day Adventist Church. Pastor Masoka used to be invited to preach at national services of worship during Independence celebrations. He claimed that he felt much safer to preach according to the dictates of his conscience in the presence of the head of state, Dr Banda.[38]

During the one party period the church needed to recover the power of God's liberating acts. The church ought to have resisted any attempt at being domesticated or politicised. K.R. Ross has argued that according to Presbyterian theology, inspired by Calvinism, civil society must be seen as the larger outer circle of two concentric circles the inner of which represents the Christian church.[39] Both of these circles have as their hub Jesus Christ and the proclaimed kingdom of God. In this light political activity is subject to criticism and reform in the light of the criteria supplied by the Word of God. Thus the faith has socio-economic and political implications and the church cannot but be involved in politics. Political organization is such an important activity affecting human destinies that it can not be left to politicians alone. Moreover, no political order can be regarded as absolute, rather it remains provisional. While restricting and relativising political activities Presbyterian theology also recognises that political order has divine mandate and mission.

---

[36] "A Statement on the Role of the Church in the Transformation of Malawi in the Context of Justice and Peace", Administrators Conference, Blantyre Synod CCAP, 22-23 January 1993, p. 4.
[37] K.R. Ross, "Where were the Prophets and Martyrs in Banda's Malawi? Four Presbyterian Ministers", Faith and Knowledge Seminar No. 41, Chancellor College, 1 February 1996.
[38] Int. by K. Fiedler, 12 January 1995.
[39] K.R. Ross, *Gospel Ferment in Malawi: Theological Essays*, Gweru: Mambo, 1995, pp. 31-48.

The fact that political activities must be restricted has recently been recognised by many Malawians. For example Marble Ngalande, writing from United States of America, emphatically said that God is the only divine ruler.[40] She noted that yet for 30 years Malawians had associated the then head of state with the divine ruler saying that he was our saviour. In a similar vein certain concerned Christians questioned whether there was another Messiah other than Jesus Christ.[41]

The issue that faith has social-economic and political implication was discussed by Orison Chaponda in his article 'What right has the church to intervene in politics.'[42] Chaponda preferred to discuss the issue using Matt 22:15-22, a passage which he contends has been misinterpreted by those who argue that the church should not be involved in politics. For Chaponda, the text has two purposes, firstly to expose the Pharisees' lack of sincerity. They asked Jesus whether it was right to pay tax when they themselves were benefiting from the Roman rule as evidenced by having a coin in their possession. Secondly, Chaponda maintains that Matthew did stress that the loyalty we owe to God should never be overlooked (vv.21f) as it has profound political implication. Even Rom 13:1-7 should be read in the light of Acts 5:30 where, in a context of unavoidable conflict with civil authorities, both Paul and Peter insisted that obedience to God comes before obedience to men.

For Fr. Gamba, the Matthean text is a rejection of the enthusiasm that seeks to elevate the kingdom of God into a political programme.[43] The passage teaches that there are two societies which relate to each other but are not identical with each other. The state which was previously regarded as sacral is hereby demystified, it is no longer the bearer of a religious authority. For its moral basis it must refer beyond itself to another community. This community in turn, the church, understands itself as a moral authority which depends on voluntary adherence. These communities counter-check each other and it is on basis of this balance of relationship that freedom is maintained.

God's Empowering Wisdom

According to Weber this power tradition has again three main aspects: a realistic assessment of human powers; empowered to become stewards of the earth; the powers and times, the order and beauty of God's creation. The first aspect stresses

---

[40] *The New Express*, 23-29 July 1993.
[41] *The Independent*, 12-19 June 1993.
[42] *The Independent*, 28 July-3 August 1993.
[43] *The Nation*, 5 April 1994.

the point that there are certain areas which are beyond human understanding. Such an awareness of human limitations should make one humble, open to learn and to be corrected. This awareness should also enable one to have less confidence in human prowess as the key to success. Kamlepo Kalua[44] has said that one of the weaknesses during the single party period was that the then head of state could not receive advice from other people. MacLaws Makwiti, reflecting on the results of the referendum, said that the lessons to be learned from the results of the referendum include the following: i) no leader however great or wise is greater or wiser than the people collectively; and ii) no amount of political or muscle power can silence the people's voice.[45]

The second aspect of God's empowering wisdom is that of being empowered to become stewards of the earth. In his article 'A New Dawn of Democracy' a *Monitor* writer said this regarding life under the one party system:

> Political power in practice comes into the hands of only one person who is both the president of the state and of the ruling party. He has authority to make decisions and appointments which cannot be questioned. Economic activity is mostly state controlled. This means political interest and personalities - often dictate the decisions. Large parastatals dominate the economy. Despite good intentions to develop and share the resources of the nation more equally and assist the poor, the concentration of economic activity means that just the opposite results.[46]

This state of affairs was partly contributed by the popular saying *Zonse zimene n'za Kamuzu Banda* (everything belongs to Kamuzu Banda), a saying which was used in a praise song to Dr Banda. If everything belonged to Dr Banda people were generally unable to contribute effectively to the development of the country.[47] Rev Chimkwita said that the Christian Council, in its open letter to Dr Banda called for a referendum because that would give the people of the country an opportunity to decide for themselves the future of the country.[48] In fact, the Christian Council was calling for popular participation in the development of the country. It must be noted that the slogan which multiparty advocates used in their campaign meetings in the run-up to the referendum was 'Power to the people' According to Makwiti, one of the lessons of the referendum results is that 'the state belongs to the people and not the government or the leader'.[49]

---

[44] Int. op cit.
[45] *The Independent*, 30 June-6 July 1993.
[46] *The Monitor*, 31 March-6 April 1993.
[47] Int. by K. Fiedler in 1995.
[48] Int. by K. Fiedler, 4 December 1995.
[49] *The Independent*, 30 June-6 July 1993.

One of the implications of the saying *Zonse zimene n'za Kamuzu Banda* was that even women belonged to Dr Banda and by association to the party officials as well. Peter Ngulube-Chinoko has noted that one of effects of one party system as far as women were concerned was the breakdown of morals.[50] Women used to be gathered in 'camps' in Blantyre for a week or so before Independence celebration and could also stay on for another week after the celebration. During that period most women would be taken out by party officials. It has been suggested that the rapid spread of the Aids epidemic can partly be attributed to that practice. The nation is today reaping what it sowed. Another problem in Malawi whose roots can be traced to the one party era is the problem of overpopulation. The nation was not informed of family planning methods during the one party era because it was felt that there was plenty of land. The present UDF government is trying to empower people in a variety of ways. There are a number of family planning programmes and Aids conscientization programmes which are aired on the national radio. The point is that God's empowering wisdom is one of the faith tradition which was neglected but has recently been recovered. It is an important power tradition even for the present generation.

Conclusion

In the foregoing section stress has been placed on the importance of God's liberating acts and God's empowering wisdom as the two most important biblical power tradition during the transition period. In this concluding section I would like to look at the power traditions in two documents: the Pastoral Letter and Presbyterian/WARC letter which were very significant during the transition. In their Pastoral letter the Roman Catholic Bishops used Gen 1:26 as the key passage by which to determine the church's understanding of the meaning of human life and society. Gen 1:26 is part of a unit which deals with creation (Gen 1:1-2,4a). This unit has been viewed by source-critics of the Bible as part of the so-called Priestly document which was produced during the post-exilic period. It is a document which is musical in form and is therefore appropriate to see the use of the term 'image' in Gen 1:26 in cultic terms.[51] The bishops, however did not use this term simply in its ritualistic sense, rather they recognized the interconnectedness

---

[50] P Ngulube-Chinoko, "The Experience of Women Under the One-Party State and in the Political Transition" in Nzunda & Ross, *Church, Law and Political Transition*, p. 94. Chinoko has further noted that women suffered during the one party period in that women's rights were abused, polygamy was approved by the head of state, maternal care being low, the death rate of women at childbirth was (and still is) one of the highest on the continent, and women were (and still are) the most illiterate section of the Malawian population.

[51] A. Richardson, *Genesis 1-11* London: SCM, 1953, p. 43.

between ritual and daily life. Hence their advocacy for church's involvement in the socio-economic and political life of society.

In the history of the religion of Israel, prophets are seen as the ones who argued for the interconnection between ritual and daily life. In this regard it is important to note that in the concluding section of the Pastoral Letter Micah 6:8 ('love tenderly, act justly, walk humbly with your God') is quoted. The whole passage out of which this verse is taken reads:

> With what shall I come before the Lord
>   and bow myself before God on high?
> Shall I come before him with burnt offerings,
>   with calves a year old?
> Will the Lord be pleased with thousands of rams
>   with ten thousands of rivers of oil?
> Shall I give my first-born for my transgression
>   the fruit of my body for the sin of my soul?
>
> He has shown you, o man, what is good;
>   and what does the Lord require of you
> But to do justice, and to love kindness,
>   and to walk humbly with your God.

This passage has sometimes been regarded as anti-cultic in favour of moral uprightness. It is better to see the two, cultic life and daily life as two inseparable sides of the same coin. The bishops have underlined the importance of social life by quoting Luke 4:18-19, a passage which has been described by John Chome as the manifesto of Jesus's mission.[52] The Pastoral Letter can thus be said to view God's power in terms of his holy presence.

The Presbyterian church (together with WARC) on the other hand used the Wisdom tradition of power. The passage from Proverbs 14:34 (righteousness exalts a nation but sin is a reproach to any people') is quoted. In line with the wisdom tradition there is a recognition that the government has the freedom of choice. Singled out here is the government's freedom to respond to demands made at the Paris (donors) meeting. An appeal was made to the government to respond positively to demands from both within and without the country for change in view of the then 'forthcoming meeting of multilateral donors' which was held in June 1992.

The fact that the Presbyterian church worked from the wisdom perspective of power is further indicated by their disclaimer that they were desiring any political

---

[52] *Moni*, 2 February 1994, p. 11.

power: "we neither represent nor desire any political power: we are simply trying to 'seek first the kingdom of God and His justice'" Two types of kingdom are recognised here, namely, the kingdom of God and the earthly kingdom. The power of the latter is limited by the power of the former. During the transition period there was therefore a recognition of the power of prayer and its connectedness to daily living.

3. Marching, Suspended and Stoned: Christian Women in Malawi 1995

Isabel Apawo Phiri

Introduction

This chapter is a reflection on the struggles of women in the church and in the academy in Malawi in 1995. It is a most painful and difficult chapter for me to write because it is based on personal experiences that I went through at a time when the Department of Theology and Religious Studies was reflecting on the World Council of Churches theme of 'All Exercise of power is Accountable to God' in the *Theology of Life* case study. Some of these experiences are still very fresh and painful. The approach adopted in this chapter is not to seek sympathy from the readers but to allow a healing process to take place. In the words of Dr Milan Opocensky, General Secretary and Dr Nyambura J. Njoroge, Executive Secretary, PACT Program, both of World Alliance of Reformed Churches 'we must bear in mind that for any healing process to take place, all voices involved in this matter should be listened to carefully and prayerfully. This is to say that it is necessary to expose all the wounds if these wounds are to be "dressed" with the "appropriate medicine" for healing to take place.'[1] Therefore I am going to let each group that was involved in the issues of women in the church and in the academy speak for themselves by constantly referring to relevant statements in minutes, letters and newspaper articles which they wrote. My reflection on these documents will be influenced by my commitment to God and guidance of the Holy Spirit as well as my gender.

The chapter has two sections. The first section is about the experiences of concerned[2] women in the Church of Central Africa Presbyterian[3] (hereafter CCAP), Blantyre Synod where I am a member in full communion. I was baptized in 1967 at Katimba CCAP church in the Blantyre Presbytery. I am now a full member of Zomba CCAP church which is in the Zomba Presbytery of Blantyre Synod. My interest in gender issues in the church started when I become a staff

---

[1] Dr Nyambura J. Njoroge - Rev Mphatso 16 May 1995.
[2] The term "concerned women theologians" was first introduced to refer to the Circle of Concerned African Women Theologians who run the Institute of African Women and Culture inaugurated in September 1989.
[3] The Church of Central Africa Presbyterian consists of five Synods: Blantyre Synod in Southern Malawi, Nkhoma Synod in Central Malawi, Livingstonia Synod in Northern Malawi, Harare Synod in Zimbabwe and Madzimoyo Synod in Zambia.

member in the Department of Theology and Religious Studies, Chancellor College, University of Malawi. My Department has a long standing working relationship with the churches in Malawi through the Diploma in Theology and Bachelor of Arts in Theology degree. My area of interest in research happens to be in African Women in Religion and Culture. Therefore it is my church membership in the CCAP Blantyre Synod and my job in the Department of Theology and Religious Studies that made it possible for me to intimately work together with my sisters who are in full employment of the church for their concerns are my concerns too. It is the intention of the first section to reflect on the background to the concerned Christian women's march, the march itself, the reaction of the church administrators, the response of other women in the country and in other Reformed churches outside the country, the role played by World Alliance of Reformed Churches and the role of women in the August 1995 Synodical meeting.

The second section is about the experiences of concerned female lecturers who formed a Gender Lobby Group on Chancellor College campus in the University of Malawi.[4] It is a reflection on the deterioration of morals on campus and its effects on the female students; the organization of seminars by the Chancellor College Lobby Group, the research on Rape and Sexual Harassment on the Chancellor College Campus; the reaction of a section of the Chancellor College male and female students and the administration; and the response of the Malawi public to the whole episode.

Women Issues in the Blantyre Synod

Women are not for power but justice and peace

Among all the Synods of the CCAP, Blantyre Synod is well known for taking a progressive stand on the role of women in the church. The Rev S.S. Ncozana, who was the General Secretary of the Synod from 1985 to 1995 is of the opinion 'that male dominance in the church is traditional, but has no place in the kingdom of God. It is not part of God's plan, but of human making.'[5] This is supported by the fact that in the CCAP it is the Blantyre Synod that was the first to establish a centre for women with full time theologically trained female staff. They are also the only ones who have sent women for theological training at Zomba Theological

---

The University of Malawi consists of five Colleges. The Polytechnic and College of Medicine are in Blantyre, Chancellor College is in Zomba. Bunda College of Agriculture and Kamuzu College of Nursing are based in Lilongwe.

[5] This was said in the Rev S.S. Ncozana's opening remarks when he was officially opening the Women in Theology event on Tuesday 25 September 1990 at Grace Bandawe Conference Centre.

College[6] (although they do not count more than four). Out of all the women trained at Zomba Theological College, Blantyre Synod is the only one so far whose candidate has been accepted to pursue a Bachelor of Arts degree in Theology at the University of Malawi.[7] Furthermore, since 1987 Blantyre Synod is the only one that has been inviting female clergy from other countries to act as role models. The first to be invited was the Rev Peggy Reid from the Presbyterian Church of Canada. Her major role was to help with consciousness raising of men and women, laity and clergy, about women working in full time church leadership roles. It is not surprising therefore that by the time the General Synod of the CCAP held its first seminar on *Women in the 1990s* which was held at Chilema from 6-9 December 1988, Blantyre Synod was able to send more delegates than the other synods.[8] It was a Blantyre Synod female theologian who was the main speaker at the seminar.[9]

The 1988 seminar is very important in the history of women in the General Synod of the CCAP because the women participants made very powerful resolutions concerning the participation and the empowering of women in the church. These included the following:

(a) When women are appointed to and/or ordained to a position, *all* the responsibilities/rights/privileges therefore be permitted (i.e. women elders, session clerks, youth organizers).
(b) Women should be represented on Sessions, Presbyteries, Synod and General Synod levels.
(c) Women be granted all voting privileges that go with their responsibilities.
(d) General Synod (should) consider the ordination of women as pastors.
(e) Women's committee and officer be established within the general Synod of the CCAP to co-ordinate the women's work within the Synod.
(f) Within this committee there should be equal representation from all synods.
(g) The committee to work towards uniformity in the structure for women's work in the Synod.
(h) The General Synod should encourage the synods to send women to study at the theological college and to encourage those women who have already begun their studies.

---

[6] The fully trained Zomba Theological College graduates from the Blantyre Synod are Mrs Gertrude Kapuma, Mrs Mercy Chilapula, Mrs Mirriam Chipeta Banda and Miss Grace Kulupando.
[7] Mirriam Chipeta Banda is the first woman to study for a degree in Theology after having completed a diploma in theology at Zomba Theological College.
[8] Out of seventeen participants, fourteen came from Blantyre Synod, one each from Nkhoma, Livingstonia and Harare Synods.
[9] Gertrude Kapuma gave the key-note address at this conference.

(i) The General Synod should sponsor a women's meeting once every two years.[10]

These resolutions formed the basis of women's charter in the Blantyre Synod. It is also important to point out that this meeting was held within the period when the World Council of Churches had declared that 1988-1998 should be the Decade of Churches in Solidarity with Women. The purpose of the Decade was as follows:

> Empowering women to challenge oppressive structures in the global community, their country and their church.
>
> Affirming - through shared leadership and decision-making, theology and spirituality the decisive contributions of women in churches and communities.
>
> Giving visibility to women's perspectives and actions in the work and struggle for justice, peace and integrity of creation.
>
> Enabling the churches to free themselves from racism, sexism and classism; from teachings and practices that discriminate against women.
>
> Encouraging the churches to take actions in solidarity with women.[11]

The resolutions of the women were taken seriously in various ways. The General Synod accepted the proposal for the establishment of the women's desk. Mrs Christina Phiri from Livingstonia Synod became its first director. Unfortunately up to now she has no office at the offices of the General Synod of CCAP. As such she is still operating from her Synod. This could imply that her office is not taken seriously by the General Synod. At another level, the women commissioners who were attending the General Synod meetings felt that the changes that have been made were cosmetic. This became very clear in the letter of the women commissioners to the Senior Clerk of the General Synod meeting held at Namoni Katengeza Lay Training Centre from 9-13 November 1994. The women commissioners argued thus:

> Sir, we appreciate the fact that women for two consecutive General Synod meetings have been represented. However, we are not happy with the limited number of women representation. Sir, this case is not in isolation. Even though women in most cases outnumber their male counterparts in the churches, their representation on the decision making courts of the churches are very limited. It is in the light of this that we are calling the attention of the 1996 General

---

[10] See women's report on seminar on "Women in the 1990s" Chilema, 6-9 December 1988, submitted to the Church of Central Africa Presbyterian, General Synod.
[11] Brochure of *The Ecumenical Decade of the Churches in Solidarity with Women 1988-1998*, World Council of Churches, Geneva, p. 1.

> Synod to encourage the participating Synods to include women in all decision making bodies of the church and increase their number at Presbytery, Synod and General Synod meetings.[12]

The women commissioners were able to pause and note their powerlessness but at the same time speak out for themselves. Despite the small number, they managed to make a significant contribution in speaking for women. The General Synod also proposed that all the synods should debate the issue of the ordination of women. It gave the synods four years to debate on the issue. In the same letter of the women commissioners, they made the following observation:

> On the ordination of women into the Holy Ministry, we are glad that some synods are already considering the full Ministry of women and there are training programmes for women. It is our prayer that more will be exposed to Theological Education. We request the Synods concerned not to relax in their dialogue on ordination of women into Holy Ministry.

The Blantyre Synod responded to the resolutions of the General Synod women's seminar by accepting to fund a follow up seminar after a period of two years. This was held in September 1990 at Grace Bandawe Centre. The aim of the follow up seminar was to get together all Malawian women in theology to know each other and identify their concerns so that they could make their voices heard in the church and society. The invitations were sent to all members of Christian Council of Malawi. This could have meant an ecumenical group. However, the women who responded to the invitation were sixteen, mainly Presbyterians from Blantyre Synod. The women theologians felt the need to repeat the themes that were raised in 1988. Their emphasis was on consciousness raising of other church women to support other women as they propose to start negotiating for increased participation of women in the church leadership and decision making positions in the church. This was crucial because women are in the majority in the church and yet for a long time they have been conditioned to look up to men only for leadership. In some cases women have opposed the inclusion of women in leadership positions in the church. This comes from women who have internalized their own oppression in the domestic sphere and in the church. They asked the churches to reconsider their stand on the ordination of women to eucharistic ministry. They asked that women who are called by God to ministry be given space to respond to God's call. They also demanded that the role of single women in the church be accepted and defined even though Malawian culture does not

---

[12] **Women commissioners'** letter 11 November 1994, signed by Mrs C. Phiri, Mrs D.K. Kumichongwe, Mrs E.F Mtika and Mrs C.M. Chibwana. Rev Alice Kyei-Anti was in attendance but was not allowed to sign.

recognize them. They demanded that the church should take a stand as regards the legal rights of women in relation to ownership of property and land.[13] Besides the Rev Peggy Reid, Blantyre Synod increased the presence of women ministers from Reformed traditions in Africa to come and talk to the Synod's women so that they can see for themselves that God also uses women in leadership positions. For example, Rev Jane Kamau from the Presbyterian Church of East Africa was present at the 1990 meeting. Her attendance was intended to encourage women in the church as she shared her experiences. In practice however the story was different. Despite the increased participation of women ministers from other Reformed traditions, when the Right Rev Ncozana tabled the ordination of women on the agenda of the 1991 Synod meeting, he was not supported by the majority of the church leaders of Blantyre Synod. He failed to get the majority needed for a positive decision on the ordination of women.

However this was not the end of the struggle for women. The Blantyre Synod women organized yet another women's conference at Grace Bandawe Conference Centre where they explored the theme of Justice and Peace in the Church in the light of women's experiences. At this meeting, three important recommendations were made. These were:

1. A letter be written to the Synod as a special request for women to meet the Church leaders during the Synod meeting.
2. The ordained women be exposed to the Presbyteries so that people should know them - not in institutions only. With or without ordination the group strongly recommends that women be encouraged to train as theologians, and that the Church make resources available for training women.
3. The group observed that there are very few women who are in the decision making bodies or courts of the church. The group therefore recommends that the Church makes sure to include women at Congregational, Presbytery and Synod level decision making.[14]

The church women sent their report to the church leaders through the women's desk in the Synod but no meeting was called for. In fact there was no acknowledgment that they had received the women's report despite the fact that the women followed the right procedures of the Synod.

When Rev Reid's contract come to an end she was replaced by Rev Alice Kyei-Anti from the Presbyterian Church of Ghana. As part of her job description, she conducted seminars for the different Presbyteries in the Blantyre Synod to

---

[13] Report of the Malawian "Women in Theology Event" Grace Bandawe Centre, Blantyre, 1990.
[14] Report on Women's Conference 14-18 September 1993.

conscientize church members on the ordination of women. This was to be in preparation for the General Administration Committee which was held on 21-26 March 1994.[15] As one of the speakers at the seminars,[16] my observation was that the voices of women were under represented. The meetings were for church leaders. The highest position for women in the Blantyre Synod at a congregational level is church elder. At the same time there are very few women elders in all presbyteries. Therefore three quarters of the voices that made a decision were of male members. Furthermore, although there was freedom of speech in the discussions that followed the presentations, it was the Presbytery Moderator and Clerk who had the final say. At both seminars that I attended their summaries were negative towards the ordination of women while the general discussion was positive. Therefore while in the Presbyterian tradition the voices of the members has weight, in this particular case the leadership of the Synod exercised their power to make a negative conclusion.

This mode of exercise of power also manifested itself at the General Administration meeting of 1994 when the issue of the ordination of women was discussed. The conclusion of the discussion by the moderator of the Synod was that the Blantyre Synod is progressing very well on the issue of promoting partnership between men and women in the church. However, time is not yet ripe to discuss about the ordination of women.[17] It is with this attitude that the Blantyre Synod leadership went to the General Synod meeting of November 1994. It was therefore not surprising to read in the *Monthly Ecumenical Bulletin of The CCAP Synod of Blantyre* that at the General Synod of CCAP, Blantyre Synod has said no to the ordination of women. The reporter said:

> During the same meeting the issue of the ordination of women cropped up during which Livingstonia Synod reported a major breakthrough that it has endorsed that women can be ordained. They argued that there was no adequate ground for the restricting women to be ministers of word and sacrament.
>
> Blantyre Synod however reported that the matter was discussed but still the majority were of the opinion that time is not ripe for the ordination of women. Nkhoma Synod ignored the issue altogether, while Zambia reported that the matter was has not yet been discussed. Harare reported that they have just started accepting women deacons.

---

[15] Rev Alice Kyei-Anti - I.A. Phiri, 18 January 1994.
[16] I was one of the speakers at Zomba and Domasi Presbyteries seminars on 4 and 15 February 1994. The title of my paper was "Patriarchy: Its effect in the Church and Society"
[17] I was invited to speak on my thesis by the Right Rev Ncozana who was then General Secretary of the Synod.

The meeting ruled out at this juncture that the matter would be left out to the separate synods themselves. Those who find it fit to ordain women can do so and the rest can consider their positions as they see fit.[18]

The news about the ordination of women in the Livingstonia was received quietly in the country. Considering that this was a breakthrough after more than hundred years of the Presbyterian tradition in the country, one could have thought that it could make headline news of church reports and national newspapers. But this was not the case. The fact that Livingstonia Synod was the first to make a move in that direction when Blantyre Synod had been importing women ministers to conscientize its members made a big statement. My observations are that, firstly, the arguments against the ordination of women are limited to timing and not the Bible. Secondly, there is a cultural element to it as well. Livingstonia Synod is in a predominantly patrilineal society, the male members do not feel threatened by sharing leadership power with women members. In the other synods, this is not the case. Therefore basically this comes down to a power struggle in the church which has nothing to do with obedience to the message of Jesus Christ who is the Lord of the Church.

The planning of the peaceful walk organized by the Blantyre Synod concerned church women followed after the General Synod meeting. Whatever the women planned was a result of constant frustration at the way the Blantyre Synod had handled women's issues since 1988. The women were confused with the Blantyre Synod's stand because at one level they were given the impression that all was progressing well. Yet at the same time they felt frustrated with the argument that time is not ripe yet for the ordination of women. What would be the signs that time is ripe? Who is going to make the decision that time is ripe? This statement is vague to say the least.

The march that made history!

At the end of every year, Chigodi Women's Lay Training Centre calls for a meeting of all its workers in order to make an evaluation of its work. At the 30th November 1994 meeting, the women workers reflected on the theme of Peace and Justice in the church. The outcome of their reflection were presented in the form of a document. The contents of the document were not new. The women were highlighting the issues that had been raised since 1988. The concerned women were reminding the church leaders about what they had said at the Administrator's conference held at Grace Bandawe Conference Centre in January 1993 on the role

---

[18] CCAP Synod of Blantyre Bulletin Vol. 2, November 1994. This report was written by H.S. Vokhiwa.

of Church in Transformation of Malawi as a nation. The women observed that while the church was concerned about Justice and Peace in the country, there was no example coming from the relationships within the church between men and women. They said that:

> we have observed that the barriers which divide women and men within the church communities continue to widen. There is no partnership between men and women in the church, for example:
>
>> (a) Women are under-represented in the decision making bodies of the church at all levels even though women are in the majority in the church.
>> (b) The few women who are in the decision making bodies of the church are treated as tokens and in most cases are chosen by men.
>> (c) Even in women organizations (Mvano), women have no power to make decisions even on matters affecting them, e.g. fund raising, and women's programmes.
>> (d) There are inequality in training opportunities. Lay women are not given a chance to go for post graduate studies (even training for Leadership).
>> (e) Conditions of Service for men and women with the same Theological education and are in full employment with the church are different, e.g.
>
> Women contribute towards their pension while their male counterparts with the same qualifications do not.
>
> The lay women contribute more percentage towards their health care.
>
> - Some of the houses occupied by the women employees are below standard e.g. a senior staff and her family at Chigodi have been living in a guest house of only one room for the past two years.
>
> In Likhubula two female senior staff at the time were sharing a house.

Violence against women

> The church is turning a blind eye to violence against women in the church and society e.g.
>> Women being battered by their spouses
>> Women receiving no security from church and community.
>> Women and widowhood rights/inheritance.
>> Male infidelity.

Leadership role

> The church has failed to recognize the gift and talents of women for Ministry, and has not involved women fully in leadership and authority in the life of the church at all levels, e.g. there are certain positions in the church which are occupied by the laity, but women have not been considered i.e. Session Clerks, Treasurers, Parish Chairmen, Education Secretary/Agency, Conveners of Presbytery and Synod Committees. Presbyterial youth directors, School/hospital Chaplains, Music directors on Congregational/Presbytery level.
> In the light of the scriptural declaration of the oneness of women and men in Jesus Christ (Galatians 3:28)[*sic*]. All women are denied ordination to the Holy Ministry on the basis of seemingly weakness of individual women.[19]

The statement was concluded by recommendations on how Justice and Peace can be established in the church when in Partnership between men and women. The original plan of the concerned women was to invite the Deputy General Secretary of the Synod to come and listen to the petition of the concerned women. However the invitation was turned down. It was only thereafter that the women thought of organizing a peaceful march from the Synod offices to the Grace Bandawe Conference Centre where the Synod and Presbytery Administrators were going to have a two day meeting. Since the intentions of the women were peaceful, they took all the necessary measures for that to happen. 5th January 1996 was declared to be for prayer and fasting on the issue. Arrangements were made to inform the police and the press.

While the majority of church full time workers were present at the initial planning meeting, the actual writing of the statement was left in the hands of a sub committee.[20] Their task was to reflect on past documents and check what progress had been made and raise new issues that affected women as they worked and worshipped in the church. A look at the past documents from the women show that there is not much new ground. What might be considered new was raising issues on conditions of service and violence against women which were in line with the concerns of women nationwide. Contrary to the Ecumenical Bulletin development report of March 1995, none of the participants was 'professional and politically minded' All the women were concerned Spirit filled women of the church voicing

---

[19] See the Church of Central Africa Presbyterian, Synod of Blantyre, A statement by women representatives meeting at Chigodi Women's Centre from 30th November to December 1994 on Justice and Peace in the Church.

[20] The sub committee included myself, Rev Alice Anti, Mrs Violet Chavura, Mrs Gertrude Kapuma, Mrs Mercy Chilapula, and Mrs Mary N. Saukila.

out their concerns in a peaceful manner. All the members of the sub committee are in full communion in the Blantyre Synod. The actual march was carried out only by a small group of eleven women mainly due to some logistic problems. The placards that were carried by the women highlighted Human rights messages. The placard which caught the eye of the press was one of a church minister carrying a placard which called for Human Rights in the country while he is standing on a church woman lying down and calling for help. Upon reaching the venue of the Administrators meeting, the Deputy General Secretary refused to accept the petition. He argued that the women did not follow the acceptable channels to present a petition. His arguments could have been valid if one was not aware of the fact that the women had been following the right procedures since 1988 without any success. The reaction of the Administrators should also be understood in terms of what was being discussed at the meeting. They were facing a crisis on 'Being Born Again' At this meeting the Blantyre Synod and Presbytery Administrators prepared a letter to be read in all its congregations informing all its members who claim to be born again to leave the church.[21] The comparison of how the church handled the Born Again issue with the crisis with church women is enlightening.

Punish the concerned church women!

The immediate decision of the Synod and Presbytery Administrators was to punish all the church workers. The heaviest punishment went to Mrs Gertrude Kapuma, then Director of Chigodi Women's Center. Through a letter dated 11 January she was informed that she was suspended with half salary as from 12 January 1995 and that "a Sub Committee had been set for the inquiry of the demonstration.[22] In a separate letter written on the some day, Mrs Kapuma was further informed that all Chigodi programmes should be suspended and that the Chigodi Vehicle be withdrawn and packed [sic] in the Synod Office garage.[23] Besides Gertrude Kapuma, all the other full time women church workers who were part of the demonstration were also given letters to inform them that they are on suspension. The Commission of Inquiry which was set up was comprised of three Church ministers and two elders. Their mandate was to 'find out what prompted the women to carry that extra ordinary demonstration.'[24]

Within a short time the Commission of Inquiry submitted its report to the same committee that set it up. The recommendations of the report were as follows:

---

[21] Synod Office - all congregations, 11 January 1995.
[22] Deputy General Secretary - Mrs Kapuma, 11 January 1995.
[23] Deputy General Secretary - Mrs Kapuma, 11 January 1995.
[24] Report of the Commission of Inquiry dated 1995.

(i) Mrs Getrude Kapuma should be transferred from Chigodi after reprimanding her and should not be associated with women in the Synod. Chigodi should be manned by minister as head of the centre and one lady theologian should be at the centre as a tutor.
(ii) Rev Alice Anti should go to Ghana with immediate effect.
(iii) Dr Isabel Phiri should be told not to interfere with the affairs of Blantyre Synod and if she has got some knowledge should go and propagate that gospel in Nkhoma Synod where she is hailing from.
(iv) The work of the women in the Synod should be restructured with immediate effect.
(v) Chigodi Management Committee and Synod Work Committee should be reshuffled with immediate effect.
(iv) Mrs Meriam [sic] Chipeta Banda should be called to clarify what she meant when she said that the Administration of the Synod is unfair and poor.
(vii) Mrs Mercy Chilapula should be called and reprimanded severely.
(viii) Some Full Time Workers should be given retirement on public interest.

The reaction to the report of the Commission of Inquiry can be divided into five sections. The first section will deal with the response of the Blantyre Synod Administrators, the second section with the response of the CCAP General Synod, the third section with the response of some church women, the fourth with the response of women organizations, and the fifth with the response of church women outside Malawi, fifth, the response of World Alliance of Reformed Churches.

The response of the Blantyre Synod Administrators

The Blantyre Synod Staffing and Nominations Committee met and agreed to all recommendations of the Commission of Inquiry. Gertrude Kapuma was informed to take up hospital chaplaincy duties at once.[25] Mrs Mercy Chilapula was told to take up the post of acting Director at Chigodi. All the women workers who were suspended in January were told to begin work again. Rev Alice's position was to be discussed by all the churches responsible for her coming to Malawi such as the Presbyterian Church of Ghana, the Presbyterian Church of the United States of America and the General Synod of the CCAP. As part of the restructuring of the women's work in the Synod, the Staffing and Nomination Committee recommended that ministers should be appointed in Presbyteries to be Directors of Women's work. These recommendations were submitted to the April General Administrators' Committee (GAC) of Blantyre Synod for approval. Since the GAC

---

[25] According to Mrs Gertrude Kapuma, Rev Chitsulo came to her house in Chigodi to deliver the message. When they asked about accommodation, the Reverend told them to continue staying at Chigodi, which Gertrude refused because the house was for the Director of Chigodi and not for the hospital chaplain.

is composed of the same Synod Administrators who refused to accept the women's document of January, the concerned women were not hopeful for a proper hearing at GAC.

The response of the General Synod of the CCAP

The response of the General Synod of the CCAP was expressed in a letter from the Senior Clerk, Rev J.J. Mphatso, to the World Alliance of Reformed Churches. Written more than two months after the march, it starts with apologies, and explains that everything is under control.

> The leadership of the Blantyre Synod informed the Standing Committee that the Synod has arranged for the appropriate Committees to discuss the matter with the concerned women. They assured the Standing Committee that the situation was going to be redressed with a solution acceptable to all parties concerned.

What the women did wrong was to demonstrate. They knew very well the proper procedure, but "the good ladies absented themselves without apologies from their Synod and Presbytery Administrators' Annual Conference where they could present their grievances for discussion at the conference or referred to appropriate committees."

Rev Mphatso further pointed out that, of all the five CCAP Synods, Blantyre deserved a "well done" in regard to women affairs, being several steps ahead of the other Synods, for example in continuing to train women theologians even after the Synod had rejected women's ordination with a 5:2 vote of the Presbyteries.

> Blantyre Synod was encouraged to continue working together with male folks as well as female leadership in programmes of conscientizing the congregations on the subject of ordination of women which appeared to be the main cause for their anger which led them to ignoring their Church's established and accepted practice and procedure.

In concluding his letter, Rev Mphatso thanked WARC for their interest and mentioned that they were "organizing seminars on partnership of women and men", and that he would keep in touch.[26] The impression that one gets from reading this letter is that the concerned women from Blantyre Synod have no agenda because that particular Synod is already doing a lot for women. If one had no background information one would be compelled to support his letter.

---

[26] Rev J.J. Mphatso - Dr Nyambura J. Njoroge, WARC, 26 March 1995.

The response of the church women

At the March meeting of Staffing and Nominations Committee, all the church workers were invited and after the reading of the report of the Commission of Inquiry, the women were asked to apologize one after the other. It is interesting to note that one of the subheadings of CCAP Synod of Blantyre ecumenical bulletin read 'Women Workers Forgiven After Apologizing for Controversial Demonstration'.[27] Mirriam Chipeta Banda was asked to explain what she meant by her statement that 'the Administration of the Synod is unfair and poor' which she did. Her explanation made the members more angry than before because her true stories were taken as challenging the Synod Administration's power. All the women were asked to go outside while the administrators debated on the issue. To the surprise of the women, they remained outside for six hours before they were invited in again to be told what would happen to them. Since Mirriam was staying far and could not wait up the end of the meeting, she was told that she would receive a letter to tell her what her punishment would be. Up to now that letter has not come.

As for the other church women in the whole country, there was no organized support. The only voices of support and protest were heard through the Commission of Inquiry's report. According to the report, only a handful of women supported the petition, the peaceful march, and the decision of the Synod to punish the concerned women. It is only Chiuta Presbytery which gave a positive response. This is the way the Commission of Inquiry reported the information:

> Mr Moderator Sir, and the House, when contracted by the Commission of Inquiry Chiuta Presbytery Women's Work Committee shown (sic) its colours by saying that there was nothing wrong with demonstration. The women have got rights to be exercised in the church. Studying the cloth which came in 1988 for Women's Decade the women had every reason to march because they are running out of time seeing that there is only three years to go for their decade. Therefore Chiuta Presbytery Women's Work Committee is solidly behind the demonstration of the women.[28]

The way Chiuta Presbytery is being presented here suggests that it was wrong for them to support the concerned women. This is one example of the biased nature of the report of the Commission of Inquiry. Secondly, the response of the Chiuta women indicate that they were viewing the issue at hand in a wider context. This comes out clearly by their reference to the Decade of Churches in Solidarity with Women.

---

[27] *Ecumenical Bulletin*, March 1995, p. 4.
[28] Commission of Inquiry report, 1995, p. 5.

Other responses came from individual concerned Church women. My letter to the Synod, of which I include sections here, is one example. I started by stating my identity, replying to the Commission of Inquiry's assumption that I did not belong to Blantyre Synod:

> I am writing as a member in full communion in the Church of Central Africa Presbyterian (CCAP) of Blantyre Synod. According to the constitution of CCAP, one's membership to a Synod of CCAP is not based on where one comes from as mentioned in the recommendation of the Commission of Inquiry's report on page 8. While I come from Dedza, I was baptized at Katimba CCAP church in the Blantyre Synod. I am now a full member of Zomba CCAP church, Blantyre Synod. I have no intentions of leaving the church unless I am asked by the church court to do so. My life has been lived in the grip of the Church. I have my roots in the CCAP.

Then I explained that I do have connections to Nkhoma Synod, both through my grandfathers and through my research which I did for my Cape Town PhD Dissertation[29], and that some of my research findings are valid for other CCAP Synods, too. Then I expressed my dissatisfaction with both the Administrators' Committee and the Commission of Inquiry:

> I wish to contend that the Administrators Committee that set up a Commission of Inquiry of 11th January 1995 is not a court of the Presbyterian Church and therefore it was unconstitutional for it to set up such a Commission of Inquiry.... The Commission of Inquiry was composed of five men. I cannot explain adequately the pain that I, as a woman, experienced when I was being interrogated by the all male commissioners. I want to contend that the commissioners were chosen for their negative attitude toward the petition of women on justice and peace in the church. Therefore, the choosing of who was to be in the Commission of Inquiry was biased and it confirmed exactly what the women in their petition were complaining about.

I was convinced that, just as much as the Commission's composition was biased, so was the mandate "to go and contact people in all the Blantyre Synod Presbyteries to find out what prompted the women to carry out that extraordinary demonstration" But isn't Presbyterianism based on the right of any individual to petition the Courts of the Church? And even if the methods of the petitioners could be labelled inappropriate, wouldn't their concerns still stand? But the Commission

---

[29] "African Women in Religion and Culture: A Critique of Patriarchy", Ph.D., University of Cape Town, 1992. A slightly revised version is being prepared for publication with CLAIM, Blantyre as a Kachere Monograph under the title: *Chewa and Christian: Religious Experience of Women in Central Malawi*.

of Inquiry did not address the issue whether the issues raised by the women in their petition were true or not.

On the report, I wrote that to me it was fundamentally misleading, and also that it was undated and did not mention the names of the commissioners. After reading through the report, my first impression was that it was written from a position of defence and confirms my earlier observation that the commissioners were chosen for their negative attitude towards women issues in the church.

> The report gives summaries of what was supposedly said by individuals or groups of people. Since I was one of the persons who were interrogated, I reject the way my contribution was summarized. There were a lot of positive things that I said but the commissioners only picked the negative ones.... As the report stands one wonders how much of this is the creation of the commissioners or genuine responses of the people. I find the language of the report shocking to say the least. The women who are being discussed are treated as if they are strangers or the worst offenders in the church since Blantyre Synod was established. Yet the truth of the matter is that both men and women are the church and not one group of humanity being more church than the other. The recommendations are harsh and do not compare with the supposed crime. The fact that it has been recommended that Chigodi should be headed by a minister (who is male) is yet another confirmation of the negative attitude of the commissioners to women and the more the reason that the women's petition be taken seriously.

Then I argued that the Development Committee, meeting 8 March 1995 to carry out the recommendations of the Commission of Inquiry, not being a Court of the Church, acted illegally, and that it was also wrong to call only female *staff* members of the church to appear before the Development Committee to apologize, since the petition was not only written by women in full time church employment. I concluded my letter mentioning that, if the women had not followed church procedures, the Synod administration definitely failed to do so right from the beginning, and I requested that:

1. All the previous judgements on the methodology of presenting a petition, the contents of the petition, the suspension of all female church workers on half salary from January to March, the demotion of Mrs Gertrude Kapuma, and dismissal of Rev Alice Anti be withheld until the case is brought before the Synod's court for a fair hearing.
2. A Commission of Inquiry be set by the appropriate body of the Synod.
3. The commissioners should be a mixed group in equal numbers of those who are for and against the contents of the petition of women on Justice and

Peace in the Church. Men and women should be represented in equal numbers.
4. The inquiries should be tape recorded.
5. The report should be in verbatim.
6. The report should be made available to all who will be interviewed.
7. The report should be submitted to the Synod's court for a fair hearing.

I closed my letter thus:

8. I am willing to raise the necessary funds to make this possible. It is in the spirit of seeking justice and peace in the church and through our Lord and Saviour Jesus Christ, that I humbly submit this appeal.[30]

This letter met with anger from the CCAP General Synod:

> With new developments on the women's issue as raised by Dr Isabel Apawo Phiri, in her letter to Blantyre Synod leadership and copied to your office as well as all the traditional partners of that Synod, I will personally be the most disappointed to see that the demonstration by the women of Blantyre Synod and the way that particular Church is handling the issue should drag us all into confrontation. Such confrontations, I feel, will only serve to put salt in the healing wounds.[31]

This letter shows that the church thought that by punishing the concerned women the case was closed. Anyone who questioned the way the issue was handled was considered to be challenging the church's authority.

Response from the Malawi public

The only open support that the concerned women received was from the Women's Voice which wrote a press release which was published in the only woman owned newspaper, *The Independent*. The Women's Voice believed that:

> these Christian Women had a point to deliver to their male colleagues and had the right to be heard, and may be through discussion come to some agreement... the church had persistently portrayed itself as the lamp of society during the pre post referendum period in Malawi and was a shining example on human rights issues when it was condemning the Malawi Congress Party The women's Voice is calling upon the Synod to reinstate the women that have been suspended and the activities of Chigodi Women's Centre

---

[30] I.A. Phiri - The Moderator, Blantyre Synod, 21 April 1995.
[31] Rev J.J. Mphatso - Dr Milan Opocensky, General Secretary of WARC, 5 May 1995.

so that they continue to render the much needed services to society.[32]

The Women's Voice is a notable women's organization in Malawi. Its founder and Chair-person is Dr Vera Chirwa who is a very committed member of CCAP and a lawyer by profession. Therefore the press release should be taken as coming from professional women who are mainly Christians. By comparing what the church did during the referendum and the way it treated its women workers, the women's voice is raising a very important issue which was also raised by the women petitioners. Can the church demand democracy from the nation and deny the same democracy to its own female members? The church was being told that discrimination of its female workers was breaking the law of the land. Does the law of the land have authority on the church? When the church is practising discrimination against women, is it a sin against God?

Janet Karim, the owner of the Independent, answered in the affirmative in her open letter to Rev Chitsulo, entitled 'Every Woman a Child of God, Saved by the Blood' Whereas the church leaders had argued as administrators, Janet Karim argues as a theologian, being convinced that in this case man-made dogma is overriding God given principles.

> Understand that one of the reasons given why women cannot take on positions of authority in your church hierarchy is because women are sinners. Their sin derives from the sin of Eve in the Garden, so the reasoning goes. Subjecting women to the sin and burden of Eve, suggests that it is only men whom Jesus saved on the cross. But my Bible tells me in I Peter 1:18-18 that I have been purchased from my empty and sinful way of life with the precious and incorruptible blood of the lamb of God - there is no differentiation between male and female in the salvation programme for God's people because God is not a respecter of persons, male and female .... Jesus - God made flesh - came to this world through a woman. God's perfect plan to use women in spreading His Word completes the circle when the resurrected Messiah appears first to a woman Mary Magdalene. This woman, Jesus commissions to go and spread the Good News that Jesus Christ is risen Women have both the authority and power from God to be His servants. Does any mortal being possess any other greater authority and power to strip women of these God given talents?[33]

---

[32] See *The Independent* 19-24 January 1995 under the headline, "Women's Voice (Liu la Amai) condemns Blantyre Synod"

[33] *The Independent*, 19-24 January 1995.

Response from women outside the country

Women from the Reformed family did not keep quiet when they heard about the troubles that had fallen on their sisters in the Blantyre Synod. As a sign of solidarity, they wrote letters of protest to the Deputy General Secretary of Blantyre Synod. A woman from the Swiss Reformed Church sent the following letter:

> That a demonstration of women, who feel that they must resort to this course of action to make their just demands felt, is punished in this severe way, will only contribute to a climate of distrust and profound disappointment. I hope you will take all necessary steps to restore the dialogue, and to establish the conditions for a just community of men and women in the church.

There were many such letters sent to Blantyre Synod and signed by a lot of women. They saw that there was injustice done to the concerned women, and they pleaded for a just response as well as for a normalization of relationships through dialogue rather than punishment. While some letters were sent to the Blantyre Synod office, others were sent to the concerned women personally. One such letter came from the Women's desk of the World Council of Churches.

> We, your sisters in the World Council of Churches, have been following the struggle that you have been having in the church in Malawi. While we did not write directly with you we have been discussing our response and solidarity actions with Nyambura Njoroge, our colleague in World Alliance of Reformed Churches, as the person to keep in contact with the women and with the churches. We hope some joint response will become possible soon.[34]

Such solidarity was greatly appreciated by the isolated women. They were being empowered to maintain their stand for justice in the face of hostility at home. One important aspect is the peaceful nature of such letters. The international women as well as the locals emphasized the importance of calmness in dealing with the issue in contrast to the aggressive stand taken by the leaders of the Blantyre Synod. The concerned women in the Blantyre Synod were being encouraged to go on despite the problems faced. Nyambura Njoroge's letter puts this more clearly:

> I would urge you to avoid any steps that would inflame the process and let the Holy Spirit continue to direct your path and all those who are involved. I pray that you remain firm in your cause for justice and peace no matter what happens for Christ never gave up his mission for God's reign on earth.[35]

---

[34] Aruna Gnanadson, World Council of Churches, Unit III, Justice, Peace and Creation, Coordinator of Women's Programme - I.A. Phiri, 29 June 1995.
[35] Dr Nyambura J. Njoroge (Women's desk, WARC) - Gertrude Kapuma, 17 January 1995.

Response of the World Alliance of Reformed Churches

Perhaps the strongest pressure on the Blantyre Synod came from the World Alliance of Reformed Churches through its Women's desk. The tone of peace continued as contact was established with the CCAP on this issue. The letters showed concern to establish the will of God in the churches all over the world. The letters were not judgmental, for in obedience to the Gospel of Christ, judgement is for God. This is well illustrated in the following letter:

> We have learned with some concern the developments in the Synod of Blantyre in respect of the women. The world church in this Decade of the Churches in Solidarity with Women is naturally concerned not only to show solidarity with churches but also with women in particular. Within WARC, since 1992, we have established a program which encourages churches to promote partnership of women and men modelled in the ministry of our Lord Jesus Christ. We understand partnership to be a gift of the Holy Spirit in which there is a new focus of relationship in Jesus Christ that brings wholeness and justice in communities. I write as a program officer on partnership of women and men being aware that every story always has two sides. Please we are interested to hear your side of the story. I sincerely urge you to do everything in your power to resolve your difficulties amicably.[36]

This letter links what was happening in the Blantyre Synod with the wider Reformed tradition, reminding the church that it is accountable to the wider church and not only to the CCAP. It is this point that makes the whole issue to be responded to differently. It also highlights two other important events in the universal Reformed tradition. First, that we are operating within the Decade of the Churches in Solidarity with Women, a point which was earlier raised by the women of Chiuta Presbytery of Blantyre Synod. Secondly, that if the church is guided by the Holy Spirit one of its recent issues is to deal with the issue of partnership between men and women in the church. Both were thorny issues in the Blantyre Synod at this particular time as another letter from WARC's Women's Desk shows. Njoroge refers to the visit of Benjamin Masilo to Malawi and sends the reports from two WARC consultations on the ordination of women and on partnership in God's mission in Africa today. She asks the General Secretary to name a woman responsible for women's issues she could communicate with, hoping that "WARC can facilitate in this process of cultivating partnership of men and women in your church".[37] Her letter is empowering to women because it seeks a woman representative to have direct connection with WARC on issues that pertain to women. Unfortunately, the CCAP did not respond to the issue.

---

[36] Dr Nyambura J. Njoroge - Rev John Mphatso, 27 January 1995.

[37] Dr Nyambura J. Njoroge - Rev John Mphatso, 23 February 1995.

Nevertheless the strength of this letter lies in the fact that it is reminding the CCAP leadership that they are part of the Reformed tradition which has already started studies on partnership between men and women in the church. Thus responding positively to the needs of the women would be in line with the Reformed tradition. It could also be a sign that the church recognizes the humanity of women in the church. In his letter of 17 March 1995, Milan Opocensky, General Secretary of WARC, made it very clear that the peaceful demonstration and the issues it had attempted to address had been widely publicized in Malawi, and thereby caught the attention of the international community, and that the world church was concerned indeed.

> People who are aware of WARC's involvement in Malawi during the political transition are inquiring from us what we are doing to address the injustices the women have expressed in their petition to the church leadership in Malawi. Since Dr Njoroge has not received any response from your office, I kindly urge you to treat this matter with utmost priority, and send the report of the inquiry as soon as possible .... I am sure that you are aware that the implications of this whole affair go far beyond the issue of suspension. We are requesting the church to look seriously into how the whole church treats women and deals with their concerns. Justice delayed is justice denied. The church has the responsibility of "breaking the chains of injustice", as the theme of the next General Council of WARC attests. The credibility of the local as well as the world church is at stake if concrete action is not taken to address the issue at hand: discrimination of women in the church and society.[38]

This letter shows that the church cannot take a double stand when it comes to issues of justice. If the church took a stand during the period of political transition in Malawi, it ought to maintain the same standard even on women's issues. If the church has a mission of 'breaking the chains of injustice' then it has to be all chains irrespective where they are coming from.

When the Commission of Inquiry's report, sent 13 March, reached Geneva, WARC was far from satisfied. Milan Opocensky pointed out the issue of women's role and position is of world-wide interest, and that churches have to come to terms with reality, since "everywhere else in engineering as in medicine, in university professorship and studentship women have been taking their place" He then mentions that they have anyhow been thinking of a pastoral visit to the New Malawi, and that they would share the Blantyre story with their constituency,

---

[38] Dr Milan Opocensky, General Secretary of WARC - Rev Mphatso, 17 March 1995.

who might ask their own questions.[39] The suggestion of a pastoral visit could not have come at a better time. It was mentioned that the visit was wider than the women's issue. However the fact that the visit coincided with the women's issue is of paramount importance. This is particularly true when one considers that the WARC was responding after reading the Commission of Inquiry report and the reaction of the church leaders to my letter dated 21st April 1995. WARC assumed the role of mediator because the conflict in the church was between people with different power. The church leaders had all the power but their stand was not in line with WARC's programme of partnership between women and men in the church and the society. On 16 May, Opocensky wrote again, thanking for the welcome extended for the pastoral visit. He referred to my letter, accepting the possibility "that there were irregularities that occurred during the process of inquiry" and advising "to expose all the wounds if these wounds are to be 'dressed' with the 'appropriate medicine' for healing to take place" I think that it was with these thoughts in mind that he was encouraged to learn that the Synod was planning seminars and workshops to address the issues.[40]

Accountability pays off

The Blantyre Synod did not maintain a negative attitude toward the issue of women. Seminars were held at Grace Bandawe Conference Centre. Of special interest was the fact that the women refused to take the petition and its aftermath as an example. This should be appreciated from the fact that the Blantyre Synod was facing other problems such as the issues of being born again, and financial management. Therefore the women felt that what was needed was to learn the principles of conflict resolution in general and at different forums apply them to each area of conflict. This meant that dialogue was required with each concerned group. Fortunately, their voices were heard and their plea was granted.

It was therefore after the seminar that the concerned women in the Blantyre Synod had an audience with the General Secretary the Very Reverend Ncozana to seek advice on how to proceed with the contents of the petition.[41] The concerned women argued that every person's attention is on the peaceful march and the punishment that the women received. The contents of the petition were not being addressed. So the women wanted to follow what the church could describe as appropriate channels to make sure that the petition was given due attention. Thus contrary to the statements of the church as represented in Rev Mphatso's letter dated 5 May to WARC which gave the impression that the whole issue was

---

[39] Dr Milan Opocensky and Dr Nyambura J. Njoroge - Rev Mphatso, 12 April 1995.
[40] Dr Milan Opocensky, General Secretary of WARC - Rev Mphatso, 16 May 1995.
[41] This meeting took place on 29 May 1995.

resolved, as far as the women were concerned. As long as the contents of the petition were not discussed, the issue was still on. After a fruitful discussion with the General Secretary, the women were asked to summarize their requests and submit them to the Development Committee. The summarized and prioritized version of the women's petition was as follows:

1. *Partnership*

   For the church to achieve positive development there has to be partnership between men and women. The results of equal participation of both men and women in any development endeavour are rich and fulfilling. In the light of the above, the following issues are brought forward for action.

   (a) Conditions of service: we would like the Synod to lay down the Conditions of Service which should take into account: the pension, housing and medical schemes for all its employees considering their educational qualifications, training and position, regardless of gender.

   (b) There should be equal opportunities for both men and women to go for postgraduate studies, training for leadership and more women studying theology.

   (c) Women should be included in the decision making Committees of the Church at all levels and have voting powers.

2. *Violence Against Women:*

   The Church should take a stand on the acts of violence against women happening in the church and in society e.g.
   - Women being battered by their spouses
   - Women lacking security
   - Women and widowhood rights/inheritance
   - Male infidelity

3. *Leadership role:*

   The Church should recognize and encourage the gifts and talents of women for ministry, and provide those gifted women chances and room to exercise their call. Those women who are capable, should be considered for the following positions; Session Clerks, Treasurers, Parish Chair-persons, Education Secretary/Agency Conveners of Presbytery and Synod Committees, Presbyterial Youth Directors, School/Hospital Chaplains, Music Directors.

4. *Ordination of Women:*

   In the light of the scriptural declaration of the oneness of women and men in Jesus Christ (Galatians 3:28) we would like to request the Synod to consider the ordination of women to the Holy Ministry on basis of their "Call and Training" so that human resources are utilized fully.

An analysis of the summarized version of the petition still indicates that what was at stake are issues of justice not women being hungry for power as suggested by the Commission of Inquiry. It also makes valid the comments of the Women's Voice and WARC that what is at stake here is injustice being practiced by the church on other church members on the basis of gender. The item of ordination was categorized as the last one in order to emphasize the same point that women are not hungry for power but would like to be treated fairly. The summarized petition was received by the General Secretary who delivered it to the 'appropriate committee' The concerned women were expecting to be invited for dialogue with the leaders but the day never arrived. I received a phone message to meet the Synod Moderator and the Deputy General Secretary on 4th July 1995 at the Zomba Presbytery Office to discuss my letter to the Synod leaders. The meeting never took place because it was postponed indefinitely.

Finally it was the pastoral visit of a team of six from WARC that made dialogue between the church leaders and the concerned women possible. The team from WARC met the concerned women on 2nd July at Chigodi Women Lay Training Centre to hear what they expected the role of WARC to be. The concerned women saw WARC as having the power to influence the church leaders. Therefore they looked at WARC as the one to foster dialogue between the two groups. They were concerned that the committee which had been set up to look at the restructuring of women's desk might not be the best instrument of dialogue, since the women were in a minority of two against three, with only one of the women being of the "concerned" group. So the hope of the concerned women was that the visitors might arrange for a better venue for the needed dialogue. The team from WARC managed to mediate with the church leaders so that a meeting was arranged for 8th July. The meeting was attended by six representatives from the church leaders, six from the concerned women and six from the WARC team. The opening statement from the team leader of WARC was most striking. He said 'wherever we are people are looking and they can make a decision for or against Jesus Christ' What makes this statement crucial is the fact that it gives power to both men and women and the way we treat each other for evangelism. Issues of justice in the church are also issues of evangelism to non believers. Both groups were given equal opportunities to voice out their concerns and defend themselves. The concerned women raised the issues mentioned above. On the part of the church, they explained that the Synod's Policy committee has a subcommittee that has been given the responsibility of restructuring the women's desk. This is a Synodical committee which was established according to the constitution. Their mandate is to look into the paper prepared by the concerned women. The subcommittee was to present its findings to the Synod meeting which is an open court of the church. The church leaders accepted that they too made some mistakes in the way they handled the women's issue and they also see dialogue as a good starting point. The concerned women were advised that they were welcome to attend the meeting of the subcommittee as observers. On the issue of restructuring the women's desk, the church administrators pointed out that it had been pending since 1992 and they felt that this was as good as any time to implement it. Nevertheless, since the concerned women objected to that decision, the church administrators agreed to shelve it for the time being.

The concerned women felt that despite the fact that the church administrators had power, they were comfortable with the discussion. They did not feel threatened. However it was at congregational level where the concerned women felt much damage was done. The report of the Commission of Inquiry had not been withdrawn. The concerned women were not treated with integrity at the congregation level. The responsibility of bringing change was still left in the hands of the church administrators because it was argued, the local leaders get their cue from the Synod administrators. The need for civic education for all the leaders on women and men in partnership in the church was voiced. This could help to change attitudes. The change was suggested to start with the theological institutions. Both sides recognised that this is a historical moment. It is a challenge to church leadership to create an enabling environment. While it is easy to talk about what should be done to improve relationship between men and women, shortage of finances was seen as a stumbling block. Nevertheless, it was pointed out that there are some changes that could be done at no cost to the church. For example, there was no need for the church to look for a resource person from other countries on women in the church when I am qualified to teach that at university level. How come the male members of the Department of Theology and Religious Studies at the University of Malawi can teach full courses at the church's theological college but not me?

Vote for a woman friendly General Secretary!

While not much progress has taken place in the implementation of what was discussed, the greatest impact was felt at the 1995 Blantyre Synod August meeting. At this meeting, the highlight was the demission from office of the Right Rev Dr Ncozana as General Secretary and the election of new one. The four prospective candidates for the position were Rev Saul Chitsulo, the then current Deputy Synod General Secretary, Rev Tom Hunter Kapengule, resident minister at St Columba congregation, Rev Misanjo Kansilanga who was until 1994 General Synod's

Senior Clerk, and University Theology Lecturer Rev Dr Felix Chingota.[42] What makes this election special was the fact that since the establishment of Blantyre Synod, for the first time the women participants were given a vote. Rev Dr Ncozana successfully convinced the delegates that according to the constitution of the Synod, there was no clause to bar women participants from voting. The women participants who were 18 lobbied among themselves to vote for a candidate who had made a clear positive stand on the Synod's women's issue. Out of the four candidates, sixteen women[43] voted for Rev Misanjo Kansilanga who won the elections to the post of General Secretary.

The role played by Rev Dr Ncozana to make it possible for women to vote cannot be underestimated. In his interview with *The Nation* reporter, Rev Dr Ncozana counted this as one of his great achievements. He said:

> I am also happy because we've been able to resolve the three heavy issues which were at hand: that is the issue of Women Empowerment and that of B.A.s (Born Again) and the Women to vote (General Secretary). When the women marched to Blantyre they were called fundamentalists. On women issues empowerment, he says all women who had their money held have been reimbursed and there is a committee to look into their grievance. 'I have been fed a communion by a woman reverend somewhere else and its no different from how men do it. I've listened to them preach and some are even better than men. After all other countries are doing it in their Presbyterian churches so who are we to stop our women? Believe you me, very soon you're going to hear that the same has started in Malawi.[44]

Rev Ncozana expanded on what he thinks should be the direction of the Synod on Women issues when he went to introduce the new office bearers to President Bakili Muluzi. He said:

> The CCAP church has said the door is not closed to having women as pastors in the church. The Rev Silas Ncozana, outgoing General Secretary of Blantyre Synod, on Thursday told President Muluzi in Lilongwe. The Synod was discussing the possibility of ordaining women.[45]

Such statements put pressure on the new office bearers to see through the issue of justice for women in the church. With Rev Kansilanga holding the top position of the Synod's General Secretary, the women are positive that their struggles have not

---

[42] CCAP Synod of Blantyre *Ecumenical Bulletin*, March 1995.
[43] There were eighteen women participants at the Synod meeting.
[44] *The Nation*, 7 September 1995.
[45] *The Nation*, 4 September 1995

been in vain. This is confirmed by Rev Kansilanga's newspaper interview where he is quoted to have said that:

> One of his tasks is to make sure that the dispute which arose between the Synod and the women recently is settled amicably and that the women's "demands are met favourably."[46]

At the same time they are aware that in the Reformed tradition, one cannot put too much hope on one person. What is required is to lobby the clergy at grassroot level for it is now clear that in the CCAP the clergy are very influential although we are made to believe that it is the members of the congregations who have power to make decisions. My experience in the CCAP has proved that on the issue of women in the church, the power to make decisions lay with the leadership.

Violence Against Women at Chancellor College

The controversial paper

On Monday 19 July 1995, at 4.00 pm, I presented a paper entitled "Violence Against Women in Educational Institutions: The Case of Sexual Harassment and Rape on Chancellor College Campus", at the annual conference of the University Research and Development Committee, held at Sun and Sand Holiday Resort in Mangochi. The paper presented findings of research conducted in June/July 1994 by myself, Linda Semu from the Sociology Department, Flora Nankhuni from the Economics Department and Nyovani Madise from the Statistics Department. The four concerned female lecturers form the Chancellor College Gender Lobby Group. The research had aimed to "determine the level of sexual harassment and incidence of rape on female students at Chancellor College Campus" In this context we wanted to find out who was responsible for harassment and rape, if the levels were increasing or decreasing, how the victims reacted and to whom they reported and also if sufficient support structures existed.[47] Questionnaires had been sent to all 364 female students on Chancellor College campus. 202 returned the completed questionnaire, which were all anonymous, and no names were to be mentioned in the replies.

The results were that 23 students (12.6%) reported that they were raped, of them 48% by a boyfriend, 17% by a friend and 6% by others. 67% (125/186) of the

---

[46] Dickson Kashoti, "Blantyre Synod Women Assured of Equal Rights" *Malawi News*, 18-24 November 1995, p. 10.
[47] See I. Phiri, L. Semu, F Nankhuni, N. Madise, "Violence Against Women in Educational Institutions: The Case of Sexual Harassment and Rape on Chancellor College Campus" unpublished research paper, 1995.

ZABWEKA...

respondents reported that they had been sexually harassed on campus, with "unwelcome sexual advances" being the most frequent form mentioned (49.6%). Persons mentioned were: friends (55.7%), boyfriends (5%), male lecturers (5%). Outside campus male lecturers were mentioned with 28.7%, strangers with 45%. Outside the campus "to grant sexual favours" was the most frequently reported type of sexual harassment. The survey did not produce conclusive evidence about a rise or decline in sexual harassment. Two thirds (61%) of the students raped did not report to anyone. Out of the 39% who reported, 22% reported to their parents and 38% to friends, none to police or College administration. The others seem to have reported to friends. Fear and lack of knowledge of where to report were the reasons for not doing so. On sexual harassment 64% shared their experience with someone, only 4% reported to the College administration, none to the police. The implications we found were problems with the students' performance, depression, mental torture, pain and an attempted suicide. As authors (supported by answers in the questionnaires) we recommended that the University should produce a policy document on sexual harassment and rape, that this policy should be effectively communicated to all concerned, that each campus should have a Gender Lobby Group composed of lecturers and students and that the University should appoint counsellors to assist victims.

The paper was generally accepted, critical comments included that the possibility that women invite rape on themselves was not included, that women may buy their way to the top through sex and that the definition of sexual harassment employed was too broad. Reporters from Malawi Broadcasting Corporation, who had been invited by the RPC, interviewed me the next morning together with other presenters. The interview was aired by MBC on newsreel just after the main 12.30 news. Of the many interviews given, only mine was aired, after mentioning that many papers had been presented.

The paper had been presented on Monday, the interview was aired on Tuesday, on Wednesday students demanded air time on MBC to make a nationwide statement to refute my report and demand an apology on MBC "to the student body and the public for the ethically sensitive information dissemination" [48] The SUCC Chairman was driven in a college vehicle to the MBC studio in Zomba and read the statement.[49] A large group of students staged a demonstration to the MBC studio. On their way a sizable group of them attacked my house by throwing heavy stones into the sitting room and the bedrooms and damaging the door and the roof of the house and my car. My son (seven years old), my nephew (six years old) and

---

[48] Report "Students Demonstration" from Chairman, Students Union of Chancellor College, to Principal, 21 July 1995.
[49] No copy of the text read has become available since then.

my mother were in the house. From there they proceeded to damage my office in Chancellor College. This was done at about 12.30pm. In addition to material damage, verbal damage was done. My life and those of my child, my nephew and mother were threatened, when the students said they would come back with petrol to burn the house.

At 2pm the Principal phoned the RPC coordinator and me at Mangochi and informed us about the extent of the damage and about the demands of the students, asking the Coordinator to rerun the taped interview and to comment. He told me to come back to Zomba immediately, but there was no transport. At the conference the tape was rerun, and the representatives of RPC stated that the tape contained what had been presented in the conference room and made a statement condemning the violence.[50] When I returned to Zomba the next day, no alternative accommodation had been arranged for me and my family, nor any security been provided because no guards could be spared. Together with the Head of Department I visited the Principal at his home in the evening to ask for accommodation, whereupon we were granted one night at Government Hostel. This is what happened. What were the reactions?

The College Administration: placate the students and blame the victim

This was the approach taken by the administration, clearly reflected in the Principal's letter to the Vice Chancellor, written the day after the attack. He wrote:

> Since the students were reacting to Dr I. Phiri's radio interview which was on the air on Tuesday, 18th July 1995 on the ground that her statements amounted to defamation and that the students challenge the validity of her findings, it is necessary that your office should without delay, set up a committee to carry out, inter alia, the following activities: (a) Evaluate the questionnaire against the objectives of the survey. (b) assess the sampling (c) analyse the responses (d) interpret the data (e) compare their findings with those of Dr I. Phiri (f) assess to what extent the information broadcast was distorted, if at all (g) assess the effects of the information broadcast (h) make appropriate recommendations to your office.[51]

Obviously I was blamed and the students were, as the letter continues, "an aggrieved party" There was no hint in the letter of any condemnation of the students' violence, but a clear distrust in the quality and validity of the research.

---

[50] This statement was to be released only *after* the students had finished their examinations, three weeks after the event.

[51] Principal, Chancellor College - Vice-Chancellor, University of Malawi, 22 July 1995.

There was no defence of academic freedom either. What was important was to protect the interests of the students.

This was later confirmed when at the meeting of Heads and Deans at Chancellor College, the Principal informed everyone that it was difficult for him to bring to book the students who were involved in vandalizing my college house, office and personal car. However he asked for the formation of a Commission of Inquiry of Deans to examine the questionnaire, methodology and interpretation of the paper that I presented. He also said that I should appear before the commission to answer charges of acting irresponsibly by giving a radio interview on a sensitive paper. A letter was sent to me by the College Registrar informing me to appear before a Committee of Deans on 7th August to answer charges in connection with the radio interview. By the time I presented the conference paper, I had already applied to go to attend two conferences in South Africa from 1st to 12th August. I wanted to retain my academic freedom to attend conferences so I suggested to the Principal that I appear before the deans after the conferences for which permission had already been granted by the Principal and Vice Chancellor. Neither did I want to forego the compassionate leave that I had applied for which included attending my brother's wedding in South Africa. So I suggested to appear before the Deans after I came back. The Principal reluctantly agreed:

> Dr I.A. Phiri The meeting with the Committee of Deans will take place early September when you return. I have talked to the Chairman, who was able to talk to two other Deans. They are not happy that they cannot meet you until September. E. Fabiano[52]

Despite the fact that the research was done by four people and in my case with resources from my Department, the Principal demanded that I appear before the committee of Deans alone. In the Principal's memo of 3rd August, he argued in the following way:

> 1. As Principal of this College, I am and have to be interested in the contents of any document that discusses the welfare of my staff or students at this College.
>
> 2. The paper that was presented at the Conference is not on Theology or Religion and was not coauthored by staff in the Department. Therefore, it is not a Departmental issue.
>
> 3. The College Administration is not going to take instructions from the Department of Theology and Religious Studies on how to manage College Affairs.

---

[52] Full copy of the text written on a note "With the Compliments of the Principal", 31 July 1995.

4. You are entitled to your opinion but please note that running away from a problem is not the same as solving a problem. Your supporting reason for the holiday that "I need to leave the country for a while until the students have finished writing their examinations and the concerned male lecturers have cooled down" implies that you are not prepared to face reality. The students will be back next academic year and note that cooling down is not the same as forgetting or forgiving. Therefore, the sooner the differences are solved the better.[53]

This letter obviously was meant to emphasize that I was the one to blame for all that went wrong after the presentation of the researched paper. To this I replied to the Principal in the following way:

I wish to apologise for giving you the impression that I do not recognise your authority as the Principal of Chancellor College. That thought never entered my mind. I acknowledge that as a head of the institution you have the authority to protect the welfare of this community. However, so far I am wondering why my welfare has not been your concern. I also acknowledge your power to institute a committee of Deans although they are also part of the aggrieved male lecturers ...

As the Principal of Chancellor College, I acknowledge your authority to demand that I appear before the committee of Deans alone   Without giving you the impression that I am telling you what to do, or that I do not want to face the committee of Deans, you may wish to note that separating the research paper from the radio interview will be very difficult and might prove to be frustrating to me and the committee of Deans   I wish to humbly inform you in advance that I will not answer questions on the research paper before the committee of Deans because I do not have the mandate to do so from the co-authors. Although the charge before me is on defamation, in my opinion, what is at stake here is doing research and disseminating information in the field of Gender. Sooner or later it will be important to establish whether lecturers who have specialized or are interested in Gender issues have academic freedom to do research and disseminate information in the University of Malawi...

I also wish to acknowledge your authority as Principal of Chancellor College to interpret my asking for a holiday from 13th-31st August as 'running away from problem' 'not being prepared to face reality', 'and thinking that people will forget and forgive' By using this kind

---

[53] Principal's memo "Violent Demonstration by Students" 3 August 1995.

of judgmental language, I get the impression that I have already been found guilty without a trial   You may wish to note that it is not in my nature to run away from academic debates channeled through academic forums as long as I am not subjected to acts of violence. Hiding from danger is not the same as 'refusing to face reality' as you put it in your memo'...[54]

My letter was never replied to and no new date was proposed for the meeting with the Deans. I was left in suspense and my movements were still restricted as I did not know what was happening. It was later learnt that meeting with the Committee of Deans was cancelled because the Malawi Broadcasting Company refused to release the tape containing my radio interview. Since the meeting was precisely based on that, then the Deans had no concrete material to work with.

The Department: the integrity of the University depends on the exercise of academic freedom

This was the position adopted by the Department of Theology and Religious Studies to which I belong. As soon as news reached members of the Department that the students had attacked my College house, personal car and College office, the Department showed its solidarity by writing a memo of protest to the Administration. Their basis for support was not just because I am a member of that Department but to defend academic freedom. They expressed surprise that it did not occur to the College Administration that they should have issued without delay a clear statement to condemn the student's unruly behaviour. They also placed my safety and that of my family on the college administration. A demand was made to the College Administration to take disciplinary action against the culprits. They further demanded that "the College ensures that academic freedom of research and expression is safeguarded and that dissent over research findings is expressed in non-violent ways."

The Department also took responsibility for making and publicizing corrections to the report that appeared in the *Daily Times* of 20 July 1995. They made it a point to poster the corrections on the notice boards on campus to show the University that they were reacting to wrong information. Copies of the researched paper which was presented at the conference organised by the Research and Publication Committee were placed in the Library, posted in the student cafeteria, both staff senior and junior common rooms. Personal copies were sent to the Chairperson and Vice Chairperson of the Chancellor College Student Union as well as the Chairperson of the University Student Union. It was the Department that went to the police to report on the damages and harassment of members of my family.

---

[54] I.A. Phiri - Principal, Chancellor College, 5 September 1995.

When the College administration could not provide security guards on the night after the vandalism, it was the Department that hired such facilities. When no alternative accommodation was arranged after my return from the conference, it was again the Department that went to the Principal's house at night to plead for my accommodation which was reluctantly provided.

The stand of the Department should be understood in the context of the Principal's memo of 21 July addressed to members of Staff of the Department of Theology and Religious Studies. The Principal argued that:

> As you will have read in my memorandum to the Vice Chancellor and my verbal responses to your memorandum, the College Administration is doing what is possible and best under the present circumstances and by taking into account other factors which we are aware of. Thus, most of the issues you have raised are under control. However there is a limit to what the College Administration can do.

Thus what the Department was doing was to fill in the gaps in the areas that the College Administration implied were outside its limits. It also decided to take full responsibility for the research paper[55] which did not please the College Administration. When the College Administration was quiet about the whole issue in the months of September and October, the Department at its meeting of 12 October decided to pursue it through the Vice Chancellor.[56]

The Vice-Chancellor: condemn the violence and catch the perpetrators

When the Principal of Chancellor College informed the Vice Chancellor on the phone on 19th July that students wanted to demonstrate, the Vice Chancellor's initial reaction was to 'query the wisdom of such a demonstration' When the Vice Chancellor saw that it was a big demonstration, he again got in touch with the Chancellor College Principal to explain what was happening. After the damage caused by the students to my College and my property, the Vice Chancellor was one of the first people to visit the vandalized scene and offer apology to my mother. He was shocked to see the great damage caused and later commented that 'I fear what would have happened had Dr Phiri been at the house then' I would hate to see this College degenerate into a Campus of thugs. I will do everything in my power to restore a sense of dignity, civility and responsibility to this once model institution.'[57] As a matured person who had worked in the University for

---

[55] Department of Theology and Religious Studies, Departmental Meeting of 28 July 1995, Minute 11.

[56] Department of Theology and Religious Studies, Departmental Meeting of 11 October 1995, Minute 5.

[57] Vice Chancellor - Mrs J.M. Walker, 24 July 1995.

29 years, he did not support the actions of the students but demanded that the Principal of Chancellor College should condemn the violence and catch the culprits. It was in this vein that the Vice Chancellor refused to set up a committee to examine the research paper in question. He argued that this was a College matter which should be settled by the College.

As the opening of the new academic year was approaching, the Head of the Department of Theology and Religious Studies and myself paid the Vice Chancellor a visit. The purpose of the visit was to inform him that the Chancellor College Administration had not yet taken any disciplinary action against the students who attacked me. This gave me the impression that I am a legitimate target for violence and made me feel very vulnerable to go back to work. It was after this visit that the Vice Chancellor arranged that there should be a meeting to discuss the issue. The meeting was attended by the Principal, Dean of Humanities, Head of Department of Theology and Religious Studies. One is left to wonder as to what could have happened if no attempt was made by the Department to initiate talks before the opening of the new academic year.

The Research and Publications Committee: the issue is too complex

The University Research and Publication Committee (RPC) reacted in two ways to the intimidation and violence that I experienced. The information about the vandalization of my property was relayed to the Coordinator of RPC while the conference was going on by the Principal of Chancellor College by phone on 19th July. The Principal gave RPC the mandate to listen to the taped interview that I made for their comments. The Coordinator duly convened a meeting of RPC faculty representatives who were present at the conference. I was part of the meeting in my capacity as representative of the Faculty of Humanities and Chairperson of RPC. Fortunately the MBC reporter was still at the conference, he therefore made the tape available to the RPC Coordinator to rerun it. I was consulted by the reporter before he surrendered the tape. He informed me that I had the right to say no if I did not want RPC to listen to the interview. Since I knew that what I had said during presentation was the same with what was contained in the paper, I had nothing to hide. I therefore gave my permission to rerun the tape. When this was done, RPC agreed to release a statement to condemn the student violence and uphold academic freedom to do research and disseminate information. It was also agreed that the statement be released after the students had finished writing their end of year examinations. The examinations were to start a week after the students vandalism. It was hoped that the RPC statement should not be used as an excuse to promote more violence and therefore disturb the commencement of the examinations.

To my surprise even after the students had gone for holidays, RPC did not release the agreed statement. Therefore the issue was further deliberated at RPC meeting of 17th September 1995. It was at this meeting that the Research Coordinator informed everyone that:

> The statement had not been released because judging by the intensity and extent of the debate, it appeared that the issue was more complex than had been assumed at the ad hoc meeting in Mangochi and that the full RPC Committee needed to give mandate to the Research Office on the suitability of releasing the statement of action regarding the students.

Following a lengthy debate the committee agreed that the issue appeared to be very complex and RPC would find itself in a mess if it got mixed up in the debate and therefore resolved that the statement should not be released.[58] It becomes clear here that by not condemning the action of the students in order to defend academic freedom, RPC was implicitly sending a message to the students that it is alright to disagree in a violent way when one is not happy with results of research conducted in the University of Malawi. One may want to know as to what makes the issue to be too complex. This becomes clear with the examination of the reaction of Chancellor College staff.

Academic Staff: a mixed reaction

The first time I went to Chancellor College campus after the presentation of the research paper was on 8th September when I attended a research presentation by the Chancellor College Principal. This was the first time to actually experience the intensity of hostility from a substantial section of the academic staff. Since no one actually came forward to accuse of anything, it was difficult to pin point what exactly it was that offended the academic staff. However, at the meeting of Heads and Deans of Chancellor College, my issue was tabled on the agenda. The Principal simply informed the participants that a decision had already been made that I should appear before a Committee of Deans. Three outstanding comments from the local male academic staff at the meeting agreed with the Principal because 'I had acted irresponsibly by disseminating sensitive information on the air', thus 'she brought the intimidation and violence from the students upon herself' and 'she is only after power to become Principal of Chancellor College'.[59]

The academic staff who were in support either came in person to show their support or wrote to the Vice Chancellor and the Principal of Chancellor College to

---

[58] See Minutes 92/95 and 93/95 of Minutes of the 122nd meeting of Senate Research and Publications Committee held at the University Office on Tuesday, 17 September 1995.
[59] Verbal report from participant.

condemn what had happened. Two of such memos came from the Head of the Law Department and a member of the Department of Education Foundations.[60] Both letters were calling the University to support academic freedom. For example, the Head of Law Department argued that:

> I would like to reiterate that unless strong measures are taken to deal with such terrorism as that displayed by those who attacked Dr Phiri's property and family, the future of academic freedom at this college remains bleak and the integrity of the University as a whole is seriously jeopardized.[61]

This group of academic staff showed that by calling the University to discipline the concerned students, we would be making a statement that academic freedom is valued at this university.

Unfortunately when the paper was presented, two co-authors were out of the country, Nyovani Madise was in Europe and the Flora Nankhuni was in Zambia participating in a conference. Linda Semu was out of Zomba in the field conducting another research project. I was therefore left alone to present the paper and bear the consequences. Nevertheless, when Linda read about the vandalism, she sent a fax to express her solidarity. Flora came back when I had gone to South Africa. During this period, the Principal of Chancellor College invited her to his office to tell her to keep off the issue for people are not interested in the co-authors but the presenter of the paper.

Nyovani wrote to the Principal to argue that 'all four of us had equal responsibility of the execution and presentation of the research findings.' She further argued that 'since this was academic research, conducted with the approval of the University of Malawi Research and Publications Committee and the female respondents, I find it very strange that people should express their dissent through violent action. Such behaviour is not only intimidating but crippling to the future of research at the University of Malawi'.[62] She therefore queried the wisdom of inviting one co-author to appear before the committee of Deans as if I am the only one responsible for the paper. She also queried the action of criticizing academic work in a court-like session with threats of disciplinary action afterwards. She did not see why the Principal wanted to set up a committee to evaluate the questionnaire against the objectives of the research since this had already been done by RPC. She reminded the Principal that RPC had already seen the abstract of the paper and approved that it should be presented. She questioned the composition of the all male Committee

---

[60] Prof J.R. Minnis - Vice Chancellor, 20 July 1995.

[61] Head of Law Department (F.F Kanyongolo) - Principal, 21 July 1995.

[62] Dr Nyovani Madise - Dr E. Fabiano, 20 September 1995.

of Deans. She concluded by stating that the Committee of Deans had the academic freedom to examine our paper. But she opposed the idea of singling out one person to appear before this committee as if an offence had been committed. If indeed the Committee of Deans can prove that an offense has been committed, then all four co-authors should be invited to answer the charges. The Principal is yet to respond to this letter.

The students: who is she to tarnish our image?

According to a report written by the Chairman of the Students Union of Chancellor College (SUCC) and submitted to the Principal, after the broadcast the students began to sensitize each other. They "became so nervous and worried about what most of them called their 'image' outside the campus to their parents, guardians, relatives and mates, that tension mounted".[63] Therefore to defend their 'image', the students met and agreed to demonstrate and "refute the report made by Dr I. Phiri using the same mass media and that she apologizes to the student body and the public for the ethically sensitive information dissemination".[64] To achieve this, the Executive of SUCC was in consultation with the Principal and asked him to provide transport.

At the MBC studio, the chairman and vice chair person "expressed the concern of the student body challenging the 67% research findings as scientifically and statistically unreliable and invalid. I (chairman) concluded by demanding that Dr I. Phiri should furnish us with information on how she carried out her research; the representative nature of the research sample and how she operationally defined sexual harassment and rape." These demands were made before any of the students had read the research report, and most of them hadn't listened to the broadcast either. It is in the mood of wrong information that a group of the demonstrators branched off to attack my house. The Executive of SUCC disassociated themselves from the vandalism on the basis that they returned to campus by the same vehicle that had been provided by the College Administration. The chairman of SUCC finished his report by stating that 'The SUCC Executive however, feels incapacitated to grapple with such an issue of criminal nature because of self evident lack of proficiency. We therefore recommend to the College Administration to bring this issue to the attention of professionals in criminology to subject the matter to scrutiny.'[65] It was on this note that the students went to their homes for the long vacation.

---

[63] Chairman, Students Union of Chancellor College - Principal, 21 July 1995.

[64] *Ibid.*, p. 3.

[65] *Ibid.*, p. 6. Neither this nor any other dissociation from the violence was made public.

The newspapers

The *Daily Times* was the first newspaper to report on the issue. It is their report that fueled more tension because it was also based on wrong information. The story was put on front page and the bold headlines read 'RAPE SURVEY CAUSES HAVOC: CHANCELLOR COLLEGE STUDENTS DEMONSTRATE' The title of the paper that I presented at the conference was said to be 'Rape and rapists at Chancellor College' I was quoted to have said 'there are 67% rape cases on Chancellor College campus which are committed by male students and male lecturers'.[66] It is important to note that *Daily Times* enjoys the largest circulation in the country. The members of staff of the Department of Theology and Religious Studies phoned *Daily Times* to protest for the wrong information. As a follow up, the *Daily Times* sent another reporter[67] to interview the Chairman of SUCC, a member of the Department of Theology and Religious Studies, another senior lecturer and two students. The information appeared in a small corner on page 1 of the Friday July 21 *Daily Times*. The title was 'Student' Vandalism Condemned'. The story continued on page four with a new title, 'Lecturer's property vandalized' It also carried two photographs of my damaged vehicle and house. No apology was made for the wrong information published the previous day.

The Nation which has established itself as a strong competitor of *Daily Times* did not pick up the story initially. However it contained debates by the public on the nature of the research. Some of the writers took the side of the students to challenge the validity of the research even though they too did not read the paper. It was argued that the report was 'unrealistic and questionable'.[68] However there were others who argued against that kind of stand. For example one writer argued that: "If the research was seen as not to be credible, why don't the students and/or staff conduct an independent survey on the question of rape at the college. This is what academia is competent of doing - proving and disproving established and non established theses and dogma."[69] There were also more reports of rape and sexual harassment in different institutions.

Of great value to me was the vote of readers of *The Nation* which declared me 'WOMAN OF THE YEAR'.[70] The front page of the newspaper carried my full-page portrait and the caption read "Phiri: lived through a male student onslaught,

---

[66] *Daily Times*, 20 July 1995, frontpage article by Sitha Katumbi.
[67] The second reporter from *Daily Times* was Ranken Nyekanyeka.
[68] See the article by Justin Kalima in *The Nation*, 6 September 1995, "Women are Sexual Offenders"
[69] See the article by Janet Karim in *The Nation*, 19 November 1995, "Someone Found Women Guilty"
[70] *Saturday Nation* 30 December 1995 - 5 January 1996.

survived a scrape with the CCAP clergy, came through with minor scars and keeps her spirits undaunted." The full story was carried on p. 5 as a special profile. An outstanding comment of the feature by Jika Nkolokosa was: "She rides tall among them all, yet so humble. She fights like an Amazon for women's rights. The battle is still on, but slowly, surely victory is hers." This was a great honour to me because it taught me that I had a big support from men and women in this country. My suffering is not in vain. Secondly, the newspaper article came out a day before the new academic year started. Therefore, it gave me the courage to go to work with my head held high to meet the student and staff community of Chancellor College for the first time after the July incident. I felt that the public had declared me 'NOT GUILTY' I was vindicated.

A case worth hiring a lawyer

Due to the criminal nature of the case and also to defend my academic freedom, I was forced to hire a lawyer to represent me. I wanted to be represented by a female lawyer, but there was none readily available. They are either working for the government or are employed by private companies. However the male lawyer that I hired started very well. He reminded the college administration that besides the damage caused on personal property, there was also physical as well as mental damage caused on my child, mother and myself. He argued that:

> Our client and her colleagues, by presenting the paper after conducting a thorough research, merely exercised their freedom of expression academically, a thing that ought to be encouraged at a place of learning. The academic community should not run away from expressions of truth and the public ought to know what is actually happening in our institutions of higher learning.[71]

He reminded the College Administration that their role is to work hand in hand with the police in order to bring to book those who were involved in vandalism so that nothing of this sort should happen again in the University of Malawi. He also demanded that I be given another office. Since the College Administration were failing to come up with the culprits, he demanded that the College should bear the responsibility for everything which included compensating me for harassment, the irreparable physical and mental shock suffered by my family and for repairing my car.

I felt that I was not ready to face a court case therefore my lawyer and I agreed that the settlement should be done out of court. The University agreed. However the University lawyer left on leave of absence before the settlement was finalized. Therefore the University has put the case on hold like all cases against it until they

---

[71] Chizumila, Msiska and Co - Principal of Chancellor College, 20 September 1995.

employ another lawyer. The initial reaction of the College was a total disbelief that I had hired a lawyer against the University. On the positive side, the College Administration allocated to me another office.[72]

The church and fellowship groups

The day that I returned from Mangochi I was visited by my church minister who offered his apology and explained to me what he observed and heard from the student demonstrators. He prayed with me. I took it as a sign of solidarity. It was then that I also learnt that I had missed my chance of being blessed to join the women's guild. For one year I had attended all the Mvano classes and sat for the oral examinations in June 1995 which I passed with no difficulty. All the Mvano students were just waiting for the church minister to choose a day for dedication. When I left for Mangochi conference I was not aware that the minister had chosen the same Sunday I left for the dedication of new members. I therefore missed my chance. On the day that he came to see me I mentioned to him the possibility of choosing another date for me and two others who were also left out. I was told that everything was to be conducted after he had returned from holiday in October. When I went to see him in October, I was told that I had been put on hold because of the Chancellor College issue. I was only going to be dedicated after I was cleared by my employers. I asked him why he did not inform me of the church's discussion and I wanted to know whether there was a committee that had been set up to conduct an investigation as to whether I was in the wrong or not. He said no to both issues. Seven months have passed since then and nothing has been communicated to me as to what the findings of the church were and whether I can be dedicated as a member of the women's guild or not. When I went to ask for a transfer letter, I was told that the minister had gone to his village on sick leave and that he had not communicated to anyone about his decision that I was on hold or that anyone should investigate my case with my employers. Contrary to the stand taken by my church minister, the new General Secretary Rev Misanjo Kansilanga visited me at home in February 1996 to inform me that I had his support in all that I was going through at work. Even though he did not find me at home, he left a message of encouragement to me as a member of Blantyre Synod CCAP. I appreciated that a lot. My greatest spiritual support during this difficult period was at a Charismatic fellowship in Chitawira, Blantyre known by the name of Holy Ghost Christian Fellowship. I shared with them my burden and they fought with me in fervent prayers. It was through this fellowship that I experienced the love of Jesus Christ when in trouble. I also experienced Jesus Christ who solves people's problems in concrete terms.

---

[72] College Registrar - I.A. Phiri, 31 October 1995. I never took up the office because it was being used by someone else

Analysis

Not a new issue

The experiences of the women in the Blantyre Synod of CCAP showed that the issues that they were raising were not new issues. They had addressed the same issues in different fora before and had tried to bring them to the attention of the church leaders. This is the same with the Chancellor College issue. The first forum was a one day seminar that was organised by the Department of Theology and Religious Studies and the Department of Sociology held on 12th February 1994. This seminar was on Violence Against Women and it was attended by both female students and female members of the Zomba community. It was at this seminar that the Chancellor College female students complained about the kind of violence that they were experiencing on campus. A week after the conference, a mob of fifty male students came to my house to insult me for being one of the organisers of the conference. Since they came in the early evening, it was difficult for me to identify them. However, there were people who managed to do that and through the efforts of all academic staff, the culprits were brought to book. My College house became an easy target for the students because it happens to be the first one after the College campus.

Accountability again

In the case of the church, there was pressure coming from the International Reformed body that forced Blantyre Synod to enter into dialogue with the concerned women. This contributed a lot to the positive outcome of the case. However in the case of the University, there was no such accountability. Most of those who wrote to protest were foreigners within the country but no international body was involved. As a result, the University did not feel obliged to defend academic freedom.

Can a moral judgment be made?

The nature of the institutions involved in this paper matters as to whether a moral judgement was made or not. In the case of the Church, although they started with a negative attitude, later they were made to see the evil of what was happening and therefore changed its stand by apologizing to the concerned women. In the case of Chancellor College, no apology was offered at all. At a meeting with the Principal in November, he made it very clear that he had no apology to make because whatever he said was influenced by the mood of the occasion. The College Administrators did not consider to look at the recommendations that we had made which are of help to the running of the College and the lives of female students. We had recommended that the University should have a policy on sexual harassment and rape that would be made available to all students and staff in order to have a yardstick on how to handle future cases of rape and sexual harassment. All that was ignored.

Positive effect

The incidents in the church and the university have had positive effects. In the church, although Gertrude Kapuma was harassed the most, as a result of what happened to her, the University of Fort Hare offered her a place to study for a degree in theology. It should be borne in mind that she did not qualify for entrance into the University of Malawi. She started her studies in February 1996. Although ministers of Blantyre Synod who come to study for a degree in theology at the University of Malawi get funding from Holland, it was not extended to Mirriam Chipeta Banda. However, during the period of conflict with the church, her plight was heard by the international church bodies and friends of Blantyre Synod. Therefore a group of former missionaries of Blantyre Synod based in Scotland raised funds for her to complete her Bachelor of Theology. In the case of Chancellor College, female students have reported to me that there is a great improvement in the relationship between male and female students. The female students have been conscientized as to what are their rights on the issues of rape and sexual harassment. Most of the female students have learnt to be assertive without being aggressive. They have said with confidence that the college has now become a learning centre with friendly atmosphere for both male and female students.

As for me I was forced to apply for sabbatical leave so that I can sort myself out emotionally and psychologically, to give our son space to heal as he is still afraid of crowds of people and particularly students. My application for sabbatical leave which is one year was converted to leave of absence which can be extended up to four years. This was done by the University Administrators. Positively this is a welcome move as I did not qualify for either. However, giving me an option to be away for a longer period raises questions as to whether they think my going away is better for them. The continued debate in the newspapers on issues of rape and sexual harassment is a welcome development because the Malawi nation is being continually conscientized on gender issues. It has also become clear that the major problem with the dissemination of our research findings was the failure to differentiate between rape and sexual harassment. In the Principal's memo to the Vice Chancellor, the Student's report, as well as in the first article that appeared in the *Daily Times*, it was made clear that rape and sexual harassment were combined to 67%. This mistake was enough to raise an alarm to whoever heard or read about it. But when the correction was made, no apology was offered. In both church and college, the methods of the women were condemned, but what about the contents? The church was forced to consider the contents but in the case of Chancellor College there was total rejection of the research.

4. Young People: Participation or Alienation? An Anglican Case

James Tengatenga

Introduction

The aim of this chapter is to ascertain the outlook of young people in Malawi in regard to their participation and/or alienation in church and society. It seeks to establish who are perceived by young people as having power, how they understand such power to be exercised, what power they feel that they themselves have and how they use it. The survey was conducted among Anglican young people in both rural and urban parishes in Lilongwe, Nkhotakota, Ntchisi, Mangochi, Blantyre and Zomba. It sought to embrace both the educated young people and those who are excluded from formal education. The Anglican Church is one of the so-called mainline churches. It is the fourth biggest church after the Seventh Day Adventist, Presbyterians and the Roman Catholics (in ascending order) in terms of membership. If it is growing at all it is at a very slow rate. Its perceived stature in the eyes of many Malawians is bigger than it really is. It is part of the colonial legacy that it is seen as an influential church. It is, therefore, chosen to be a sample of the influential churches. Apart from a different denominational polity the youth work in these churches is similarly organized to the extent that when one has seen one, one has seen them all. This latter assertion is based on the fact that the Christian Council of Malawi used to have a very active youth department which coordinated the work in the member churches (of which work I have first hand experience having been the convenor of the committee that advised that department for three terms of office).

By the terms "young people", "the young" and "the youth" I mean people aged 15-29. This term will consistently be contrasted to the term *adults*. Generally speaking all people who have reached the age of majority, 18, are considered (and they consider themselves) adults. This obviously leads to a difficulty in my use of terms. The term *adults* is preferred to *senior* which may mean anybody older than one, even among infants and in some respects conjures up ideas of geriatrics. The term *elders* is also not used because it may be understood in the same way as senior in the former definition and may also be confused with the title of some church officials. The *elderly* is also not suitable as it also has geriatric connotations. In youth work the 20+ bracket of young people is usually called *young adults*, and work among them is considered youth work. For purposes of this discussion the 18+ are young adults and therefore adults will be the over 30s which is the bracket from which those in authority come.[1]

The demography of Malawi indicates that young people make up about 25% of the population;[2] which stands at over 10,000,000. This would, therefore, suggest that they are an important component of society and that their contributions to it are of vital importance. One would assume that ministry to and with them would be a matter of course. However, the opposite is true. Gerontocracy, with no representation of the young people, is the order of the day. Because of their numbers and energy they are exploited by the powerful for the latter's gain. If they are noticed at all it is as apprentices and they are not taken seriously.

What do the young people themselves say about this situation? What do we make of it in relation to power and the exercise of it? If all power is accountable to God is this a responsible exercise of it? What is the place of youth in the church and in the world?

In order to hear the young people's views an open-ended questionnaire was used for group interviews. The groups were the traditional Anglican youth group gatherings. It was decided to use this method because it was less intimidating for the young people and it reduced the fear of being drawn into what can be used against them as individuals. This is something that Malawians are very cautious about in the wake of the Kamuzu era. This method also provided the opportunity for girls to be included without being isolated. The open-ended questionnaire made it possible for the young people to say what they felt like saying without thinking that there is a specific answer required.

The Role of Young People in Church, Society and Politics

Church

Their response was that they sweep and clean inside and outside of the church building, sing in the choirs, serve at the altar during the Eucharist, read lessons during the service and occasionally lead services. The latter occurs more in the rural areas than in the urban. They mend fences and dig pit latrines. Some are

---

[1] However, since the age for joining Holy Orders is 23 some of the adults are really young adults! By virtue of being in the Holy Orders they automatically become *adults* - people with authority.

[2] *Malawi Demography and Health Survey 1992*, Zomba: National Statistical Office, 1994. In most studies the figure usually quoted is over 65%. This seems to include children which figure, according to this latest demography, is 71.8% (i.e. ages 0-14 [47.3%] + 15-29 [24.5%]). The age bracket of interest here is the 15-29 which totals 24.5%.

Sunday School teachers while others are involved in local congregation drama initiatives. As just indicated in some rural areas they are the virtual Lay Leaders doing the leading of worship and some pastoral work. In contrast to these, those in town have not such a chance and they even have a hard time in getting permission to lead the hymn singing, which permission is generally not granted. When it comes to representing themselves in the Parish Council and Synod they also do not have a chance. They are represented by the leaders who are themselves adults.

Apart from the few differences indicated, there is not much difference between the rural, town and educated youth in their experience. When their involvement is analyzed it is clear that the rural youth, who seem to be more involved, do so by default. It is not by design. It is because they are the literate ones and so can lead services: they can read. The pastoral work they do is also because in some areas there are not enough elders to do it. During church services they are not allowed to lead the hymns because that is a major thing not to be left to the minors. They can entertain the congregation with their choirs and fill up the silences but not the 'real' worship music.[3] This they resent.

When it comes to decision making they would like to represent themselves and not be represented by youth leaders who are themselves adults. They do not like being called future leaders:

> If you say we are future leaders, then you are wrong. We are leaders already because we are executing the same job which a paid catechist is doing somewhere in the parish.[4]

From the catalogue of their involvement it is evident that they are relegated to manual work. They are made to do the jobs that adults consider to be beneath them. The comment of Clive Andrews is apposite:

> If I were asked to sum up the relationship between young people and the church, I would say that young people are more frequently wanted than loved. To love them is essential.... If young people are expected to participate in the mundane chores they may receive the impression that adults think that is all they are fit for.[5]

---

[3] Hymns are seen to be the *real* Worship music while the choir anthems are not. This seems to be the way both the young and the adults see it. This is, however, a misunderstanding of the place of music in worship.

[4] William Matuta of Matewere Village, Mangochi, interview, 18 October 1994.

[5] C. Andrews, *A Handbook of Parish Youth Work*, London: Mowbray, 1984, pp. 16, 10.

Society

They understand their role as one of helping parents with domestic chores. They are also involved in doing any odd tasks that the elders consider to be too menial for them. Among these tasks are the digging of graves and doing all sorts of errands at funerals. On very rare occasions they may help in preparing the dead body. They are excluded from decision making processes as they are considered too young to be involved. This is mainly the experience of the rural sample. The educated said that they are only needed when there are jobs to be done. They take the lead when it comes to self-help projects in the community. Some indicated that they were involved in 'mob-justice.'[6] As for town youth, it seems that there is no activity to speak of. When quizzed about it they said that they have no idea of what form that would take and that they do not see it as an issue for them.

Politics

Most of them saw their role as nothing more than just casting their vote and those eligible said that they had done so. Others have taken it a step further and become youth members of political parties - the so-called "young democrats" During the referendum and the general elections some of them were monitors and were involved in active campaigning and singing campaign songs for the politicians. During the one party state they were used to disseminate multiparty propaganda while others were Malawi Congress Party Youth leaguers who have now changed their song to "*Zisinthe - zasintha*" (Let there be change - there is change).

However not all youth saw it as a Christian duty to be involved in politics. This was more so among the evangelically-minded ones. They have their reasons:

> Politicians want to be idolized, now where do we put Jesus? Where is his place in that kind of situation? That is why politics has to be left to politicians and Christianity to Christians.[7]

From the foregoing it is evident that in church, society and politics the youth are needed for what they can do; which is errands and menial jobs. They understand themselves as having only subservient and subordinate roles. They see themselves

---

[6] In 1994 the general public had taken to administering their own form of justice on thieves and other robbers. This usually took the form of dousing with petrol and setting the victim alight. This was not an activity of vigilantes but was usually impromptu, rather impulsive.

[7] Nixon Tembo, Mponda's, Mangochi, interview 15 November 1994. Cf. R. van Dijk, "Young Malawian Puritans: Young Preachers in a Present-day African Urban Environment", Ph.D. University of Utrecht, 1992. Charismatic youth in Blantyre who say that their kingdom is not of this world but heavenly hence they have no time for politics. Seventh Day Adventist youth claimed that they were expressly forbidden to be involved in politics by the church hierarchy. (The latter is from a small research project I carried out along with this one.)

as wielding no power. Where they are involved in power roles it is more by default than by design: they are the literate ones or it is because there are not enough adults available.

The Young People's Sense of Participation

Church

The situation in the rural areas called for mixed reactions. Where they were included it was because there were not enough elders and because they were the literate ones. They however lamented the lack of training for them to properly fulfill those tasks. Others felt that they were excluded and to make it worse whenever they had functions they received no support from the adults.

Similar sentiments were voiced by the educated youth. Some indicated that they felt included in the jobs that they did but were not happy with the adults ignoring their activities. Others felt that they are not given enough time to read during worship and are not allowed to be church elders. Whenever the church is giving parties they are relegated to cooking and serving. They felt excluded in decision making. They are rarely, if at all, included in parish council and diocesan committees. More often than not when they raise issues and concerns they are usually given partial attention or have only lip service paid to them with no tangible improvement in their situation.

Among the town youth the big cry is that they are not allowed to be in the Parish Council. Their requests are generally not attended to. They are not allowed to preach and are not allowed to lead services. For this reason they feel excluded. Because adults do not turn up to youth functions they also feel ignored. Girls felt it more than boys. It therefore seems that the general trend is the feeling of being marginalized.

Society

The young people in town generally felt excluded and ignored. The educated seemed to be rather unsure about this. Some of them felt that their involvement in funerals was not enough. However, they were rather ambivalent. The rural ones felt ignored and only noticed when there are jobs to be done. They also felt ignored and undermined by being treated as not mature enough. They also felt excluded in decision making. They thus see themselves as marginalized again. This situation has been given as a reason why young people seem to have opted out of society and have developed (and are committed to) their own youth subculture. They have thus created an alternative society complete with a language of its own.

Politics

The rural youth felt ignored in decision making but included in campaigns. The educated saw themselves as totally excluded from any meaningful positions. They are not in any positions of power. The town ones see themselves excluded and ignored and needed only for campaigns.

Reasons for Treatment Received

The young people in town have ideas about why they are treated in the way they are. They believe that it is because adults consider them as not mature and competent enough for what are seen as adult responsibilities. The young people explain this attitude of adults as a reflection of an inferiority complex among the adults. They believe that adults are really afraid that the young people will do the jobs well and thus oust them from their positions of power. They are excluded from eldership because the rule about the married being the only ones eligible for eldership marginalizes them. In fact this rule is a creation of adults which is not part of the Anglican rules and procedure. Every baptized and confirmed person aged 18 or above is eligible for election to any lay office in the church.[8] Van Dijk, commenting on a similar situation, observed:

> Of paramount importance to our discussion here is the fact that the internal power structure of the large, established and missionary churches (whether Protestant, Catholic or Pentecostal) leave the young few opportunities to assume positions of status and responsibility. Generally, the *akulu ampingo*, a body of church elders headed by an educated reverend or priest, exert widely acknowledged authority. They demand obedience in all aspects of church affairs; no initiative in religious matters may be taken without their prior consent. Governing Committees (for instance the Kirk Sessions in the CCAP) usually include every older male of undisputed standing and exclude young men and women. As I witnessed myself, even within these committees there is a hierarchy which is based on seniority as well as certain criteria. One of the most striking of these criteria is the status recognized in having been baptized by one of the early white missionaries of bygone years. In a number of respects, these bodies of elders can make their influence felt in the respective townships in ways that are either not open to the young preachers or rejected by them.[9]

Some pointed fingers at themselves, saying that it was because they themselves do not have confidence and because some of them are not well behaved and that they are ineligible on those grounds. They also pointed out that the young people

---

[8] Acts of the Anglican Council in Malawi.
[9] Van Dijk, "Young Malawian Puritans", p. 132.

exclude themselves by giving deference to adults.[10] As for political involvement they blame their lack of riches. Notwithstanding these they said that they see the big reason as the selfishness of adults who do not want the youth to enjoy the same benefits as adults gain through these positions of power.

The educated youth see their exclusion from responsibility as a result of parents' concern for their education. They do not want to disturb the young people's education. On the other hand they are aware that adults do not consider them competent enough and in some cases the adults say that the time has not yet come for the young people. They see their inclusion as mainly in "apprenticeship" capacity. The Mangochi youth who are the most involved of the sample see their involvement as one thrust upon them out of necessity. There are not enough adults and they are the literate ones. In some cases the involvement is seen as apprenticeship: preparation for future leadership. Adults do not trust them with decision making because they don't see them as mature enough.

The Young People's Sense of their own Power

The young people see themselves as a power to be reckoned with first because they are human beings and also because of what they can contribute to the church and society. If they were ignored, a lot of church projects would not happen and self-help projects would suffer, errands would not be done and messages would not be sent and political campaigns would fall flat. They see themselves as having power to disrupt society through demonstrations and civil disobedience. If they are excluded there would be no future leaders. If ignored they can withhold their vote (and theirs is a substantial vote). In the church if they are excluded they can withhold their pledge and so affect the finances of the church. Some even suggested that it is against the law for them to be discriminated against and that they can use the law against the powers that be. Others went on to point to the shortage of clergy as a reflection of what happens when the young people are ignored. They further saw their exclusion and being ignored as bad stewardship since this was under-utilizing human resources.

Young People's Understanding of Power and the Powerful

Power

It is their understanding that power is good in and of itself. It is for everyone but ultimately belongs to God. Power is necessary for government both in the church and in society.

---

[10] This is in contrast to Van Dijk's "puritan preachers" who have established themselves as a reaction to gerontocracy and in so doing inaugurating a new power base.

People with Power

Asked to identify people with power they mentioned the rich, adults, the clergy, church elders, chiefs, councillors, the president, politicians, headmasters, teachers, mayors, managers of all sorts, doctors, parents and other leaders in society. They generally regard these people negatively. They do not trust the powerful and they do not understand why the powerful treat them the way they do. They, however, acknowledge that some of the people with power are good but the weight is on the bad ones. The opposite is only true when it comes to parents! The powerful bad are seen as oppressive and most of them incompetent but still remaining in power. They see these as rather selfish and ignorant of the people's needs and problems.

The tendency, by the bishops, of transferring delinquent priests to other parishes is condemned. Priests and preachers should show exemplary behaviour. The appointed spiritual counsellors should also counsel wives of priests where necessary. If a priest commits an error or a sin he should be counselled and disciplined by the counsellors. The practice of transferring them to another parish to hide the sin committed in one parish should be stopped. There is no reason why a repentant priest cannot continue his work in the same parish. If he is not willing to repent of his sin, he should be retired from his job, not transferred to another parish. Transfers may, however, continue to be made on other grounds.[11]

The Attitude of People with Power towards Young People

People with power are predominantly seen as oppressive and not appreciative of young people's contribution. As Andrews writes: "Nothing, however, is more disheartening to the young people, than to spend time expressing their opinions if at the end of the day no adult seems prepared to listen or act on what they have said."[12] They see young people as people to be exploited for their own ends and gain: e.g. campaigns, filling in the gaps with music during worship. They are generally seen as people with no time for young people and do not listen to them. Only very few of them seem to appreciate young people. They are seen as nepotists and 'sugar daddies' (abusers of youth). They are not trusted to keep their word. They are understood as only looking at young people in terms of their future contribution and not much of the present. Young people are perceived as good for nothing but trouble, vandalism and bad behavior. Young people are not considered important enough hence their functions are ignored and chaplains (if any at all) do not visit schools. The latter can be borne out by the fact that among protestant churches I know of only two denominations that have what they call

---

[11] Resolution 5.3 and 5.4 of meeting of Soche Parish youth and their priest on 1 and 2 January, 1994. See also resolution 2.1 of the same meeting cited on footnote 13.
[12] Andrews, *Handbook of Parish Youth Work*, p. 10.

chaplains or youth workers set aside for secondary schools. (The Diocese of Southern Malawi has since discontinued this ministry.) One of these is in Lilongwe and I believe that is also the locus of this ministry. The other one is in Zomba. The Lilongwe one thus serves Lilongwe schools and that leaves hundreds of schools without ministry. In some cases we have an embarrassing situation whereby there is a tug-of-war between the chaplain and the local minister. While this 'power struggle' is going on, no ministry is happening. The Diocese of Lake Malawi seeing that it could not employ persons exclusively for this, chose to ask all parish priests to act as chaplains to the Anglican students in the secondary schools within their parishes. This solution has not worked for two reasons. First the priests have a lot on their plate. However, they can squeeze this in if they are really concerned. Secondly, there is an unspoken fear of secondary school pupils. 'Is my English good enough?' For some of them it is that they cannot honestly handle a youth situation but continue to make promises that they will make it some day, and that day never comes! I know of a particular situation where the priest did not minister to the young people because he was afraid of the dark! What I mean is that he was not willing to visit in the evening which was the convenient time for this particular group. It never crossed his mind to ask for an escort. In the very same situation the youth themselves used to come for me and escort me back to the rectory every Wednesday night! This leaves our young people uncared for.

Another side to this secondary school ministry is that, for some who actually do it, it is more like a worship community. You go and do some Bible study and some singsong or sometimes a real worship service but very little one-on-one work. In my own time as both youth worker and parish priest it was not uncommon for me to do just that. Not many, if any, would just be there and let the students come to them with their needs or make it known that they would entertain such a relationship. It is only the bold students that would stop the pastor for such ministry. There seems to be a difficulty in handling a non-worship situation.

University is another forgotten field. I also have the honour (most probably dishonour) of having been involved with the Christian Council's committee on university chaplaincy. This again sounds more like voicing my frustrations than an impartial observation. My intention here is to do the latter as far as is possible. Life Ministry (Campus Crusade) is doing something among the students but that is not church sanctioned and is more often than not held suspect by most parish clergy. Very unfortunate. At Chancellor College the Baptists have of late arisen to the task and have some ministry going. There are also a few individuals that have taken it upon themselves to do some ministry. The Assemblies of God have Oscar Johnson working on campus. Oscar also doubles as the unofficial chaplain or shall I say chaplain by default! The story is that the Christian Council could not appoint a chaplain and two campuses was too much for Stewart Lane who then used his discretion to ask Oscar to help. The Anglicans have no presence on campus. The students have organized themselves into what they call The Anglican Society. It is recognized by the diocese but no ministry is extended to it. Incidentally during the time of this research there was a scuffle between the wardens of the local congregation and the leadership of this society over *pentecostal* happenings during a meeting organized by the students. The affair was hurriedly reported to the bishop and the activities of the society were so affected as to grind to a halt.[13]

We are talking about 17 Churches (Anglicans included) failing to appoint a chaplain! They can't afford one, so they say, but are too proud to endorse Oscar, who is a pastor in a non-member church. The colleges with all the adjustment problems of the young people are left without ministry and the church in Malawi is not ashamed. The Colleges have no chaplains because no one in the West is sponsoring one. This suggests, at least to me, that the churches do not care. Why should the chaplain not have the same conditions of service as the local parish minister? Chaplaincy is seen as a 'special' ministry that requires a different set of conditions. (There may be a case for it but given the crisis, crisis management is called for.) The conditions of service are the important thing and not the youth! The youth in the colleges can forego nurture because the conditions of service are important. I do not believe that the different denominations would fail to provide this ministry if they thought it was important. I can't help but remember the Referendum time when the churches worked so hard and they deployed their clergy all over, even at the expense of parish work and at great personal risk. I know that some would say that there were honoraria given. I know from experience as one of the two Central Region Coordinators that there are a lot of clergy who never got a penny for all the work they did and for those that did get the honoraria it was not commensurate with the time put into it and the personal risk involved. The church was ready to do that, but youth work is childsplay! It can be ignored. If the churches believed that this ministry was important it would not be impossible for each denomination to have personnel deployed; each according to their resources. We would have the college campuses crawling with pastors!

Another case to illustrate the attitude of the church towards young people is again from my personal files. In the Holy Week of 1992 I was stripped of my youth work portfolio in the Diocese of Lake Malawi and was suspended as parish priest and subsequently asked to leave the diocese. My crime was that I had so empowered the youth in my parish that they were active in their own things and

---

[13] I actually went over to the campus to conduct my research during a regular society time and found only three members who told me that this was what the society had become.

some of them were active as pastoral agents and were popular with the parishioners to the extent that a lot of adults called them to their house for in-depth ministry. They also challenged some of the eldership on their moral standing in the community.[14] Most of these young people had evangelical tendencies (which are not against Anglican ethos). The elders saw themselves losing power. Most of the parishioners preferred ministry from these young people than from the elders, as was the tradition. They tried to stop the young people but could not. They wanted me to stop them but I refused and told them that this was actually a good state of affairs and that there was nothing in this which was against church tradition. They were so incensed that they decided to report the matter to the archdeacon who in turn defended my position. This annoyed them and they went to the bishop. The powerful few decided to claim that they stood for the views of the whole Parish Council and for the congregation.

The powerful few made their representations to the bishop without even letting the congregation know what they were doing in its name. The congregation on getting to know what was going on tried to make representations of their own but they were refused by the bishop. Several meetings were held with the bishop in my absence. I asked for an audience with the bishop but was denied it. Power had moved to the young and that was not acceptable. The young people had upset the echelons of authority and my facilitation of this was anathema. Since I was one of the powerful I was expected to be on their side. My betrayal of that led to my ouster. Their evangelical faith was not acceptable in an Anglo-Catholic diocese. I was finally charged with teaching doctrines contrary to the church and dividing the congregation and was also accused of being misled by the youth! So as not to pollute the rest of the diocese's youth I was stripped of my position as diocesan youth worker and was relieved of my incumbency and later asked to leave the diocese. (I was later taken back into the diocese and the relationship with the bishop has been restored and has even grown beyond what it was at any time before.) To youth work I was not reinstated and in fact up to now (1996) youth work is still banned in this parish. The eldership does not want the young to ascend to any position of power. They are willing to go to any length to hinder

---

[14] Cf. Resolution 2.1 of a meeting of youth from Soche Parish in Blantyre and their priest on 1st and 2nd January, 1994: "Authorities should endeavour to be exemplary in their conduct and should follow the rules and regulations set by the diocese. On the other hand the church should be strict with the standard of life of our leaders including the bishop, priests, and all those who hold office in the church activities. No matter their theology does not teach them that a particular behaviour is sin, e.g. drinking. If it does stumble others on the way into the kingdom, if it will stumble others in their faith, the leader should refrain from such practice. If not for his own sake, at least for the sake of the sheep. If the leader does not stop the practice after proper counselling, he/she should have their position relinquished - not only transferred from one station to another."

any attempt in that direction even if it means misinterpreting the constitution and canons of the church and conniving. That this was a sharing of ministry and thus good stewardship of gifts was not appreciated.

Yet another test for the commitment of church to the young is the way they appoint youth workers and leaders. Some of the workers/leaders are 'blackmailed' into those positions while others volunteer but both of these get very little or no training at all for the job. What Andrews observed in the English situation is also true for the Anglican Church in Malawi:

> Traditionally most workers have been appointed without any training whatsoever. To them is entrusted the development, well-being and spiritual growth of numerous young people simply on the basis that they are themselves young, that they had children, or that they could find no reasonable excuse to alleviate the guilt that would have followed a negative answer to the vicar's request.[15]

I believe that this is one of the reasons why most youth leaders are not able to represent the youth. Most of them do not understand the youth and would like to treat them as adults in young people's bodies. The young people see this and they resent it. The Southern Region Zone of the Anglican Society wrote several letters of complaint to the bishop about the schools' chaplains but those appeals were not acted upon.[16] What young people see in this is that they are not important enough. If they were, their needs would be attended to and careful consideration would be given to the appointment of leaders, workers and chaplains.

It is interesting to notice that the government launched for the first time ever, this year (1996), a National Youth Policy. A country with over 25% of its population being youth and one which in the *ancien regime* had a youth movement and prided itself of 'well behaved youth' had hitherto no policy! I had first hand experience of this when I was frustrated by the Ministry of Youth when I tried to get one in 1990 (for purposes of research) and was told that there was none. This to young people can only be interpreted as marginalization.[17] From the foregoing it is

---

[15] Andrews, *Handbook of Parish Youth Work*, p. 23.
[16] One such complaint was a resolution read out to the Zone conference participants at Malosa Secondary School in 1994. I was present at this conference as the Main Speaker at this conference.
[17] *The Saturday Nation*, 27 January-2 February, 1996 has recorded some reactions from youth and youth organizations to the National Youth Policy. They believe that it is good that the government has launched a youth policy. They are, however, not happy that when it came to drafting it they were excluded only to be invited to the launching. They argued that even if the contents of the documents reflect their aspirations the fact that they were not invited to participate is a gross oversight by the government which they would like to see redressed.

evident that there could be no kind word for the people with power. This is therefore an indictment on adults and the people with power.

Conclusion

If this sample is indicative of the general trend then the church, state and society are treading dangerously. This is a potential time bomb. It is also a sinful situation for which the church will need to repent. From the foregoing it is evident that there is not much difference in the self-understanding of the young people in the rural areas, the town and the educated ones. The only major difference comes in relation to society where the rural ones are heavily involved while the town ones seem to have no concept of involvement. On the whole the youth feel ignored, excluded and exploited and thus marginalized. It is their understanding that they are not treated as human enough (which is what they understand power to be). Their potential is under-utilized. It is also clear that they are ignored at the leaders' peril. Most of the church will, however, claim to have youth work of some kind going on. At a closer look one realizes that most of these are really choirs started by young people which then end up having an endorsement and patrons given to them by the church councils. Strictly speaking, choirs are not youth work since they can be multi-age. It is usually these that tend to gather at synod or diocesan annual conferences. In some places there are all-girl groups for girls set up by the church for them. In many cases there is also a programme for young people that is supposed to cater for all young people and is centred around Bible Study and singsong. There are also some variations to these. All this seems to be well. In fact the annual conferences are usually so well attended that one is led to believe that there is vibrant youth work going on in the country. These have a tendency to be deceptive because most of the attendees are usually not found in the local church meetings[18] and also by their nature these gatherings are a sum of the congregational groups. Youth work has more to do with the local situation than with the annual conference. The annual conference is not a good indicator of the state of youth work in the congregations. Synod and diocesan officials see these and get reports of these and thus are led to believe that there is a lot of youth work going on.

To illustrate the magnitude of the problem and thus to show how much has been left undone I will again revisit my old parish which used to be the biggest Anglican congregation in Lilongwe. This congregation is in the high population density area of the city and has over 1,000 adult members. Given the average

---

[18] In most cases it is elders' and clergymen's children and also those children who come from well-to-do families who can afford the fares and conference fees but who usually think that everyday local youth work is a waste of their time who make the majority at the Diocesan conferences.

family size in the country, we are talking about six children per family. Let's for argument's sake say that two of the children are adolescent. That will give us a youth membership of about 1,000. At the time I was the parish priest there, there was one choir with a membership of about forty, with only half of these present at any one time. That gives us 20 young people. There was also an all girls group, St. Agnes, with about 20 regular members. There was also another group of young people who were involved in drama: about 10. Finally there were some who did Bible study wherever they met. These were not more than 15. Together we had 65 active young people. These would gather once a month as one large group for singsong, Bible Study and some fun and games. The truth of the matter is that we were lucky if we had fifty at one gathering. However, by Anglican standards that is vibrant youth work. In fact we ended up meeting every Saturday. There were occasional ones who came in who belonged to none of the aforementioned groups.

What this says is that 65 out of 1,000 young people is considered vibrant youth work and an example to be emulated! In percentages this is 6.5% of the young membership of the congregation. What of the 93.5%? These figures reflect only those that do come to church. What about the many more who do not come to church at all? Of course when there is a conference you would have more than double the number wanting to go. Now if this is the most active parish in Lilongwe what is the situation in the less active ones. The story from around the diocese was that nothing really happened between conferences. The interesting thing is that church leaders do not seem to understand what these figures suggest. Maybe they do and do not know what to do about the situation. If over 90% of the youth are not attended to by the church what right does it have to blame them for their unchristian behaviour? Isn't the behaviour of our youth a cry for help more than it is a rebellion? Those who are active in the church have made their needs known but they have always got the crumbs of the cake and never a piece.

The Church and its leadership seem to be oblivious of this situation. They do not use their power to right the situation. If anything, they use it to exploit and give token appreciation. Since power ultimately belongs to God leaders and adults are accountable to God and insofar as the young people are concerned they do not score high marks. Where the young people are included it is by default: because there are not enough adults and where adults are not literate. In other instances they are included as apprentices, being trained for future leadership. Where they are active and minister according to their gifts they are chastised for it. This is not satisfactory to the young people hence they feel undermined. The young people are not interested in taking over but in partnership and recognition of mutual worth and potential. The leaders and adults understand fully well the power that the young people wield hence their use of it during campaigns and in other forms of exploitation and marginalization. One is tempted to suggest that adults are afraid of the power that the youth have hence their resolve, both intended and unintended, to marginalize them. The image of the powerful is, therefore, negative and is seen as a tarnishing of the image of God who is the ultimate Power. That being the case this is an indictment on adults and the powerful in their use of power.

Postscript

This state of affairs suggests that the church needs to rethink its relations with the young. It is possible, however, for the young to have misunderstood their church. If it is so, it still leaves the church with the responsibility to see to it that it communicates its position clearly to avoid misunderstanding. It is one thing to have a wonderful policy on the young but quite another to put it to effect and to be seen (and understood) to be doing so by the beneficiaries. Not only the church but also society at large. However, the church is called to be the light. Hence the imperative for it to do something about the situation is greater. What form should this take? What is the place of young people in the church? The church has always said that all baptized people are members of the body of Christ with equal rights, albeit with various responsibilities according to their gifts. Those that are confirmed seem to be more so. The irony in this is that the majority of those who make up the youth are both baptized and confirmed. The scripture which says that God is no respecter of persons seems to be turned on its head. God is a respector of age. Granted, young people have a lot to learn but that is not the reason for ignoring and exploiting them. It seems to be the *Animal Farm* scenario (in which 'all are equal but some are more equal than others') revisited.

The Bible enjoins that parents are to nurture their children in their faith (Deut 6:4ff). It encourages the young to 'bear their yoke in their youth' (Lamentations 3:27). In fact the whole of Proverbs seems to be written for the specific purpose of teaching the youth. It is, therefore, an abdication for adults to ignore the youth. It is also a self indictment when they express disappointment with the young. In this case the *Apprenticeship* model of youth work is in order. In the secular sphere this is what is known as the *Social Education* model in which the young are helped to grow into responsible and useful citizens.

Apprenticeship by its very nature requires that the apprentice gets a hands on experience of the skill to be learnt. It is strange that the church would like to have apprentices who are not allowed to do any practical. The church should not be surprised when the young want to be and are involved in all sorts of ministry. If it is true to its calling it would encourage such participation and would not be threatened by it. Sometimes apprentices can do such good work as to steal the limelight from their mentors. That should not be seen as usurping the power of mentors. It should be a source of pride to a conscientious mentor. Reproof and correction is also part of this arrangement. It would be presumptuous for the youth to expect not to receive any. However, all reproof and reprimand must be done in love. It must not be 'provoking the children to anger, but bringing them up in the discipline and instruction of the Lord' (Ephesians 6:4). The leadership of the church has to provide and create opportunities for the apprentices to practise. Apprenticeship also takes the theoretical base of the training seriously. Opportunities for the training of mentors should be created and facilitated. When the youth leaders return from training it would be unwise for the church to move them to other unrelated responsibilities as seems to be the trend.[19] Not only is the theory important for the mentors but it is also important for the young. It is no use complaining that the youth have departed from the way when they have never been shown the way.

Honesty is a hallmark of Christianity. Adults have a tendency to want to give the impression that their youth was saintly and is the ideal for their children to follow. This is as far from the truth as is the east from the west. A case in point is a quotation from Peter the Hermit over 700 years ago:

> The world is passing through troubled times. The young people today think of nothing but themselves. They have no reverence for parents or old age; they are impatient of all restraint; they talk as if they alone know everything, and what passes for wisdom with us is foolishness with them. As for the girls, they are foolish and immodest and unwomanly in speech, behaviour and dress.[20]

If this complaint has been repeated in the last 700 years can parents of today's adolescents honestly claim saintliness in their youth? There is a sense in which the parents of today's youth are amnesiac. They seem to have forgotten what it was like for them at that age. A knowledge of young people is called for. Not only is knowledge called for but also an understanding of the youth and an appreciation of what they are going through developmentally.

> That which the young are going through should not be seen as a disease but a normal course of events in their growth and development. Impetuous, it tends to be. That impetuousness can and should be turned to good. Youth is a stage in development during which participation is valued highly. Anglican leaders should

---

[19] Many youth workers are appointed without training but as soon as they get trained the dioceses have been known to move them to other responsibilities unrelated to their expertise. Sometimes it is argued that their age militates against their continued involvement with youth. This is a misunderstanding of what a youth worker is.
[20] Peter the Hermit (1274) cit. Andrews, *A Handbook of Parish Youth Work*, p. 5; cf. Aristotle who lamented: "When I look at the younger generation, I despair for the future of civilization"

> understand the changing times. They should show love and concern for the youth and help them in their life struggles. They should know that the youth, particularly between 13 and 25 years old are usually mentally alert. There are many changes taking place in their bodies and they have many questions needing answers. The youth should not be interpreted as rebellious when they question or challenge certain practices. The church should see the opportunities in this question-oriented intellectual development to promote Christian teaching.[21]

What the young desire is not necessarily a take over from adults. They want to participate. Youth work which ignores this is not worth the name. Participation in the body of Christ is not just participation in the worship. It is participation in the eucharistic mystery which mystery empowers 'to love and serve the Lord' as the dismissal at Holy Communion says. This requirement is not required only of adults but of all who partake of the gifts of God. This is not to say that the youth are expert. As stated before apprenticeship assumes guidance. As members of the body of Christ they too have gifts and are entitled to self representation rather than by proxy as seems to be the current situation. It is therefore important that they be included, and made to feel included, in the parish councils and any other committees in the life of the church and wherever possible be allowed to take responsibility. It is only then that the talk of them being future leaders becomes meaningful. To deny them that is to quench the gifts of the Holy Spirit. Mutual respect is called for and humility is a Christian virtue. The young need to learn it from the examples of adults.

If all power is accountable to God, the exercise of it should reflect honour to God. If the exercise of it is to the exclusion of those that are supposed to be co-workers, albeit apprentices, it does not please God. If, as the young have said, all power ultimately belongs to God then his viceregents reflect a very negative image of God. If power is also a characteristic of being human, as the young have said, then to be denied it is to be dehumanized. This would then mean that the marginalization of young people is a sin - against the young and against God who endowed them with humanity and thus with power. We are stewards of the power of God. The one who gave us this responsibility will certainly call us to account. Therefore, the Church and Society would do well to exercise their power responsibly, with respect to the young, as God will call them to account for it. We are all members of one body by virtue of our baptism and we are all called to a responsible use of the power we have so that we all (the young and adults) can reflect the image of our Lord from one degree of glory to another.

---

[21] **Resolution 2.5 of a meeting held by youth of Soche Parish and their priest at Likhubula Youth House on 1 and 2 January 1994.**

5. Muslim Perspectives on Power

J.C. Chakanza & Hilary Mijoga

Introduction: Islam in Malawi

Historically, the introduction of Islam in Malawi goes back as early as the 1840s when the first Jumbe, Salim Bin Abdallah converted the present day Nkhotakota to the new faith.[1] Salim Bin Abdullah was a representative of the Sultan of Zanzibar. Consequently, Islam established itself in three main areas: Nkhotakota, under the Jumbe who established an Islamic community of freed slaves; Mangochi, where Arab slave traders had strong contacts with local chiefs (Jalasi, Makanjila, and Mponda), and in Karonga, under Mlozi who traded in ivory and slaves.[2] The spread of Islam in Malawi can be accounted for in at least three ways: (a) attempts by Swahili Arab traders from the East Africa coast to establish petty sultanates on the shores of Lake Malawi; (b) conversion of large numbers of the Yao people; and (c) dispersal of the Asian community throughout the country. Since the turn of the century Asians, predominantly Muslims, have followed trade opportunities not only to the towns, but also into the trade centers and rural areas throughout Malawi. Generally they took with them their own Malawian workers, cooks, tailors, and storemen who were usually Yao Muslims.[3] The Yao were established traders even before they came to Malawi.[4] When they established themselves in the country, they continued their trading activities with the Arabs of the coast. During this early encounter, it appears that the Arabs made no active attempt to spread Islam among the Yao. However, the tide changed later when in the last decades of the nineteenth century Islam became a popular religion among the Yao.

There are several steps which led the Yao to embrace Islam, for example, a) the conversion of their chiefs; b) the European colonisation of East Africa and the

---

[1] See D.S. Bone, "The Christian Missionary Response to the Development of Islam in Malawi: 1875-1940," *Bulletin on Islam and Christian-Muslim Relations in Africa*, Vol 2 No 3, (July, 1984), p. 3; D.S. Bone, "Towards A History of Islam in Malawi," History Seminar 1982/83 Paper No 1, Chancellor College (1983), p. 1; D.S. Bone, "The Muslim Minority in Malawi and Western Education," *Journal Institute of Muslim Minority Affairs*, Vol 6 No 2, p. 412; I.A.G. Panjwani, "Muslims in Malawi," *Journal Institute of Muslim Minority Affairs*, Vol 1, No 2.; I.A.G. Panjwani, "Islam in Karonga District", History Seminar Paper, Chancellor College (1983) pp. 1-2.

[2] Bone, "Towards A History of Islam in Malawi," pp. 2-3.

[3] *Ibid*, pp. 3-4.

[4] Bone, "The Christian Missionary Response to the Development of Islam in Malawi: 1875-1940," pp. 3-4; Bone, "Towards A History of Islam in Malawi," pp. 2-3; Panjwani, "Muslims in Malawi, " p. 162.

reaction of the Swahili and their Yao associates to what they perceived as a threat to their mutually profitable partnership in the trade of slaves and ivory; c) led by their chiefs many Yao communities embraced Islam the more firmly as a way of asserting their tribal and cultural identity in the face of European domination; d) the introduction from the coast in the 1920s of the Qadiri brotherhood. The tenets and practices of this group were enthusiastically spread by a number of energetic young Malawian born sheikhs who had received their training on the East Africa coast. Their banners and their chanting attracted many members of the Swahili brotherhood which had come to Malawi some years earlier. Noisy controversies developed between the two groups mainly over questions of diet and the conduct of funerals. In addition to this, rivalry between the brotherhoods for adherents led to an increased interest in Islam and a heightened level of Islamic activity; e) Islam was a means of modernizing the Yao society. The trading activities with the coastalists gave the Yao the opportunity to compare and contrast their own values with those of the Arabs and Swahili of the coast; the interaction between the traditional Yao beliefs and Islamic beliefs and practices.[5] f) As a matter of fact, the Arabs did not ask their converts to abandon confidence in their mystical forces. Because of this tolerance, Islam went syncretistic until recent developments arising from the world-wide Islamic revival which started in the Middle East.

Predominant Muslim areas

By the 1931 census, Islam was established as the largest single religion in Mangochi district (45%) and the religion of a significant minority of people in parts of Machinga (38%); Zomba (18%); Chiradzulu (8%), Blantyre (6%); Mulanje (4%); Dedza (12%); and Salima (25%).[6] Blantyre, Machinga, Mangochi, and Zomba are predominantly Yao populated. These along with the Chewa dominated district of Nkhotakota, can be regarded as the districts of Islam in Malawi. In the absence of more recent census figures concerning religious affiliation, the most reasonable assumption, seems to be that the number of Muslims has increased in proportion to the increase in population in the above districts. If this assumption is justified, within the Muslim districts today the number of Muslims will be around 10-15% or even up to 30% (as some Malawian Muslims have indicated) of the population, over half of them in Mangochi and Machinga districts.[7]

---

[5] Bone, "Towards A History of Islam in Malawi," pp. 3-4; S. Kazokoko, "The Circumstances in which, and the reasons why, Islam first became a popular religion among the Yao of Malawi," Department of Religious Studies Seminar Paper, Chancellor College, 1981, pp. 1-4.

[6] Bone, "Towards A History of Islam in Malawi," p. 4.

[7] *Ibid*, pp. 5-6; Bone, "The Muslim Minority in Malawi and Western Education" (unpublished version), p. 1.

The world Umma

Malawi is now said to have the largest number of Muslims in Central Africa. Until the mid 1970s Malawi was very much cut off from the mainstream of the Islamic world with few contacts with the wider *Umma*. These Muslims are now in contact with the mainstream Islamic community. This is particularly evident in several ways, for example, young Malawians are going abroad for advanced Islamic studies. Some of the richer Muslim countries have given generous support to educational and mosque building projects. Increased numbers of Muslim scholars and speakers have visited the country in recent years and regional Islamic conferences have been hosted.[8] All Malawi's Muslims are Sunni, the Asian Muslims belong to the Hanafite school, and Malawian Muslims to the Shafiite.[9]

Muslims, Christians, and Colonial Government

At the time Christianity came to Malawi, it appears that some people had already embraced Islam. So when Christianity came, it targeted those areas which were predominantly Muslim. Their objective was to combat the slave trade by converting the Muslims. In a way, their aim was to halt the advancement of Islam. This created hatred and distrust among the religious leaders, and the communities at large. In this struggle, missionaries were at an advantage because the colonial government supported them.

Traditional Islamic education antedates western style schooling in Malawi.[10] Despite its later arrival, however, it was the western type of schooling that quickly came to dominate the education scene. The establishment of schools was judged by many Christian missionaries to be one of the most effective ways of preventing the spread of Islam into new areas and they used it as a tactic for stopping their rival religion's advance. It is not surprising in these circumstances that the overwhelming majority of Muslims reacted by refusing to have anything to do with western education when it was so much under the control of Christian missionaries who so actively used it as a means of proselytisation.[11] Because they run western education schools Christians found high positions in the capitalist economy (teaching, medical professions, technical skills, clerks, clergymen, foremen), whereas Muslims, with their madrassa education, could only work as tailors, cooks, shopkeepers, or watchmen in the Asians' business firms. In other words, the main factor which prevented Muslims from participating fully in the

---

[8] Bone, "The Muslim Minority in Malawi and Western Education; p. 412; Bone, "Towards A History of Islam in Malawi," p. 10.

[9] Bone, "Towards A History of Islam in Malawi," p. 6.

[10] Bone, "The Muslim Minority in Malawi and Western Education, p. 413; (Unpublished, p. 3).

[11] *Ibid*, pp. 413-15.

economic, professional, administrative, and political life of the nation in the highest positions was therefore, the low level of their education.[12] In the mid 1920s the colonial government decided to take some measures of control of the education system. According to this intervention, schools were to be open to all regardless of religious affiliation. It was hoped (in the government circles) that this would encourage Muslims to avail themselves more fully of the western style schooling. But this attempt failed due to at least three factors: (a) at the insistence of churches, Christian religious education was made an integral part of the agreed syllabus; (b) missions retained control of teacher training; and (c) as missions continued to provide a major share of the cost of running their schools, they were in a position to follow their own policies.[13]

Notwithstanding these attempts to obtain access to western style education, Muslims avoided this type of schooling in whatever form it was offered. The cost to them was that they were very much left out of jobs of influence, importance, and high economic reward. Furthermore, those few who did pursue western education tended to stop identifying themselves as Muslims and in this way the Islamic community lost the allegiance of some of its most able young men. However, with the attainment of independence in 1964, things changed for the Muslims.[14] Due to the favorable conditions that the new government offered, e.g., freedom of worship, improvement in communication, government taking control of education, i.e., government making it a priority to rid the education system of denominationalism, Muslims felt acceptance. Some of the changes that have taken place since include, building of modern madrassa and mosques, involvement in social development and different associations within the Muslim community, and adoption of western education which has created an Islamic elite from different colleges and universities. Though there has been this shift, the effects of the colonial past are still felt. In 1981 a major census of the peri-urban area of Lilongwe (survey of traditional housing areas in Lilongwe) showed that Muslims had the highest proportion (52%) with no education and the lowest proportion (2%) with secondary education in all religious groups. At this time also, Muslims constituted only 1% of all university undergraduates.[15]

---

[12] *Ibid*, p. 415; Bone, "Towards A History of Islam in Malawi," p. 11.

[13] Bone, "The Muslim Minority in Malawi and Western Education," pp. 415-17, Bone, "Towards A History of Islam in Malawi," p. 11.

[14] Panjwani, "The Muslims in Malawi," p. 162; Bone, "The Muslim Minority in Malawi and Western Education," pp. 415-16.

[15] Bone, "Towards A History of Islam in Malawi," p. 11; Bone, The Muslim Minority in Malawi and Western Education. pp. 416-17

Islamic Revival in Malawi

The vigorous revival that Islam is currently experiencing in Malawi is of course a manifestation of its world wide resurgence. Major sources of origin of this revival in this country include the following: (a) the Asian factor. This started when Jamaats from India and Pakistan came to Malawi and this resulted in some Asian Muslims taking a keener interest in their religion. By the late 1970s one of the major ways in which this interest was expressed was in a high degree of concern for the state of Islam among Malawian Muslims and in particular the lack of provision for madrassa and secular education. According to one Malawian Muslim, it should, however, be pointed out that the efforts of the Asians working directly with Malawians have largely been uncoordinated and their aims have been ill conceived. It should also be pointed out that the Asians have not been keen on sponsoring secular education. (b) increased amount of contact its Muslims have had with the wider *Umma*. Before the late 1970s, though individual Muslims had travelled to the East Coast of Africa for further Islamic studies and though two eminent Zanzibari Muslims came to Malawi to advise the local Islamic community, Muslims in Malawi were very much cut off from the wider world of Islam.

A significant development took place in April 1977 when seven Malawian Muslims attended the First Southern Africa Youth Conference in Botswana. The contacts initiated at this conference were followed up to such an extent that in 1981, the third Youth Conference was hosted by the Muslim Association of Malawi in Blantyre and attracted delegates from within the region and beyond. In recent years, significant numbers of young Muslims have gone abroad for further Islamic studies to Sudan, Pakistan, and Saudi Arabia and are returning with not only academic qualifications but also experience of life in Islamic states. The cumulative effect of these contacts is that Malawi is moving away from being a Muslim backwater and its people are increasingly being exposed to mainstream Islam. (c) inflow of substantial amounts of money from charitable organisations within the Arab world, notably the African Muslim committee based in Kuwait. Channelled through the Muslim Association in Malawi, several millions of Kwachas have been spent to finance Islamic projects. (d) the emergence of a small but vigorous, secularly educated Muslim elite. These are young men who have passed through the western system of secondary education, and perhaps even gained admission to one of the colleges of the University of Malawi.[16]

---

[16] J.C. Chakanza, "Islam in Africa Project and the Islamic Revival in Malawi," (Unpublished; Chancellor College, Zomba, 1989), pp. 3-4; Bone, "The Development of Islam in Malawi and the Response of the Christian Churches: 1940-1986" Department of Religious Studies Seminar 1986/87, No. 1, Chancellor College, pp. 11-13.

Obvious manifestation of the increased level of Islamic activity in the decade include the following: (a) a programme of mosque building; (b) greater interest in education, both secular and Islamic than ever before; (c) madrassa education at a primary level has been boasted by the fact that a majority of the new mosques have buildings attached to them for this type of schooling; (d) training school for mu'allims; (e) involvement in the provision of health care; and (f) proliferation of Islamic literature.[17]

Quranic teaching about humanity

The Quran teaches that God is creator and that a human being is God's creature (cf Sura 16; 96:2). Because of this relationship, a human being is completely dependent on God for guidance. Despite this utter dependence on God, the Quran also teaches that a human being is responsible for his/her actions. The Quran makes it clear that the proper response of a person to God is that of gratitude (cf. Sura 39:8). In addition to this, a person's proper response is also one of submission and of total commitment (cf. Sura 22:70). In the Quran, the most characteristic description of a person's status before God is servant or slave. God is the master (cf. the term "Islam" Muslim means one who submits). Islam, of course, came to be the name of the religion the prophet Muhammad proclaimed (Sura 3:17).

Despite emphasizing humanity's lowliness before God, the Quran gives humanity a high status over the rest of creation. Sura 2:28 calls man "God's vice-roy" or vice-regent. The special term used is *Khalifa* or Caliph. It is understood that the world belongs to God, Allah, and that in his benevolence he has created humanity to take care of it on his behalf and under his guidance through his prophet Muhammad in the Holy Quran.

Islam in democratic Malawi

Now that Malawi has a President who is a Muslim and also several ministers, parliamentarians, and leading politicians, it is necessary to assess, from the Muslim perspective, how the exercise of power is conceived in the current socio-political dispensation. The central theme around which all the questions on this issue revolve is the empowerment of Muslims here in Malawi, particularly after the change in the political climate. The main issues addressed can be summarized as follows: (a) Muslim participation in party politics, government, and in the socio-economic development; (b) educational enterprises; (c) the advancement of

---

[17] Chakanza, "Islam in Africa and the Islamic Revival in Malawi," pp. 5-6; Bone, "The Development of Islam in Malawi and the Response of the Christian Churches: 1940-1986," pp. 13-17

women and youth; (d) internal organization through the formation of associations; (e) the growing contact with Muslims in other countries; and (f) active involvement in local and international media. A survey of these issues may contribute to our understanding of the way Muslims in Malawi interpret and translate into reality their understanding of the exercise of authority which, according to their teaching, comes from God.

The Research Methodology

To obtain the views of Muslims from different backgrounds, occupations, and roles within the Muslim community, we drew up a four-page questionnaire with twenty questions. Twelve research assistants were recruited for this exercise. All twelve assistants are Muslim undergraduate at Chancellor College, University of Malawi.[18] The role of these research assistants was to distribute questionnaires to those who were comfortable with the written questions but also to conduct direct interviews, person to person, with those who could not work with the written questionnaires mainly because of (a) language problems because these questionnaires were in English and (b) levels of education among some respondents.

Problems

This research encountered some problems. Among the several complaints raised were the following:

    (a) the questions were difficult;

    (b) why Muslims were the target of the research. This was in light of the fact that when the Christians had their chance to rule, no one asked them how they felt;

    (c) others complained that the researchers only wanted to create confusion and distrust among the people;

    (d) others indicated that they were not politicians hence they could not answer the questions.

Despite all these problems, the interviews were successful.

Areas of study, number, and sex

The research covered a representative sample of districts of the three regions of Malawi: the north (Karonga, Mzuzu [Mzimba], and Rumphi), the centre (Lilongwe and Nkhotakota) and the South (Blantyre, Chiradzulu, Machinga,

---

[18] There were eleven male and one female. This was the case because she was the only one who volunteered to take place in the field research. It is interesting to note that this female research assistant was the only student from the Department of Theology and Religious Studies.

Mangochi, and Zomba). It is interesting to note that out of those districts, some of the so called Muslim districts were included in the research (Blantyre, Chiradzulu, Mulanje, Mangochi, and Nkhotakota). From these Muslim districts, there are also districts which are predominantly Yao populated (Blantyre, Machinga, Mangochi, and Zomba). From the districts visited it was noted that the three main areas where Islam established itself were included (Karonga, Mangochi, and Nkhotakota). It should also be observed that all the three cities and the municipality of the country were visited (Blantyre, Lilongwe and Mzuzu, and the Municipality of Zomba). So, apart from visiting rural Muslims, the study also covered the urban Muslims. From these few observations, it can be concluded that the research covered a representative sample of the Muslim community in the country.

Mangochi leads the other districts with a total of 25% of its population being Muslim. Earlier, it was noted that by the 1931 census, Islam was itself the largest single religion in Mangochi district with a percentage of 45% of the district's population. This is not surprising because Mangochi was one of the three main places where Islam established itself. Following Mangochi is Zomba with 18% of the total number of the respondents (cf. the 1931 census for Zomba). This large number is easily explained because as we noted above, Zomba is one of the districts which is predominantly Yao populated and the Yao embraced Islam in large numbers. Nkhotakota follows Zomba with 17.6% of the total respondents. As noted above, Nkhotakota was also one of the three main places where Islam established itself. Though Chewa dominated, as compared to Mangochi and Zomba, Nkhotakota is one of the districts of Islam in Malawi. Next comes Machinga with 15.6% of the total respondents. As indicated above, by the 1931 census, Islam was the religion of a significant minority of people in parts of Machinga (38%). It has also been noted that Machinga is one of the districts predominantly Yao populated and this explains the large numbers. Then comes Chiradzulu. Referring to the 1931 census again, Chiradzulu had a significant minority of Muslims (8%). Of the total respondents, 9.7% were from Chiradzulu. What is evident here is not unusual because, as noted already, Chiradzulu is one of the districts of Islam in the country. Blantyre follows Chiradzulu in the numbers. 3.5% of the respondents had indicated Blantyre as their district of origin. As we have already noted, Blantyre is also one of the Yao dominated districts hence its association with Islam. Dedza and Salima follow with 3.2% and 3% respectively. These two districts had significant minorities of Muslims according to the 1931 census of 12% and 25% respectively. Dedza and Salima are also districts of Islam in Malawi. Karonga, which was one of three main places where Islam established itself, had 1.5% of the respondents indicate the district as their place of origin.

It is interesting to note that some respondents indicated Lilongwe (0.7%); Nkhata Bay (0.7%); Chitipa (0.2%); Dowa (0.2%); Mulanje (0.2%); Mzuzu (Mzimba) (0.2%); and Thyolo (0.2%) as their districts of origin. By the 1931 census, these districts were not among the districts of Islam in the country. Perhaps, this indicates that Islam has spread into these areas, i.e., Islam has been gaining ground in other parts of the country. There were also Asian Muslim respondents in the research. In all, there were ten Asian respondents (2.5%): nine males (2.2%) and one female (0.2%).

The foregoing shows that most of the respondents pointed at the districts of Islam in Malawi as places of their origins (Blantyre, Chiradzulu, Dedza, Machinga, Mangochi, Mulanje, Nkhotakota, Salima, and Zomba). Out of these districts, Blantyre, Machinga, Mangochi, and Zomba are predominantly Yao populated, whereas Karonga, Mangochi, and Nkhotakota are the three main places where Islam established itself. The presentation has also revealed that Asian Muslims were also included in the research. All things being equal, we can conclude that respondents were drawn from predominant Muslims areas, Asians, and from places where Islam was unknown in the past. This gives us a representative sample of the Muslim population hence the resulting views will be representative of the general feeling of Muslims in Malawi.

The research also covered both sexes. 326 males and 78 females were interviewed, giving us the total of 404 respondents. Percentage wise, this gives us 81% male and 19% female. The relatively few women respondents could indicate, on the face of it, that Islamic teachings de-emphasize the role of women in society. However, the major reason for the disparity has to do with the conduct of the interviews and research assistants. All the research assistants were male except one; they may have been biased in favour of men. Secondly, it is likely that most of the interviews took place at work places and since most women do not have paid jobs, they were missed. All age groups (though the majority are between 18 and 35 years of age) were represented in the study: teenagers (14-19), middle ages, (20-40), and the older bracket (41-86). These age groups comprise males and females. From this, we can conclude that the respondents were a representative sample of age groups within the Muslim community. So, the views presented in the research on the issue at stake are representative views of Muslims in Malawi.

Type of occupation

We noted in the introduction that the main factor which prevented Muslims from participating fully in the economic, professional, administrative, and political life of the nation in the highest positions was the low level of their education, for with their madrassa education, Muslims could only work as tailors, cooks, shopkeepers, or watchmen. This research confirms that some of the Muslims are still involved in these types of jobs.[19] The number of the unemployed is far greater than appears on the list. We may also suspect that those who indicated that they were farmers could in fact be subsistence farmers and not real commercial farmers. If this were the case, the number of the unemployed would be much higher. Most of the people who indicated that they were business people were in fact people who sell second hand clothes or are hawkers. Everything being considered, it is realistic to say within the present economic situation in the country, that many of these business people are within the poverty bracket. Most of these business people only manage to produce money for food and some few necessities of life.

However, some new trends are emerging. The number of students and teachers is encouraging. These students are primary, secondary, and college students. Most of the teachers are mu'allims and few teach in secular schools. This raises hopes for Islamic education in the country and even secular for that matter. On the high paying jobs, there were a few people. In the list, we have such professionals as managers, clerks, university lecturer, college administrator, seismologist, and so on. It is safe to say that these professionals have gone through the western education schools which have availed them the opportunity of high positions in the capitalist economy. This might confirm what was noted earlier that the adoption of western education by some Muslims has created a Muslim elite from different colleges and universities. It would be interesting to find out whether, as was the case in the past, those few who pursue western education tend to stop identifying themselves as Muslims. But from the look of things, as evidenced by the Chancellor College community, Muslims don't hide themselves. They are no longer afraid to identify themselves as Muslims in the secular institution. In fact, they have their own association on campus. In addition to this, Muslim graduates of the University of Malawi have formed their own Islamic organisation, the "Muslim Alumni Society"

From the above we can conclude that Muslims are now fully participant in the capitalist economy. Muslims are not only engaged in cooking, tailoring, shopkeeping, or guarding but they are also involved in the professional jobs. This is notwithstanding posts like members of parliament, cabinet ministers, and the presidency. Consequently, the views expressed in this research are representative

---

[19] The types of jobs involved included: shoemaker, carpenter, policeman, butcher, unemployed, soldier, driver, painter, farmer, tailor, teacher, businessman, housewife, fisherman, builder, shopkeeper, shopowner, social worker, restaurant owner, engineer, director, accounts assistant, data processor, salesman, bank teller, typist, bus inspector, university lecturer, college administrator, messenger, watchman, seismologist, laboratory technician, librarian, radio repair, mechanic, nurse.

of a cross section of the work force in Malawi in general and in the Muslim community in particular.

Position in the Islamic community

The biggest number of respondents are ordinary members of the Muslim community (69%). However, we have also large numbers for chairmen of jamaats (7%), sheikhs (6%), and mu'allims (3%).[20] These are top or respectable positions in the Muslim community. This means that the views, opinions, and decisions of these people are well respected by the Muslim community. What it all amounts to is the fact that the respondents range from ordinary members of the community to sheikhs. The respondents also hold various positions in Islamic committees. We can therefore conclude that the views expressed in this research are representative of the views of the Muslim community in Malawi.

Islam and the Exercise of Power in Malawi

The Muslim President

Respondents were asked what it meant to them as Muslims that now Malawi has a Muslim President. One of the obvious answers given was that this was the first time a Muslim has been a president in the history of the country (6.2%). This is history made for them. This fact alone will encourage Muslims to participate in politics and contribute to social and economic development of the country (4%). To other Muslims (12%), this was an opportunity for Islam to grow and be taken seriously as a religion. This would be achieved because the president will help this to happen.

The election of a Muslim as a president means that there is real democracy in the country, but much more that there is religious tolerance. On the democratic side, it was felt by many that any citizen of Malawi, irrespective of religion, can be elected as a president of the country (4%). On the religious tolerance, it was noted that the election of a Muslim in a Christian dominated country is testimony to that fact. This we suppose goes hand in hand with real democracy. In this connection, a substantial number of respondents (29%) indicated that it meant nothing to them to have a Muslim as president. Among the reasons given were: leadership is religion blind (4%) and so the president could have come from any religion; nothing is unending (perhaps a reference to the life presidency situation); politics and Islam are two different things; it is the will of Allah (5%).

---

[20] Other positions include: treasurer of jamaat, secretary, imam, student, patron, regional secretary, Islamic scholar, student advisor, choirmistress, secretary general, legal advisor, youth coordinator, administrative officer

It was interesting to note that a sizable section of the respondents indicated that now there will be freedom of worship and freedom of expression (10%). We noted earlier that with the attainment of independence in 1964, things changed for the Muslims. One of the things that the new government professed was to have freedom of worship. The answers given indicate that, in fact, there was no freedom of worship or freedom of expression during the past thirty years as far as the Muslims were concerned. Maybe restrictions were put on how the Muslims could worship. As we shall see later, one of the factors that could have led to this state of affairs was the fear of Islamisation on the part of Christians in general and the leadership in particular. In fact, a large percentage of the leadership was Christian.

Some answers worth noting include: Muslims are no longer backward; Muslims are no longer marginalised (8%); no more inferiority complex; Muslims are no longer looked down upon; Muslims have beaten the odds; conditions of Muslims will improve, a despised section of the community has produced a president; Muslims are now educated; Muslims are now working with the Christians to develop the country; Muslims will no longer be oppressed; Muslims can do what other citizens do; Christians are no longer the favourites. All these answers may suggest that the Muslims regarded themselves as outsiders before the election of the Muslim president. It is now their opportunity to: play a role in nation building; contribute to social activities; hold important positions in the government; have access to the president and government; work hard; and promote peace. In short, with the election of a Muslim president, new prospects are now open to the Muslims in Malawi.

Opportunities in the new political environment

On the whole, some of the responses to the above question indicate the dismal knowledge that a lot of Muslims have about their own faith. Respondents were asked, if, in view of the current political environment, the Muslims have better opportunities than under the previous government. Although these respondents believe that Islam and politics are different entities, the truth is that Islam cannot fully be useful except in power. According to one Malawian Muslim, the real question for Muslims in this country when they are not politically in power, is whether they should strive for religious communalism or religious nationalism. This question had two answers: negative (28%) and positive (72%). Negatively, several factors were pointed out. One of the things that was noted was the fact that Muslims are in minority (cf. the 10-15% of the population). This means that there are few Muslims in politics and in positions of leadership. The point being made here is that their influence cannot be felt when they are in minority. To add to this, others indicated, the system does not provide opportunities for minority groups. Even if opportunities were provided to them as a minority, Muslims would be accused of favouritism (5%). In fact, others said that opportunities do not depend on religious affiliation and having a Muslim president does not mean that Muslims should be above everyone else. The question was also answered negatively because, to some, multi-party means equal participation and opportunity (10%). This also means that there are equal rights and justice in the country. In fact, the president, government, and the country as a whole are supposed to be for all citizens (7%). Other respondents pointed out that there was no chance because nothing has changed (6.8%). This is partly because Muslims are still lowly educated, Christians are many, and according to some, there were better opportunities in the previous regime. What it all amounts to is that what has transpired in the political situation is just a different way of looking at things. Others indicated that current politics do not favour Muslims (notwithstanding the fact that some politicians are Muslims). This is partly because there is fear of Islamisation on the part of some non-Muslims. As a result of this, there cannot be better opportunities for Muslims.

It was also interesting to note that other respondents indicated that there are no better opportunities now, for example, because the president is more interested in Christian activities than Islamic ones. This means that the president does not pay much attention to the plight of his fellow Muslims. Another aspect that was pointed out was the fact that it was difficult for Muslims to have access to the radio station (MBC). The access to the radio seems to be an important issue for some Muslims because it is going to appear in some of the answers that follow. On the positive side, some of the notable answers included the fact that there is freedom of expression (11%); freedom of worship (22%); and access to the radio (17%). These factors create conducive conditions for better opportunities for the Muslims. We have already noted the frequent reference to the two freedoms. It seems Muslims' advancement was hampered by lack of these freedoms. The fact that Muslims are no longer marginalised, oppressed, are better understood, and have access to the president ensures that they have better opportunities now. The Muslims are now free to approach the government, engage in business enterprises, gain access to politics, have free education, get more scholarships, relationships; introduction of Islamic education in schools; and avail themselves of the education opportunities. All these things are now possible because of the current political environment. With the present political climate, Muslims have chances to go to Muslim countries for further education and also funds from these countries are pouring in. It is also hoped that there will be development in predominantly Muslim areas under this new political dispensation. In short, things which were previously denied to them, are now available to the Muslims in the country.

Influence of Muslim countries on Malawi

Respondents were also asked how they felt was the influence of Muslim countries on Malawi. There were some respondents who indicated that there was either no influence (8%) or minimal (3%) influence by Muslims countries on Malawi. Others pointed out that they had no idea whether there was any influence or not. Those who indicated that Muslim countries have some influence on Malawi (63%) point to some of the following factors: economic aid (23%); Muslims who were expelled are now coming back; Arabic language (4%); Muslims encouraged to preach (3.8%); scholarships (9%); trade (7%); employment opportunities; education (3.8%); literature (2.9%); diplomatic ties, establishment of Islamic institutions, Islamic scholars; fear of Islamic fundamentalism that has been instilled in the non-Muslims; development projects (schools, hospitals etc) (20%). Muslim countries, e.g., Saudi Arabia, Pakistan, Sudan, etc are involved in one or more of the above. Since they are responsible for these things, it is fair to say that these countries have some influence on Malawi because when they provide these things, without doubt, there are some strings attached.

Chances for development of Islamic education

Respondents were asked what they thought were the chances for the development of Islamic education in Malawi at primary and post primary levels. Some respondents answered that there were no chances (6%) or they were not yet there (1%). The large majority (93%) indicated that there were indeed chances for such development. There are several factors which make this development possible. The political climate is one of them. It is noted that the political climate is conducive to such a development. The new political dispensation has offered freedom of worship (one of the two freedoms) (1%). This means that Muslims are now free to offer Islamic education (19%). The free education that is now being offered contributes to this development. Parents are now encouraging their children to go to school in their large numbers (2%). In connection with free education, we have also many qualified and highly trained Muslim teachers (16%) who teach in secular but also in Islamic schools. These teachers offer better chances for the development of Islamic education in the country. Funds from Muslim countries are available to build more learning centres (21%). With this goes scholarships (3%) and literature. In fact, many students are going abroad for further education whether secular or Islamic (2.8%).

It is important to note here that some respondents gave access to the radio as their answer to the question. How this access would contribute to the development of Islamic education in Malawi is difficult to say. As we noted earlier, access to the radio is going to be an important issue. Perhaps access to the radio will ensure that

Muslims are heard all over the country through programmes they may put on the radio. All the above factors indicate that chances are good for the development of Islamic education in Malawi at primary and post primary levels.

Rate of Muslim contribution to development

Respondents were asked to rate the Muslim contribution to development in Malawi. Some respondents indicated that Muslims have not contributed anything to the development in Malawi (19%). Others pointed out that their contribution is very little compared to other religious groups in the country (4%). Part of the reason for this little contribution, according to some respondents, is that Muslims are not very educated. Other respondents pointed out that Muslims contribute to development in Malawi like other Malawian citizens (74%). For example, Muslims contribute to community development like self-help projects and other projects. The Muslim community also offers scholarships to students which help to develop education in the country. Muslims engage in business, too, and other trading activities which help in the development of the Malawian economy but also, through their enterprises, they offer employment opportunities to Malawians, both Muslims and non-Muslims. All this helps to develop the country. One other notable contribution from the Muslim side is the fact that the country has a Muslim President. From these answers, it may be concluded that Muslims feel that they contribute a lot to the development of the country. The contribution is in terms of material, manpower, and spiritual matters.

Islam and political parties

Respondents were asked how they felt was the relationship between Islam and political parties. Two views were expressed on this question: negative (47%) and positive (53%). On the negative side, different reasons were given for the lack of relationship between Islam and political parties. Just because the two are different means that there is no relationship between them. In fact, there is no political party which was founded on religious principles, some respondents indicated. They also pointed out that having a Muslim president does not necessarily mean that Islam is related to political parties. In simple terms, there is no politics in Islam, i.e. Islam deals with divine issues, whereas politics deal with mundane matters. This difference is carried even further by some respondents who noted that Islamic promises are fulfilled whereas political ones are not. Furthermore, others said that Islam does not allow its members to become rulers. Other respondents noted that there is a general uneasiness and hostility towards Islam by some political parties. Some parties are not happy to see Muslims prosper. Perhaps, this general uneasiness is partially explained by the fact that some non-Muslims are afraid of Islamisation of the country if they allow Muslims to establish themselves (6%).

Though a section of the respondents answered the question negatively, others answered positively. Some respondents indicated that both Islam and political parties aim at peace, freedom, and human rights (16%); both work together for democracy and unity (6%); both are concerned with freedom of expression. All this indicates that there is close relationship between Islam and political parties. Other respondents indicated that Islam allows its members to take part in politics (6%). This explains why Muslims participate in politics. There are Muslims in the cabinet and the president himself in a Muslim, i.e., some Muslims are political leaders. This only shows that there is a close relationship between Islam and political parties. It is also noted that Islam cherishes good politics and in fact it is pointed out that some political policies are in line with what Allah wants (2%). As we have already noted elsewhere, freedom of worship and freedom of expression are mentioned (the two freedoms). Some respondents (40%) indicated that Islam and political parties work for these freedoms. On this note too, it may rightly be concluded that there is a close relationship between Islam and political parties in the country.

Islamic influence on current politics in Malawi

Respondents were asked to state the extent to which Islam is influencing current politics in Malawi. Here too, the question was answered negatively (24%) and positively (76%). On the negative side, it was reported that Islam has no say in worldly affairs (1%), as such it has no influence on what is happening politically. This is notwithstanding the fact that the president is a Muslim. On a more modest note, it was pointed out that Islam is influencing current politics as much as every religious group is doing in the country (1.1%). On the positive side, an obvious fact that was noted is that the president is a Muslim (4%). This alone creates the impression that Islam is influencing current politics in Malawi. In addition to this fact, it is reported that Islam is the originator of democracy (1%). Perhaps, this is why Muslims join political parties and, as we have seen in the case of the president, some Muslims are political leaders and others joined PAC (4%). Islam tells people to obey the government. In fact, Islam agrees with some political policies. Other respondents indicated that Islam ensures freedom of worship and freedom of expression. These two freedoms are also fundamental to some political parties. By ensuring that these freedoms are observed in the country, it implies that Islam has a role to play in the current politics in the country. By encouraging parents to send their children to school, Muslims help educate the population. To show its seriousness, Muslims even offer scholarships to the needy students. Though not directly related to politics, education plays a major role in the current politics (cf. free education policy). Muslims contribute materially to political parties. This is one way in which they influence politics in the country. The above presentation suggests that Islam is indeed influencing current politics in Malawi.

Use of public media

Respondents were asked how Muslims in the country use the various public media. Respondents gave varied answers to this question. Some indicated that they are denied access or have very little use or limited access (10%). Others (9%) pointed out that they use public media like everyone else in the country while another section of the respondents said that Muslims do not use the various public media as other religious groups. Still others indicated that improvements can always be made. On the positive side, many respondents (78%) did indicate that Muslims make use of the various public media. They said that they use the radio for preaching and prayers (77%), propagating Islam (30%), Islamic education, advertisements (44%), and strengthening brotherhoods. They use print media for disseminating Islamic literature (2%), advertisements, and also for propagating Islam. From this, it seems that both the radio and print media have a big role to play in the Muslim community, especially in the spread of Islam.

Role of Muslim women in the new Malawi

Respondents were asked to indicate the role of Muslim women in the new Malawi. Some respondents, especially the male respondents, indicated that the Muslim women have no role or they don't have a significant role or there has not been any change in their position (9%). The reasons behind these answers include the fact that the women do not seem to know their role because of their limited education and also because they are weak in preaching Islam. On the positive side (89%), a lot was said about the role of Muslim women in the new Malawi. One of the issues pointed out was the part Muslim women play in the family (6%). The Muslim women are responsible for bringing up reliable persons, because the future of Islam in Malawi depends upon the good behavior of the Muslim children. This upbringing includes encouraging the children to go to school. This means that Muslim women are educators. Perhaps the increased enrollment of Muslim children in the schools is due to this encouragement. The role of the Muslim women in the new Malawi involves being exemplary. This includes matters of dress and behavior. In addition to this, these women promote fellow women's affairs, i.e., they help to develop other women. This promotion includes fighting for women's rights. Another role that Muslim women play in the new Malawi deals with social welfare activities (6%). A major section of the respondents indicated that Muslim women are involved in charitable activities. They are involved in fund raising activities which help the needy people in the country. One of the areas which was also frequently mentioned was help at funerals.

Muslim women are also free to take part in politics (6%). They voted in the referendum and the general elections. In addition to taking part in politics, Muslim women also work in government and companies and some hold important posts in these places. In short, these women are involved in the political, social, and economic spheres of the new Malawi. Muslim women are also forming religious groups. Here, they pray and help each other in raising their families, behave properly and fight for their rights. What was very notable here is the fact that now Muslim women are free to preach (45%). Unfortunately, they only preach to their fellow women. Women do not preach to men because women are not supposed to lead men in public. This is according to the Quran. By preaching, though to women only, these women help the men to develop and propagate Islam in Malawi. Finally, these women are engaged in business enterprises. This helps in the economic development of the country, but much more, it helps to develop their families. So the Muslim women are also a force to be reckoned with in the country.

Development of Muslim youth

Respondents were asked to give changes that have taken place in the development of Muslim youth. To this question, there were two answers: negative (14%) and positive (86%). Those who answered in the negative pointed to negative developments, like very few of the Muslim youth go to school, they are not developed Islamically, they don't know what to do, they are more involved in secular education than in Islamic education (4%), they behave badly due to western influence (drugs, drinking etc) (8%). To some of the respondents, these are negative changes that have taken place in the development of the Muslim youth in the country. There have also been positive developments. First and foremost in the fact that Muslim youth are going to school in large numbers instead of engaging in early marriages (60%). Factors which have contributed to this development include: freedom of movement, free education, more schools are built, free to learn in Christian institutions; scholarships are available to them and freedom of expression. As a result of this, there are many highly educated Muslim youth today. Another positive development that has taken place is the fact that there is no more conversion of Muslim youth to Christianity (3%). The youth are aware of their Islamic responsibilities. This includes a better understanding of Islam. The Muslim youth can now lead in prayers but also can preach. What it all amounts to is the fact that the Muslim youth are now more behaved. The Muslim youth are also free to take part in politics and business (6%). We saw earlier that there were many respondents who indicated that they were involved in business activities. It is important to note here that among the factors which have contributed to the development of the Muslim youth are the freedom of movement and freedom of expression. We have already noted that freedom of expression is one of the two famous freedoms we have encountered in this research. We now add freedom of movement which ensures that the youth can travel overseas for studies, travel to any part of the country for education and business. So, this is also an important freedom.

Sources of conflict in the Muslim community

Respondents were asked to give sources of conflicts in the Muslim community. Many answers were given to this question. On the one hand, some respondents (2%) indicated that there were no conflicts in the Muslim community, on the other hand, the majority (98%) pointed at sources of conflict in the community. Leadership struggles was one of the leading factors (24%). Many people want to become leaders. The leadership position ensures respect and also easy access to scarce resources. In the process, greedy leaders take over. Problems arise when these leaders fail to share fairly charitable goods donated to the community. Mismanagement of these goods and embezzlement of funds create conflicts (10%). Many respondents pointed to this factor as one of the main sources of conflicts in the Muslim community. Another source of conflict is the presence of different Islamic sects (25%). Because people belong to different sects, within the same community, disagreement arise in terms of doctrines and practices. Related to this factor is the issue of belonging to different political parties (5%). This also creates conflicts because each party has its policies, hence conflicts between opposing parties. The usual problems in the community are also factors that lead to these conflicts. These are issues like backbiting, petty jealousies, refusing to work together in projects, selfishness, witchcraft, intermarriage, migration, lack of devotion, tribalism, opportunistic behaviour, and many more. These issues are part of everyday occurrences. Syncretism is one of the sources of conflict (6%). As Islam has been adapted to the local conditions, there is bound to be syncretistic behavior on the part of the community. Perhaps the case of Yao Muslims will illustrate the point. The Yao Muslims have adapted some of the Islamic practices to their own beliefs and practices. So, when it comes to these practices, there are going to be clashes if Muslims from the other parts, e.g. Chewa dominated areas, Asians etc were to be together. Levels of education also account for some of the differences (8%). Those who are lowly educated would tend to have different perspectives on some religious issues, different from those who are highly educated in terms of doctrines, practices, etc. In the end, the community ends up having progressive and traditional Muslims within its ranks.

Areas of cooperation between Muslims and Christians

Respondents were asked in what ways Muslims were working together with Christians. There were a few respondents who indicated either that they had no idea whether the two groups work together or they do not work together (2%). But the majority gave ways in which the two religions work together (98%). One notable way in which the two work together is in politics (30%). Obviously, the choice of a Muslim as a president is testimony to that fact. This means that Muslims and Christians are running the government together. The two groups also work together in community development projects (32%), e.g. in selfhelp projects (building schools, hospitals, roads, etc). They too work together in traditional ceremonies (3%), e.g. marriage festivals, traditional dances, etc. In connection with this, they also help each other in funerals although their burial practices are different. Some Christians and Muslims belong to same organizations e.g., political parties, PAC, and many more. They work together in work places, business, and in time of crises (16%). They both fight against diseases, poverty, and ignorance. They live together in villages. Finally, Christians and Muslims preach the word of God/Allah (11%). Although their approaches to this end differ, they have one common goal, i.e. the spread of the word of God/Allah. All the above examples demonstrate the fact that Christians and Muslims are working together in Malawi.

Ways in which Muslims and Christians do not work together

As part of the above question, respondents were asked to point out ways in which Muslims and Christians do not work together. The overwhelming majority noted that the two do not work together when it comes to religious beliefs and practices (77%). The Christians have Jesus as their prophet whereas to the Muslims, Muhammad is the prophet of God. Others indicated that the two groups do not work together in running religious schools, e.g. seminaries, madrassas (1.5%). Each does its own business. Still others complained that Christians consider Muslims as pagans, hence Christians do not recognise Islam (1%). The two also do not work together in burial procedures (.8%) and when it comes to converting new followers (.4%).

Help from Muslim institutions

In the first place, respondents were asked to state ways in which Malawi has profited from outside Muslim help. Some respondents indicated that Malawi has profited nothing or not very much (3%). Others (97%) however, pointed at several ways in which Malawi has profited from that help. One area has been in community development projects (schools, hospitals, etc) (50%). Many learning institutions have been constructed and this has contributed to the physical development of Malawi. Islamic literature and education have been made available to the country. This has helped develop religious education in the country. Employment activities have been created in the country through the help given by these Muslim countries (3%). There have been business activities which have created jobs for Malawians. Some Malawians have also found jobs in the Muslim countries. The economic assistance given to Malawi has profited the Muslim community as well as the rest of the country. The poverty alleviation programme has also received assistance from these countries. In this way, many Malawians have profited. Many Muslim students have received scholarships to study within but also abroad (10%). This is helping the country in terms of literacy. These students are doing Islamic as well as secular education. In the final analysis, we end up having a literate society. Malawi is, therefore, definitely profiting from this assistance.

The second part of the question asked the respondents to give problems that might have risen as a result of this outside help. Some respondents indicated that there have been no problems or if there have been any, then they are not noticeable (10%). However, others pointed out a number of problems that have arisen as a result of the help that the country has received from Muslim institutions and countries (90%). Poor leadership, greedy people, nepotism, corruption, mismanagement of funds, and lack of accountability are some of the problems (40%). This has created jealousies, enmity, and hatred in the Muslim community. Another problem has been the conflict between the Muslim community and the previous government (9%). The previous government was interfering in the affairs of the Muslims. The government was suspicious of the help. The bottom line was that there was fear of Arab dominance through the aid that was coming in, i.e. there was fear of Islamisation by non-Muslims (9%). The Muslim community had also problems in maintaining the infrastructure that was created as a result of the assistance. Many schools, mosques, etc were erected, but to maintain them, it was very difficult. This problem was created because sometimes the aid was reduced and the Gulf crisis also contributed to this reduced aid (0.5%). Dependency syndrome was created. The Muslim community depends on help from outside. This is a problem because when no aid comes, the community suffers as was the case during the Gulf crisis. This dependency is also a problem because the community does not do anything on its own. This is not a healthy situation especially when it comes to development. The above are, therefore, some problems that have arisen as a result of the help that has come from Muslim countries.

Relationship with Muslims in neighbouring countries

Respondents were asked to indicate ways in which Muslims in Malawi are working together with Muslims in neighbouring countries of Africa, like Tanzania, Kenya, Mozambique. Some respondents said that these countries do not work together (8%). Perhaps those who answered this way had no idea of what goes on in their community especially when it comes to international relations. In actual fact, some indicated that they had no idea. An overwhelming majority indicated that these countries work together (92%). These countries work together in spreading Islam (8%). They exchange preachers and pray together (43%). They share ideas (4%) by exchanging visits (5%), scholars (5%), and by meeting together in international forums (13%). The Muslims in this region belong to the same regional Islamic organizations. They also work together in regional offices. They also exchange students (14%). Scholarships are offered so that these students can learn in each other's country (6%). They also exchange Islamic literature (70%), which promotes Islamic education and strengthens brotherhood. Other respondents indicated that there was trade among these countries and they help each other economically. They also involve themselves in fund raising activities which help the poor of these countries. In other words, they work together in times of crises and provide relief to the victims of these crises. Muslims in these countries work together in promoting peace and justice in their countries. So these are some of the ways in which Muslims in this part of Africa work together.

Conclusions

This study has revealed that Islam has now spread from the three districts (Karonga, Mangochi, and Nkhotakota) to almost every part of the country. Muslims, therefore, are a force to be reckoned with in Malawi. Malawian Muslims are no longer cut off from the mainstream Islamic *Umma* as it used to be. The research has also brought up a number of issues. It will suffice here to reflect only on four of these. First, some respondents have raised the issue that the president likes to attend or get involved in Christian functions more than he does in Muslim activities. This Christian association worries some Muslims because these people had hoped that the present would be their leader in the strict sense of the word. Is the president aligning himself with the dominant Christians at their expense? The president has not said why he likes to attend Christian functions more than Muslim ones, but one would speculate that it is a matter of policy and, perhaps, putting it crudely, it is because the Christians put him in power. If he was too close to the Muslims, Christians would accuse him of favouritism and the fear of Islamization of the country would not be far from the truth. If this is a matter of policy, is he not alienating himself from his kind? The president is obviously in a dilemma here although we should have expected him to be impartial as the head of state. Second, there has been mention of freedom of worship. In the previous regime, Muslims were not very often called to participate on public occasions. This could be due simply to the style of the Muslims not to mention, e.g., Kamuzu in their prayers. To them Allah is the name, whereas to the MCP, it was the Ngwazi. Perhaps, the Muslims did not want to be involved in idolatry by mentioning someone like the president. This might have been one of the reasons why they were excluded from many public functions. With the new dispensation, they are free to worship without being called upon to pray for the president. In fact in many of their prayers, Muslims do not mention the president unlike the Christians. Third, there was mention of freedom of expression. One thing that is very obvious now is that Muslims have at least two newspapers. This was unlike in the previous regime when this was not the case. Finally, there was the issue of access to the radio. Symbolically, this is access to power that was not there in the past. Now, they can be heard as all other religious groups. Access to the radio is also one way of strengthening unity among themselves. They can now speak with one voice. So freedom of worship, expression, and access to the radio are channels of power and equality to them.

6. Power at the Receiving End: The Jehovah's Witnesses' Experience in One Party Malawi

Klaus Fiedler

The Refusal to Constitute Power

When national independence came to Malawi in 1964, it meant a transfer of power: from colonial authority to national leadership, from a non political administration to a political government, constituted by the majority party in the national Parliament, which was elected by the people. Thus every Malawian could have a share in constituting power in the land, and as an independent nation Malawi would then rule itself for the benefit of all. So far the theory. By the time of the Cabinet Crisis it became clear that freedom of choice meant to support freely what Kamuzu chose, and even before formal political independence it had been made clear that Congress Party demanded the allegiance of *all* Malawians.

In the Party's conflict with the Jehovah's Witnesses the issue at stake was not which party could win power, and if so, how to organize it, but the refusal to share in political power. The Congress Party expected everyone to support its power, and by doing so, constitute that power (and possibly share in it). The Jehovah's Witnesses did not struggle to achieve power, nor would they want a share in power. They refused to constitute power. In their turn, first the Party and then the government made it abundantly clear that every Malawian, babies included, has to do her or his part in constituting power. On the practical level the issue was: What kind of society is independent Malawi to construct for itself? Is it to be pluralistic or unitary? And if it is to be unitary, will there be room for individual deviation? The answer soon given was clear: Society must be politically unitary, and no deviation is allowed. The individual is of no value in itself, its value is to help in constituting the larger whole. But how that larger whole is to be, will not be decided by the contributing individuals, but by the leaders and owners of that larger whole, namely the party leadership and ultimately by their leader and owner, Kamuzu Banda.

The message of the new power to the people of Malawi was freedom. Freedom from colonial rule and from the stupid Federation and its racism, and even in 1993 during his last public performances Kamuzu would shout: "*Ufulu*!", to which the crowds had to respond enthusiastically: "*Ufulu*!" To put emphasis on the message, shout and response were repeated several times. So freedom was and remained high on the agenda of the Malawi Congress Party all the years it remained in power. The touchstone of political freedom is religious freedom. If one is allowed to live according to one's deepest religious convictions, this entails a lot of political freedom. The constitution of Malawi granted religious freedom, and Kamuzu proclaimed it again and again. In addition he prided himself in being a Christian, and not just nominally so, but with full involvement as a church elder. He also emphasized repeatedly that he had read the Bible from beginning to end. But in spite of all this, religious freedom in Malawi would, during his time, belong to the realm of the constitution, not to the realm of life, as the Jehovah's Witnesses were to experience.

The Jehovah's Witnesses

The Jehovah's Witnesses are an international religious organization, which was started in America by Charles Taze Russel in 1881 as the Zion's Watch Tower Tract Society. It formed an extreme wing of the broader pre-millennial movement, which had changed evangelical eschatology dramatically from about 1820 onwards. The missionary movement that was born in the Great Awakening and which changed the religious map of Africa so drastically in the 19th century, was "postmillennial" The term means that they expected the second coming of Christ to take place *after* the millennium, during which the church would "reign gloriously" for a thousand years. The millennium would be brought about by divine intervention at the end of a process of missions and social reforms gradually encompassing the whole world, and thus making it a better place to live in. The premillennialists did not expect the world to improve with time, but rather to deteriorate. Then, and probably quite soon, Christ would return to usher in the millennium and rule it as its visible king. This general premillennial conviction had come to be shared by 1870 by almost all the newer Protestant missions as well as by many missionaries who, before, had held postmillennial views. While most evangelical Christians were convinced that the return of Christ was "near" or "imminent", some groups started to calculate the date of that event by using ingenious combinations of apocalyptical and historical time reckoning.[1] One group

---

[1] The apocalyptic time reckoning was taken from Daniel and Revelation. These two books were combined, and then certain apocalyptic events, dates and personalities were identified with historical events, dates and personalities. The false prophet was, at times, identified with Muhammad, the antichrist was identified either as a certain pope or as the papal system etc. Based on these identifications and on a certain concept of prophetic language, so that a week in the book of Daniel would be taken to mean seven years ("a week of years"), timetables of past and future events could be developed. The first modern European theologian to fix the date of Christ's coming was the German Pietist leader Johann Albrecht Bengel (1687-1752), who fixed the date of Christ's second coming as 18 June 1836.

to do so were the Millerites who fixed the date as 1844,[2] another group to do so were the Jehovah's Witnesses, who chose 1914.[3]

Right from the beginning it was not Russel's aim to start a new denomination, but a new movement, a movement of Bible students who prepare for the end soon to come. Christ did not return to earth in 1914, Russel died in 1916, somewhat bewildered, but the organization he had started lived on, consolidated and spread. No precise date for Christ's return was ever set again, though the date of the beginning of his invisible presence was moved to 1914. The event of 1914 was now seen as a heavenly event, marking the *beginning* of the final stage in world history, which would not take longer than one generation.[4] The Watchtower Movement then developed from a somewhat loosely structured organization into a tightly structured religious group, centrally directed from headquarters in Brooklyn, New York. The Jehovah's Witnesses do not see themselves as one church among so many others, and they do not even accept that they *are* a church. They see themselves as the Theocratic Organization, whose members will be saved in the final battle of Harmagedon. The have no fellowship with Christian churches.

The Jehovah's Witnesses in Malawi

The Jehovah's Witnesses (then Watchtower Society) originally came to Malawi in 1908 through the preaching of Elliot Kamwana.[5] The link to Russel in America was Joseph Booth in Cape Town, who, before and after his allegiance to the Watchtower Society was a Seventh Day Baptist. Booth had visited Russel in 1906 in the USA,[6] returned to Cape Town as a Watch Tower representative, trained Elliot Kamwana there as a Watchtower missionary and sent him back to his native Malawi, where he had great success among the Tonga, baptizing about 9,000 people within three months.[7] Kamwana preached the coming of the millennium for 1914, and seems to have added to the general Watchtower message about the

---

[2] On William Miller's life, evangelism and teaching see R.W. Schwarz, *Light Bearers to the Remnant*, Mountain View/Oshawa: Pacific Press, 1979, pp. 31-57.

[3] This calculation was based on N.H. Barbour's assumption that Christ had been present invisibly since 1874, and that he would usher in the millennium after a period of testing of 40 years.

[4] This concept is based on Matthew 24.34 which says: "I tell you the truth, this generation will certainly not pass away until these things have happened" (NIV).

[5] See J.C. Chakanza, "From Preacher to Prophet: Elliot Kenan Kamwana and the Watch Tower Movement in Malawi, 1908-1956", in: J.C. Chakanza, *Preachers in Protest*, forthcoming in the Kachere Series (Blantyre: CLAIM).

[6] H. Langworthy, "Africa for the African": The Life of Joseph Booth, Blantyre: CLAIM, 1996, pp. 195-196.

[7] *Ibid*, pp. 195ff.

millennium some anticolonial touches. On the suggestion of Livingstonia missionary MacAlpine the government deported him to Southern Malawi.[8] Later he was deported to Chinde and finally to Mauritius. In spite of his absence the congregations he had started continued, and attempts by Joseph Booth to make them Seventh Day Baptists failed.[9]

In 1934 the international Watchtower Society, now under the name of Jehovah's Witnesses, sent a representative to check on the state of affairs in the Watchtower movement in Malawi. He declared almost all Watchtower members to be heretical, accepting only 30 as genuine. Starting with this small group the international Jehovah's Witnesses built up their organization in Malawi, until at the time of independence it had about 17,000 members. The expelled Watchtower adherents continued as Watchtower Mission (Native Controlled). When Kamwana finally was allowed to return in 1937, his branch became the Watchman Healing Mission. For this chapter it is important to keep in mind, that, though the two movements have a common root, they do not recognize each other, and in the following text the name Jehovah's Witnesses only applies to those who belong to the international organization under that name.

The Jehovah's Witnesses are represented in most countries of the world, counting presently more than 4 million members worldwide, many of them in Africa. Their organization is strictly centralized. Therefore their Bible studies, magazines and books are the same everywhere, being translated usually from English, and displaying a style strongly reminiscent of some religious subculture in America.

Now we can speak

While working for the Theology of Life Project, we felt that a record should be made of those who suffered through the exercise of power and because of the denial of religious freedom. So during the Easter vacation 1995 students were encouraged to record the experience of Jehovah's Witnesses, usually in the students' home areas. I had been aware that the Jehovah's Witnesses had been banned in the country, and that many had fled to neighbouring countries, but I was shocked by the horrible details which these stories, randomly collected, contained. There was no record of it, yet, but a record there should be, for the sake of truth, to remember those who died in the fight for religious freedom, to make clear what national unity meant for those on the receiving end. Let those speak who still can because they survived.

---

[8] *Ibid*, p. 219.
[9] *Ibid*, chapters 13 and 14.

In the Theology of Life Project it was my task to pay special attention to the "smaller" churches. Though the Jehovah's Witnesses would refuse to be called a church, they somehow belonged to my remit. Having lived in Malawi less than four years now, I did not witness any of the physical persecution, and as someone who did not live through this period himself, I must be careful not to be judgmental. I can only surmise what I would have done, thought and felt in those days. I must also be careful, not to forget that as a German I come from a nation with one of the worst human rights records, which did not only cause the most horrible war in world history, but also killed six million people for no other crime than being Jews, not counting hundreds of thousands of other people like Sinti and Roma ("gypsies"), the mentally ill, the politically dissident and thousands of Jehovah's Witnesses.

I am not guilty of those crimes, simply because I was not around then, being only three years old when Germany was liberated by the Allied Forces, and I do not believe in collective guilt. But I feel shame, and I do believe in collective shame. After 1945 the German nation decided to face its horrible past, and not to attempt a new start by forgetting both victims and perpetrators. I am convinced that Malawi neither should start a new era by "forgiving and forgetting", but should face its - far less horrible - past, remember it, relive it to some extent, face the truth and thus seek healing, forgiveness and a new start. I wish that this chapter, written by one who shares the collective shame of *his* nation, may help to heal.

One nation, one party, buy your card!
Worldwide the Jehovah's Witnesses have some convictions which a state can easily take objection to: in their first decades they saw the state as such as evil, but receiving newer light the Jehovah's Witnesses leadership ("the wise and faithful slave")[10] changed the teaching on the state so that it is now seen, according to Romans 13, as not bad in itself. Even before this change in teaching Jehovah's Witnesses were law abiding citizens, but the change of teaching removed any doubts about the propriety of paying taxes, sending children to school etc. On the other hand, Jehovah's Witnesses continue to refuse military service, and they refuse to take any part in politics. Since they always paid their taxes, and since military service was voluntary, the major area of conflict in Malawi was politics, and the nationwide symbol of political involvement was the "party card", signifying membership in the Malawi Congress Party.

Persecution started in 1963 in the run up to the elections that led to independence. At one place the Kingdom Hall was burnt three months before the election, Jeho-

---

[10] **Based on** Mt 24.45-47

vah's Witnesses fled to Mozambique to a village close to Chiromo, and children were barred from attending primary school because they did not have a party card.[11] "Mr Simoni and other Jehovah's Witnesses were beaten very severely. His property was destroyed, his house was set on fire. All maize seedlings in his field were uprooted by the Youths."[12] These persecutions were too organized and too widespread to be seen as public outbursts against those who do not help in the struggle, and they took place while the Jehovah's Witnesses were perfectly legal. What was done were criminal acts according to the laws of Malawi, but no report of legal persecution of the criminals has come to light.[13] It seems that even at that early stage in the history of free Malawi the judicial system was less than free.

Peaks and Valleys of Persecution: 1964, 1967, 1972

After the elections of 1964 the persecution decreased somewhat.[14] Some report that they could pray freely and without interference.[15] Refugees were encouraged to return, "since everything was over,"[16] but they were still pressurized to buy the card.[17]

Mzuzu 1967

The Mzuzu 1967 Malawi Congress Party Convention brought the first major peak in the persecution. The convention made this resolution, which the Ngwazi heartily endorsed in his closing remarks:

> 8. Recommend strongly that the Jehovah's Witnesses denomination be declared illegal in this country as the attitude of its adherents is not only inimical to the progress of this country, but also negative in

---

[11] Int Faison S. Chimphepo 14 April 1995 [Ashanie Gawa].

[12] Int Macdonald Simoni 14 April 1995 [Charles Eliyasi].

[13] Since several houses were set alight with the people in them (Int Jevis and Chrissie Kapanda 15 April 1995 [Rosemary T. Muhuwo]), criminal charges might even have included murder.

[14] In the material collected there is no case of severe persecution reported for 1965 or 1966.

[15] Int Cecelia Mazibuko 21 April 1995 [Munthali].

[16] "In 1965 all the Malawian Jehovah's Witnesses who went or fled to Mozambique were forced to go back home. The Malawian government and the MCP assured them that everything was over but that was not the truth. After returning to Malawi, they were subjected to similar problems as before and they were still forced to buy party membership cards (Int Langton W. Mukhwapa 1 May 1995 [Charles Eliyasi]).

[17] "Despite this freedom granted to them while in Mozambique Mr Simoni and his family were not comfortable in Mozambique because it was foreign land. Such being the case he came back to Malawi together with the other Jehovah's Witnesses in 1966. They were not welcomed in Malawi. Even chiefs did not like them except for some few close relatives. They were still forced to buy MCP membership cards" (Int Macdonald Simoni 14 April 1995 [Charles Eliyasi]).

every way that it endangers the stability and peace and calm which is essential for the smooth running of our state.[18]

In his closing remarks Kamuzu mentioned that Government "may pass a law in such way that every area district can decide itself whether it wants Jehovah's Witnesses or not. If people in any area said 'No' then there would be no Jehovah's Witnesses there." Such a law was indeed made by government in October, but it banned the Jehovah's Witnesses outright, leaving the people of given areas no choice, and threatened to punish anyone trying to keep the movement going with 14 years in jail.[19]

Long before these legal niceties had been completed, the MCP had taken the law in its own hands and launched a ferocious onslaught on the Jehovah's Witnesses. In this onslaught the youth wing of the party, and in some areas the Malawi Young Pioneers, were prominent, acting obviously under the direction of higher party officials. At Gowoka, the area chairman told the youth leaguers to hunt down all Jehovah's Witnesses. One was Mr Phiri. The Youths surrounded his house at night, ordered Mr Phiri out, then entered the house and threw his sleeping wife out and started to beat both of them. Their books were torn to pieces and scattered on the way. Then they pushed them to walk, while singing a mocking song:

Mwawamboni kutenthena muleke!	Witnesses, don't be afraid!
Mwafwa mwafwira chiuta winu.	If you die, you die for your God.
Iyi ninkhondo mwayiona.	This is war as you see.
Mwa wa youth kuthenthena muleke!	You Youth, don't be afraid!
Mwafwa mwafwira chalu chinu.	If you die, it is for your country
Iyi ndi nkhondo mwayiona.[20]	This is war as you see.

After arriving at a school, both were undressed (except underwear), they had to run around the school blocs so that the Youth Leaguers, encircling the bloc, could beat them. Soon others were brought in and were subjected to similar treatment. Torture of women was discontinued in the morning, for men it continued till midday, with sticks with sharpened metal pieces being used in the exercise. Some were left for dead, but they had only fainted. None could be taken to hospital, because the Jehovah's Witnesses were not allowed to use "Kamuzu's hospitals" But still they would not buy party cards.

Major methods of persecution were the burning of houses (preferably with the inhabitants inside), the slashing of crops in the fields, general beatings and more

---

[18] Printed in *Malawi News* 19 September 1967 "On Jehovah's Witnesses the President said that they were causing trouble everywhere."
[19] *The Times*, 23 October 1967
[20] Int Syton E. F Mumba for Amosi Phiri 20 April 1995 [Munthali].

exquisite forms of torture. Sometimes this killed, but sometimes murder was consciously included.

> He and other Jehovah's Witnesses were beaten severely by the MYP and Youths for refusing the membership cards. His relative ... was killed on the spot for the same reason. He was cut into pieces as a demonstration to others to scare them but they were not.[21]

Persecution brought benefits to the persecutors: they would serve their country, experience the pleasures of power, and could distribute the movable property of the persecuted among themselves. In such a situation, even the corrugated iron sheets of a roof were easily removed.[22] The land they had been cultivating, though not movable, could still benefit others. Part of it was taken by the persecutors, part of it was allotted to relatives. In spite of this severe persecution, most Jehovah's Witnesses continued to refuse to buy party cards, and they would meet at night in private houses in smaller groups or even in the bush. Despite many Witnesses fleeing to neighbouring countries, their numbers did not decrease, as their faith continued to be attractive. In 1968 there was, just as in 1965, a certain relenting of the persecution.[23] Not that it stopped, but it was less severe. In the cities persecution took place,[24] too, but was generally less severe than in the countryside. In Chithawira (Blantyre) they were able to meet openly and in 1969/70 even to build a major Kingdom Hall.[25]

Zomba 1972

The renewed persecution was launched with new and much stronger resolutions passed by the convention, with Kamuzu again, and this time much more clearly, endorsing them. The resolutions were published in both Chewa and English, and for resolution c. it is worth comparing the two since the Chewa version is much less guarded than the English version.

---

[21] Int Samson Gresham 12 April 1995 [Charles Eliyasi].
[22] Int Stewart Kumbanyiwa 2 May 1995 [Charles Eliyasi].
[23] Int Cecelia Mazibuko 21 April 1995 [Munthali].
[24] After the publication of the ban in the Gazette, eight expatriate Witnesss were deported ("Banned Sect Heads to Go. Four Remanded", *Malawi News* 10 November 1967).
[25] This was built with money from wellwishers in USA and UK, and with money and labour of the local members, close to Chitawira Primary School. Before they had been meeting sometimes in the grounds of the school (Int N.N. 9 April 1995 [Aloisious Nthenda]).

"Zitakambirana mwatsatane - tsatane pa zobvuta zimene ziletsa chitutuko cha Chipani ndi cha dziko, nthumwi.

a) Zidakhumudwa poona kuti anthu ena a liuma a zipenbedzo zobuta, zooneka ngati mpingo iya woletsedwa wa Mboni za Yehova, atanititsa chitutuku cha ndele ndi chuma mdizko lino.

b) Zidegwrizana kuti mamembala onse a mpingo ya anthu obvuta chotere amene ali pa ntchito m'kampani achotsedwe ntchito lerolero, ndipo ngati kampani iriyonse siitsata zimene talemba pa mfundo ino, kampani imeneyo ilandidire laisensi.

c) Zidapangana kuti mamembala onse a mpingo yobvta chotere amene adalebedwa ntchito ndi Boma achotsedwe ntchito msanga-msanga, ndiponso kuti aliyense wa mpingo yotere amene ali ndi ntchito yakeyake, ngakhale ndi ya bizinesi yakeyo kapena ya ulimi, bizinesi yakeyo kapena minda wakewo ulandidwa.

d) Zidapangana kuti onse a mpingo yotere amene akale ku midzi apirititsidwe kumidzito,[26] ndipo zidapempha Boma kuti lisabvute anthu a Chipani amene azilimbana ndi anthu a mpingo yotere.[27]

Having discussed in great detail the problems that confront the Progress of the Party and the Nation, delegates

a) Deplored the fact that certain fanatical religious sects which operated like the banned Jehovah's Witness sect,[28] hindered the political and economic development of the country.

b) Resolved that all the members of those fanatical religious sects employed in Commerce and Industry should be dismissed forthwith, and that any commercial or industrial concern that does not comply with these resolution should have its license cancelled.

c) Resolved that all the members of those fanatical religious sects employed by the Government should be dismissed forthwith and that any member of these sects who is self-employed either in business or farming should have his business or farming interests discouraged.[29]

d) Resolved that all members of those sects who live in the villages should be chased away from there, and appealed to government to give maximum possible protection to members of the party who deal with the adherents of these sects.[30]

---

[26] At the same conference Kamuzu emphasized the importance of good behaviour: See caption page 5. *Malawi News*, Friday 22 September 1972. "Commenting on the resolution, the Life President emphasised the importance of good manners in keeping with our tradition."

[27] Mfundo za ku Msonkhano Waukulu wa Chipani (*Malawi News* Sunday 10 September Saturday 16 September 1972).

[28] Though here groups "like the Jehovah's Witnesses" are mentioned, the resolution was applied to the Jehovah's Witnesses and to no other group.

[29] The English version of this paragraph is [intentionally?] vague: "should have his business or farming interests discouraged" The Chewa version clearly states: "bizinesi yakeyo kapena

The last clause in resolution d) shows that those who drafted it must have been aware that what they were intending was illegal, even in Malawi. The persecution of the "banned sect" was not to be done by the appropriate authorities like police and judiciary, but by the party. Therefore they would need legal protection for their illegal actions. But do you need legal protection for illegal acts if they are done on behalf of Kamuzu? No, as became clear immediately.

At the end of the convention, Kamuzu made it clear that nobody "dealing" with the Jehovah's Witnesses had anything to fear. He endorsed the resolutions wholeheartedly, as recalled by one Jehovah's Witness:

> Kamuzu consented to the idea of torture and persecution of the Jehovah's Witnesses. Kamuzu's part of the speech was like this, "The Jehovah's Witnesses claim to know God's Word, but I read the Bible from Genesis to Revelation and if at all there is somebody to enter heaven, then its me. They refuse to buy party cards but when in trouble they rush to police, whose police? Therefore I order them to prepare a ladder that will lead them to heaven, but it shouldn't be placed on the country's land because my ants shall devour them". Since his word was like an established law, persecution started on the very same day, 18th Sept.[31]

Malawi News also reported that Kamuzu made it abundantly clear how he rated the Jehovah's Witnesses: "They are the Satan's or the Devil's Witnesses". He also made clear that there was no difference between party and government:

> when they are in trouble, "they complain to the police, the DC or the Chief. These are government. These are government but they refuse to pay taxes to the government.[32] Why do they not go to the church and ask for help from God when in trouble."[33]

At a mass rally at Zaone, just after the close of the Zomba convention, he made it very clear: "They are stupid."[34] On the same day as Kamuzu gave his endorsement, a new wave of persecution started, more widespread and more terrible than the preceding ones.

---

munda wakewo ulandidwe" This must be translated: "His/her business or field must be taken away (by force)"

[30] *Malawi News* 19 September 1972 [Tuesday]

[31] Int Mr M. Kaleso 16 April 1995 [Hanna A. Bonzo].

[32] I have no evidence whatsoever that Jehovah's Witnesses refused to pay taxes. Obviously Kamuzu, ignoring the subtle differences between party and state, understood the party card to be a tax.

[33] *Malawi News*, 19 September 1972 [Tuesday].

[34] *Malawi News*, 22 September 1972 [Friday].

William Clark, the leader of the Jehovah's Witnesses in the whole country, living in Chigumula, Blantyre, was given 24 hours to leave the country.

> When he left in the morning of 19th Sept. 1972, there came a multitude of MCP members to steal and share all his property.[35] His workers were commanded to leave. Failing to do so, they would be burnt.[36]

Expatriates were usually treated more generously. Malawians had no other home than Malawi. All civil servants were dismissed from their jobs, and even private employers were forced to dismiss their workers who were Witnesses. In Blantyre, again, the situation seems to have been a bit easier. A Jehovah's Witness, owning a barber's shop in Ndirande, had his shop demolished by "unknown persons" in September, but no harm was done to him, and on 5 October the local MCP chairman came to his house and gave him 12 hours to leave "since Kamuzu had directed that they should vacate the country."[37]

In rural areas less subtle ways of persuading the remaining Jehovah's Witnesses to "vacate" the country were applied. The Mazibuko family had their maize store burnt, the father was taken to the chief where he was beaten to the point of death.[38] On 25 September MYP came to Mr Mkandawire's village. They

> were told to come out of their houses, and neighbours were leaders in this act. Properties were taken away from them and those which were of no value to them were burnt to ashes. At midday of 25th Sept. Mr Qabaniso Chibambo who was by then MCP minister in the Northern region called all the J/W members for a meeting. He said that the govt. had decided that they must buy MCP cards and must join the party. If not they must be killed or chased away immediately. He gave them two days to think but they were not left alone since the Youths and Pioneers were there forcing them to buy the MCP cards by beating them, young and old, male and female. While they were at the meeting, their houses were burnt to ashes.[39]

> Mr Mkandawire's grandfather Mr Mhango who had two shops seeing that his house was burning to ashes managed to run from the group and hid his two sewing machines in the bush but unfortunately he was seen by the MYP and as a result was beaten to death. They

---

[35] The crowd showed a very similar behaviour the morning after the army had dislodged the MYP from their Zomba base. The actual armed attack produced little damage compared to the looting afterwards.
[36] Int Michael Kovuluva 15 April 1995 [Hanna Bonzo].
[37] Int Mr C.J. Nekonda 10 April 1995 [R.M. Soko].
[38] Int Cecelia Mazibuko 21 April 1995 [Munthali].
[39] Int Aaron Mkandawire [Mirriam Chipeta Banda].

> were left without any property and were forced to stay in the bush since their houses were burnt. They were not regarded as human beings but animals e.g. they were not allowed to visit hospitals, buy food at the markets, cross bridges, go to the maize millers. They lived in the bush for 3 weeks and they survived by eating potatoes which they used to harvest at night in their gardens which no longer belonged to them since they were taken away from them.[40]

The 1972 persecution surpassed in cruelty and scope the persecution of 1967. Most Jehovah's Witnesses seem to have left Malawi then. Some managed to remain by giving up their faith or by somehow compromising it, others remained without doing either.

Dzaleka, 1975

After the 1972 peak the persecution did not relent much. But in 1975 a change occurred in that now the judicial system became officially involved. This was in some ways a hardening of the persecution. But the advantage was that now the pattern became regular: Jehovah's Witnesses would be brought to court at Dowa to be accused of treason and plotting to overthrow the MCP government. The judge was always Muhango, who would always find them guilty and sentence them to two years imprisonment with hard labour. The prison to spend these two years was always Dzaleka, where in the "Jehovah's Witnesses section" up to 3000 were housed. Dzaleka was no holiday resort, and cruelties not included in the term "hard labour" could also not be excluded, either.

> At Dzaleka they were given hoes and were told to level down a hill which was nearby. They were forced to work all day long whether under intense sunlight or rainfall. They were not allowed to rest and were constantly being beaten at the back while working. Many people were dying, in a week six to ten people could die. They were working from 6:00 am to 7:00 pm. They ate at 12 midnight without washing hands. They could stay for two or three months without taking a shower.[41]

In the camp it happened that elders who taught anything resembling Jehovah's Witnesses teaching were given additional punishment, and any Jehovah's Witness, who was caught reading one of the prison Bibles, would have to stay on two extra months. But Dzaleka, hard as it was (and not everyone survived), had the advantage that the time was clearly regulated. After two years you would be given a warrant to travel home, and there the party was not to trouble you unduly.[42] The Jehovah's Witnesses could not meet openly, but they were normally not to be

---

[40] Int Aaron Mkandawire [Mirriam Chipeta Banda].
[41] Int Michael H. Nambera 11 April 1995 [Charles Eliyasi].
[42] Int Jenifa Moyo 18 April 1995 [Munthali].

persecuted when they met unofficially, first usually in the bush, later also in private houses. In addition somewhere during this time (1975-1977) prison conditions improved, and all children (up to 18 years) were released unconditionally. Various accounts report that the then Inspector General of the Police, Kamwana, made these arrangements.[43]

The relenting of the persecution (1978)

The year 1978 was marked by a considerable change in the experience of the Jehovah's Witnesses. They remained as illegal as before, they could not meet openly, land taken away was not returned, and they could expect various forms of harassment at any time. The Youth League continued to be active, but the level of harassment changed. Children could attend school again, and when in 1986 six were dropped for not having a party card, the police immediately reinstated them.[44] Forced selling of party cards was still an active pursuit, but instead of beating, stealing, raping and killing, they would arrange for a forced exchange: When party cards were due for renewal, they would come and take by force (which Jehovah's Witnesses would not resist) what they considered the equivalent in value, be it chicken, chair or other movable property.[45] This "muted" persecution continued until the referendum brought the defeat of the one-party system. In September 1993 Parliament rescinded all restrictions on the Jehovah's Witnesses. In the spirit of forgetting instead of forgiving no effort was made to address the injustices done.

Lands of Refuge

One advantage for troubled Malawians is that the country is small and that a border is never very far away. This was a way for many of the Witnesses to save their lives, and for the government a convenient way to get rid of the undesirables.

Mozambique

Due to its geographical proximity, in many areas Mozambique was the land to flee to. The borders were not really controlled, sometimes not even clearly defined. But even where a river like the Ruo marked the border, crossing it was rarely difficult for people who knew the area. In the wake of the 1963/64 persecution, refuge in Mozambique was more an individual issue. Numbers were limited, and those who sought refuge often knew their way around the area. In the wake of the

---

[43] He also visited the camp to hear prisoners' grievances. He arranged for example that mothers with small children were given three blankets (Int Mrs Nekonda 11 April 1995 [R.M. Soko]).
[44] Int John Henry Mwase [Esnat Mdolo].
[45] Int Lydia Shawa 19 April 1995 [Munthali].

1967 persecution, numbers were bigger, but they were biggest in the wake of the 1972 persecution. The main area of refuge in Mozambique was Milanje, just across from Mulanje in Malawi. "The people of Mozambique were amazed with such unruly and unbecoming actions and as a result welcomed them."[46] But it was not easy to help all when, like on 9 October 1972, 1,000 people arrived in one go.[47] As soon as administratively possible the Mozambiquan government, then still under Portuguese rule, began to assist.[48] The Jehovah's Witnesses were given refugee status, and the United Nations assumed responsibility.[49] The refugees were housed in large camps, where they would be able to receive assistance and then gradually establish their own agriculture. There in the camp they had full religious freedom, they would build their Kingdom Halls and witness to their faith. They were free to move, and a number even made their permanent homes in Mozambique.

Colonial freedom, though, came to an end with the coming of political independence to Mozambique. Instead of the MCP it was now Frelimo which demanded signs of allegiance, like shouting "Viva Frelimo" or "Viva Samora Machel." The Malawi Government seems to have taken advantage of the change of government in Mozambique and therefore seems to have arranged for forced repatriation.[50] The Witnesses, anyhow, were told by the Mozambiquan government that "they had been called by their Kamuzu" But when they came, there was no friendly welcome: "Mwatipezanso" (you have found us again) and party cards as usual. Forced repatriation and Frelimo demands were not the only problems. War made things worse. Renamo was not keen to elicit a show of support for national symbols from the refugees, but they wanted them as carriers in the war, and that was not welcome to the Jehovah's Witnesses who were conscientious objectors. In addition Renamo was renowned for its random cruelty. The war, then, forced many refugees back into Malawi, and the international Jehovah's Witnesses' authorities even seem to have advised a return in 1977. Some were clever: They fled to Malawi as Mozambiquan refugees. As such they were received well, and in the camps supervised by the UN, there was full religious freedom.[51]

---

[46] Int Mr R. Nivalo 19 April 1995 [Hanna Bonzo].
[47] Int Michael Kovuluwa 14 April 1995 [Hanna Bonzo].
[48] Special mention is made of the DC of Vira District (Int Mr L. Mkwayira 22 April 1995 [Hanna Bonzo].
[49] The refugees numbered about 19,000 (Int Mr M. Kaleso 16 April 1995 [Hanna Bonzo]).
[50] It is not fully clear which government was the driving force in the repatriation.
[51] Some Malawians even took advantage of this from their side, going into the camps for their prayers (Int Mapulani Alufeyo 16 April 1995 [Ashanie Gawa]).

Zambia: Nsindamisale

In 1972 the biggest exodus went into Zambia, where they were received into a camp at Nsindamisale. By November about 21,000 people had reached the camp.[52] Nsindamisale was a place of refuge, but also of death. The camp was ill equipped, the number of people was too large, and the sanitary conditions terrible. Hundreds died of waterborne diseases, ascribed by some even to the MCP poisoning the sources of water:

> After a week of their stay in Zambia [according to the source this was six weeks after the persecution started at the convention], Malawi sent spies who managed to survey their source of water and poisoned the water. As a result of drinking poisoned water, many of the brothers and sisters died and they buried them in mass graves without coffins.[53]

The illness probably was cholera, but can one blame refugees who had gone through so many atrocities of putting the blame on the MCP for just one more?[54]

Zambia, though, did not like to keep the refugees, in spite of UN responsibility. It negotiated with the government of Malawi a forced repatriation. In mid December the refugees were put into buses and lorries and driven back to Lilongwe Old Airport, where they were welcomed by Mr Kumbweza, the Regional Minister of the MCP for the Centre. The welcome was most unwelcoming. They were requested to shout "Kwacha" (which they refused), were searched for weapons (how should they have got them?), and Kumbweza told them:

> Munapita nokha mwabwerakonso nokha, kodi mudzatsata zofuna za chipani? [You went on your own, and you have come back on your own, will you now do what the party wants?]

Some were made to feel the welcome physically. They were searched for guns while naked,[55] their books were confiscated, some were beaten up,[56] a number of elders were sent to Maula Prison.[57] Those who did not live too far from Lilongwe were told to go home and behave themselves, the rest was transported in the direction of home on army lorries. Those going north were all dropped at Pyukuru

---

[52] *The Times* (London) 19 December 1972, referred to in an anonymous paper, written possibly 1993: "The Watchtower Movement in Malawi: Its Origin, Development and Persecution (1908-1993).

[53] Int Aaron Mkandawire April 1995 [Mirriam C. Banda].

[54] *The Times* (London) 19 December 1972 reported that 342 had died so far

[55] "Ndipo anthu a akazi ankawasecha kumaliseche ali abisako mfuti choncho nkavulidwa kuti aone ngati sali ndi mfuti" (Int Chief Josamu Kwendanjati 14 April 1995 [Rosemary T Muhuwo].

[56] Int Alabia Barnard 18 April 1995 [Rosemary T Muhuwo].

[57] Int Alabia Barnard 18 April 1995 [Rosemary T Muhuwo].

(Mzimba) on command of the minister of the Northern Region, Mr Chibambo. They were told to respond to the "Kwacha" slogan, but nobody responded,[58] and they were threatened with massive shooting.[59] Pyukuru Hill then was a lonely place, with lots of lions. They were given no provisions, but local people helped them on their way.

Return to new persecution

The general pattern after this forced return was new persecution. When going to find some sweet potatoes in what once used to be their gardens, the Youth might hide and frighten or torture them.[60] Nothing was given back to them. On Christmas Day 1972 e.g. the MP for the Makhanga area, commanded that the Jehovah's Witnesses assemble at Makhanga School where they whipped them severely and asked them why they ran away to Zambia on their own choice and returned again.[61] Many returnees, realizing that they had been cheated and that nothing good was in store for them, immediately or very soon after fled again, this time mostly to Mozambique via Mlangeni.[62] But some fled back to Zambia, where they were allowed to stay, too.[63]

International Power

The Jehovah's Witnesses suffered for their refusal to create national power and thereafter from the excessive and illegal use of this national power. This national power was legally sheltered by the concept of national sovereignty and the concomitant concept of non-interference in national affairs.[64] This meant that international power did not bring much relief to the suffering Jehovah's Witnesses, and possibly it increased it. The fact that there were competing national powers around Malawi made it possible for the Witnesses to find refuge. An exception here is Tanzania, where the Jehovah's Witnesses were banned, too.[65] If countries like

---

[58] Int Mr Nyasa Moyo 12 April 1995 [Ashanie Gawa].
[59] Int Syton E.F. Mumba 17 April 1995 [Munthali].
[60] Int Mr Nyasa Moyo 12 April 1995 [Ashanie Gawa]
[61] Int Mr Nyasa Moyo 12 April 1995 [Ashanie Gawa]. In 1973 things were quiet.
[62] "They were forced to leave on that day and they went to Mozambique where they camped at Mlangeni. They were protected by the police on their way to Mozambique (Int Chief Josamu Kwendanjati 14 April 1995 [Rosemary T. Muhuwo]).
[63] Int Peter, Matthew and Phodo 14 April 1995 [Rosemary T. Muhuwo].
[64] Cf Klaus Fiedler, "National Sovereignty. An Outdated Concept?" Faith and Knowledge Seminar No. 43, Chancellor College, 29 February 1996.
[65] I lived at that time in Songea in the Ruvuma Region. I never heard of any active persecution. The only Jehovah's Witness I personally knew was a carpenter, frequently working for us. He made no secret of his religious adherence, had access to Jehovah's Witnesses' literature, and in

Mozambique and Zambia offered refuge indeed, thus helping the persecuted, they also helped the persecutors by providing a place to which the Jehovah's Witnesses could be expelled to. The concept of national sovereignty made it possible to "solve the Jehovah's Witnesses problem" in Malawi by dumping the unwanted members of the nation elsewhere. That was much cheaper than to put them all in Malawian prisons and much easier than to kill them all.[66] The concept of national sovereignty made it also possible, after changes in government, to negotiate forced repatriation schemes.

It is important to note that the powerful nations of the West, so strong in their allegiance to democracy and freedom, found the extreme denial of both democracy and freedom in Malawi not to be a big issue. In writing this chapter I had very little access to international sources, but it seems that at least the British Government made some verbal representations to the Malawian government through its ambassador. But little power seems to have been attached to these representations, because Britain (and the other Western powers) continued to support Banda and often even to praise his able leadership, wisdom etc. The Western powers, as protagonists of the fight for freedom and democracy, supported (not by their few words, but by their actions) the suppression of the Jehovah's Witnesses' religious freedom (and of other freedoms) in Malawi because they had located the enemy of freedom (rightly) in worldwide Communism, and then (wrongly) concluded that any enemy of the Soviet Union must be treated as an ally in the West's fight for freedom, so that freedom in that country would not matter much.

Some relief through international power came to the victims of persecution through the UN, which cared well for the refugees and granted them the religious freedom they treasured so highly. Though the political powers in the West took little notice, international organizations fighting for human rights did in documenting many of the atrocities. But the influence of these organizations was limited, and since the Jehovah's Witnesses had no high profile cases of human rights abuse, the international human rights organizations concentrated their efforts on cases like that of Vera and Orton Chirwa and that of Jack Mapanje. The international churches seem to have been hampered also by the concept of national (church) sovereignty. The Church of Scotland was committed to the policy of the independence of the national church, which meant that it would act only on request

---

his village not far from Songea he had build a nice little Kingdom Hall. There was nothing secret about it, only that he did not put up a sign post "Jehovah's Witnesses Kingdom Hall"

[66] Other nations like Germany in the Jewish Holocaust, Turkey in the Armenian Massacres (1915) and Kampuchea (under the Khmer Rouge) used that "solution" with a combined total of about 10 Million murdered.

of the local leadership.[67] But the national churches never requested the use of international power to help those who suffered. Things only changed when, with the demise of Communism, concepts of national sovereignty limited by human rights developed, so that international power could help to bring about a change to democracy in Malawi and thereby also to restore to the Jehovah's Witnesses the religious freedom that had been their human right all along.

The Character of the Persecution

Since persecutions differ from case to case, it may be good to point out some characteristics of this one.

Its public character

In many cases persecution of opponents is a hidden activity, with anonymous hit squads claiming their victims at night, the criminals covering up their steps. This practice was not unknown in Malawi under Kamuzu, but was not made use of in the Jehovah's Witnesses' case. Their persecution was public, and intended to be so. It was to have a deterrent effect.

Its extrajudicial character

No persecution for religious reasons can ever be legal. During the first peak of the persecution (1963/64), there was not a shred of a legal base for persecution. In 1967 a legal pretense for persecution was produced, providing for a ban and for prison sentences for those who contravened the ban. But the persecution started as soon as Kamuzu had made his remarks, it did not wait for legal niceties to be completed. And once they were there, they were disregarded. The beatings, paradings, killings, destruction of crops, humiliations and expulsions were carried out without any reference to the legal system, until 1975.

The extrajudicial character of the persecution was officially emphasized at the Zomba 1972 convention, which appealed to government "to give maximum possible protection to members of the party who deal with the adherents of those sects".[68] This protection was given to the maximum. The party was taken to be the highest legal authority, its members could act freely as investigators, accusers, judges and executioners. This protection seems to apply even under the new

---

[67] Kenneth R. Ross, in reply to questions during the Faith and Knowledge Seminar No. 46, 13 June 1996 "Does Malawi (still) Need a Truth Commission?" at Chancellor College, Zomba. The only time that the Church of Scotland intervened (without being requested to do so) was in the case of Vera and Orton Chirwa.
[68] *Malawi News* 19 September 1972 [Tuesday].

government. None, to my knowledge, has been asked to account for crimes committed against Jehovah's Witnesses.

The extra cruelty

Taking the situation for what it was, some of the persecution of the Jehovah's Witnesses could be taken as lawful because there was some kind of legal base for it. By government order, the Jehovah's Witnesses were banned, and by the same order clandestine activities were threatened with punishment by up to 14 years in prison. In 1972, by party resolution, expulsion and expropriation of property was added. Local MCP leaders may have seen this as a legal base for persecution. But the sufferings inflicted went in most cases far beyond what was provided for in this "legal" base. There was no provision in it for torture, public parading of victims, slashing of crops, burning of houses, murder. All these were extras, executed with intensity and delight, and with random crowds participating in the show.

> One Youth Leaguer held an extended piece of the rope in one hand. The other was busy blowing on his whistle. By the time we had reached Chitakale, about 3 kilometres from Mulanje boma, a crowd followed behind me. The whistling Youth Leaguer prompted the group into a song: "Wopanda card sachidya, sachidya, uyo chimubvundira".[69]

Shame and sexual violence

In Malawian societies proper behaviour in order not to be shamed is considered to be of high value, and Kamuzu, at the Zomba 1972 convention, emphasized very much the need for the youth to follow traditional cultural values of good behaviour. In the persecution the party members were obviously encouraged to break the taboos of decency.

> Arrived at Gowoka 7 p.m. in June 1972 and here they were told to buy cards but they declined.... So, they were stripped of their clothes and put outside their houses for all to see. Stayed outside from 9 p.m. to 2 a.m. without clothes. They were six of them i.e. him, his wife, and the founder Mr Amosi and his wife and some other two ladies.[70]

Sexual taboos are even stronger in Malawi than those of shame, with the incest taboo being the strictest. Attempts to force Jehovah's Witnesses to publicly violate this taboo were a frequent aspect of torture inflicted:

---

[69] "The one without card will not eat it [the maize, the food], will not eat it, that one it will rot for him" (Int Harris Nakhumwa 11 April 1995 [Peter Mitunda]).
[70] Int Winston S.B. Neba 18 April 1995 [Munthali].

> [After having been paraded round the village naked] they were put in lines and fathers were forced to face their daughters while naked, similarly mothers were asked to face their sons while naked.[71]

> They undressed us completely men as well as women and our children. After undressing us they could take a man and his daughter to have sex. When we refused they could whip us like cows.[72]

Pregnant women were spared neither shame nor abuse:

> By then, she was pregnant (7 months), but when the Youthmen came to her home, they got hold of her and beat her severely. Thereafter they raped her in her own house all five of them. After that they let her go while crying bitterly. When she came out of the house she found her father literally naked having been beaten heavily.[73]

The Role of State Organs

The police

In the persecution the police played different roles. The police's role is to protect people against those who break the law. If anyone is apprehended doing so, it is the duty of the police to secure the evidence and hand over the law breakers to the judiciary system. For the period 1963/4 I found no evidence that the police (colonial or independent) did anything to stop the forced selling of party cards, nor did I find evidence for this later. This suggests that the police colluded in the persecution. The police also seems to have shared in it in other ways, like keeping detained Jehovah's Witnesses and, on occasion, beating them, too.[74]

On the other hand it is very clear from the records that often the police protected the Jehovah's Witnesses[75] or assisted them. Sometimes police cars ferried them to safety,[76] and in one instance at least the police, in a night action, witnessed by the DC of Nsanje, Harry Ghabu, ferried Jehovah's Witnesses back to safety in

---

[71] Int Frank Homela 11 April 1995 [Charles Eliyasi].
[72] Int Mchima Msuku 10 April 1995 [Esnat Mdolo].
[73] Int Alabia Bernard 18 April 1995 [Rosemary T. Muhuwo].
[74] To Mr Karioti's surprise, he was taken to Bvumbwe Police station instead of being taken to Mrs Chitalo. There he was beaten badly by a certain police constable by the name of xxx (Int Mr Karioti 12 April 1995 [R.M. Soko]).
[75] A randomly selected case: "The police officer, Mr Lidamlendo, showed sympathy. They, together with his family, were released and sent home with a police escort" (Int Mr Meke Ndege, 17 April 1995 [Ashanie Gawa]).
[76] Int Mr L. Chikopa, 9 April 1995 [Peter Kalawa]; Int Chief Josamu Kwendanjati 14 April 1995 [Rosemary T Muhuwo].

Mozambique, from where they had been taken previously by the MCP.[77] The police both assisted in the persecution *and* assisted Jehovah's Witnesses against their persecutors. It is understandable that Kamuzu preferred that MCP and MYP deal with them.

The army

In the available material there is no evidence that the army shared in the persecution, except that it provided some of the vehicles used for the forced repatriation from Zambia. On the other hand there is evidence that they helped transport fleeing Witnesses to safety, and prisoners from Dzaleka, who had to serve part of their sentence working for the army, were treated very well.[78]

The Role of the Christians

In the material accumulated so far there is no evidence of active involvement of any church (as an organization) or of any higher church leader like ministers or priests. Also there is no evidence that the top church leadership of any denomination publicly opposed the violations of human rights.[79] On the less official level there was often a feeling that the Jehovah's Witnesses got what they deserved, or, more frequently, that they had drawn it upon themselves.[80] When I discussed the persecution of the Jehovah's Witnesses in a group, the first question after my presentation was: "Do you think that it was right for the Jehovah's Witnesses to refuse to buy party cards?" The Jehovah's Witnesses were rivals to the Christian churches, and there was also some feeling that it was not too bad to have these rivals out of the way. Beyond such feelings of antipathy there was a lot of active participation in the persecution. The Jehovah's Witnesses, living almost exclusively in the Christian areas of Malawi, would be persecuted by MCP members, most of whom would be members of various Christian churches. Some of them even held positions like deacons and elders. In a number of cases there was support from Christians in various positions. One example are priests from Thunga Parish and Nantipwiri Pastoral Centre close by who helped as they could,[81] as did their neighbour, the Italian Mr Dondi.[82] After the MYP had

---

[77] Int Mr Meke Ndege 17 April 1995 [Ashanie Gawa]; cf. p. 55 above.
[78] Int Sidreck Khoromana 13 April 1995 [Charles Eliyasi].
[79] I heard that the Catholic Bishops tried to influence the government through representations, but I have not found the evidence yet.
[80] "Christian churches felt that the problem of Jehovah's Witnesses was of their own making and had to solve it single handedly. The Christians often said to hell with their uncompromising doctrine" (Int Mr Governor Chisale 1 April 1995 [Aloisious Nthenda]).
[81] Int N.N. 13 April 1995 [Aloisious Nthenda].
[82] Int Mr Karioti 12 April 1995 [R.M. Soko].

attacked the Jehovah's Witnesses congregation meeting at Chithawira Kingdom Hall in Blantyre in June 1972 and beaten and scattered the worshippers,[83] "some Catholics and CCAP... could hide them in their houses, tell them when the MYPs were coming and provided hiding and food."[84] There are other cases where help from Christians is reported, but the overall picture is very mixed, as it seems with more shadow on it than light.

Those who Helped

In the dreadful picture of persecution from verbal harassment via shame and torture to murder, there are some (though too few) bright spots. How many sympathized with them and were too afraid to do anything is difficult to assess. Then there were others who did not help them, but in no way would they have done anything to harm them. If there had been more of these people, less persecution would have happened. Direct help the Jehovah's Witnesses often received from relatives. Some of them were members of either MCP or the Youth League, and they would warn the Witnesses of impending attacks. Sometimes the warnings came even from MCP members who were not related to the intended victims. Due remembrance should also be accorded to those who were in the system, and from there tried to lessen the suffering, like one woman MCP secretary whose name was forgotten but who is still remembered for "emphasizing on reducing the persecution ordeal on the Jehovah's Witnesses like stopping the people from beating them so much."[85] In some cases holders of competing authority with the party used it to help Jehovah's Witnesses. The chief of Chiendausiku "ordered that in his village no house was to be set on fire and nobody was to be harassed."[86] Since he could not keep the Witnesses safe, he had to advise them to flee to Mozambique. Other chiefs did not reveal that there were Jehovah's Witnesses in their villages.[87] On Chisi Island in Lake Chirwa the Jehovah's Witnesses were never molested.[88]

Help from Christians, from the police and from the army has already been described earlier. Israel has created a special category and a memorial for those non-Jews who helped Jews against their persecutors. I think even in Malawi those

---

[83] "The witnesses were beaten like hell. Some broke their legs, arms and the situation was worse for nursing mothers and children. They could not run very fast and were the victims of the day" (Int N.N. 9 April 1995 [Aloisious Nthenda]).

[84] Int N.N. 9 April 1995 [Aloisious Nthenda].

[85] Int Mr I. Malindadi 17 April 1995 [Hanna Bonzo].

[86] Int Mr L. Chipoka 9 April 1995 [Peter Kalawa].

[87] Int Mr Banda/Miss B. Banda [Bernadette S. Banda].

[88] Information from Joe de Gabriele, 15 May 1996.

who helped, secretly or not so secretly, should be given due recognition, MCP members included.

Responsibility

Kamuzu knew nothing!

On Friday, January 5, 1996, the *Daily Times* came out with a banner headline: "Kamuzu apologizes, urges reconciliation". In this "apology" he made it very clear that he had known nothing about the cruelties inflicted and that, if indeed "suffering was caused by anybody in this country in the name of nationhood", he had known nothing of it. Kamuzu did not claim that he had lost his memory of it, he claimed that he had never known about it. I think it would have been good if the *Daily Times* had also proposed a revised song for popular consumption:

Mtsogoleri: Zonse	Leader: Everything
Onse: Zonse zimene n'za Kamuzu Banda	All: Everything belongs to Kamuzu Banda
Mtsogoleri: Zonse	Leader: Everything
Onse: Zonse zimene n'za Kamuzu Banda	All: Everything belongs to Kamuzu Banda
Mtsogoleri: Misewu yonse	Leader: All the roads
Onse: ya Kamuzu Banda	All: [belong to] Kamuzu Banda
Mtsogoleri: Misewu yonse	Leader: All the roads
Onse: ya Kamuzu Banda	All: [belong to] Kamuzu Banda
Mtsogoleri: Koma kuzunza	Leader: But persecution
Onse: Koma kuzunza anazunza ena.	All: But persecution, others did it.
Mtsogoleri: Koma kuzunza	Leader: But persecution
Onse: Koma kuzunza anazunza ena.	All: But persecution, others did it.
Mtsogoleri: Zonse	Leader: Everything
Onse: Zonse zimene n'za Kamuzu Banda	All: Everything belongs to Kamuzu Banda.
Mtsogoleri: Zonse	Leader: Everything
Onse: Zonse zimene n'za Kamuzu Banda	All: Belongs to Kamuzu Banda
Mtsogoleri: Masukulu onse	Leader: All the schools
Onse: a Kamuzu Banda	All: Belong to Kamuzu Banda
Mtsogoleri: Masukulu onse	Leader: All the schools
Onse: a Kamuzu Banda	All: Belong to Kamuzu Banda
Mtsogoleri: Kupha Amboni	Leader: To kill the [Jehovah's] Witnesses
Onse: Kupha Amboni anapha ndi ena.	All: Others kill the [Jehovah's] Witnesses
Mtsogoleri: Kupha Amboni	Leader: To kill the [Jehovah's] Witnesses
Onse: Kupha Amboni anapha ndi ena.	All: Others kill the [Jehovah's] Witnesses

Mtsogoleri: Zonse	Leader: Everything
Onse: Zonse zimene n'za Kamuzu Banda	All: Belongs to Kamuzu Banda
Mtsogoleri: Zonse	Leader: Everything
Onse: Zonse zimene n'za Kamuzu Banda	All: Belongs to Kamuzu Banda
Mtsogoleri: Koma zoipa	Leader: But evil things
Onse: amachita ena	All: Others have done them.
Mtsogoleri: Koma zoipa	Leader: But evil things
Onse: amachita ena	All: Others have done them
Mtsogoleri: Iye Mkango	Leader: Him the Lion
Onse: Iye Mkango, iye samadziwa	All: Him the Lion, he did not know
Mtsogoleri: Iye Mkango	Leader: Him the Lion
Onse: Iye Mkango, iye samadziwa	All: Him the Lion, he did not know.

Though Kamuzu is clever, his attempt to make himself blameless by putting the blame on his subordinates for whom he was responsible, did not work. The attempt can, following the example of so many in Germany, also be made the other way round: "Yes, we committed some atrocities, but it was all on orders, it is the higher authorities that are responsible." Though it is possible that occasionally an MCP member may have acted under direct pressure from higher authorities, the many cases of violence seem to have been carried out usually by people quite happy to do so, and quite eager to get their profit out of it, be it in terms of fun, sadism, material benefits or political favour.[89] That non-participation in these outrages was quite a possibility is shown by men like Chief Chiendausiku.

Healing the Nation

The crimes against the Jehovah's Witnesses were committed under the guise of achieving the unity of the nation. But by now it has dawned on most people that neither the unity of the graveyard nor the unity of the prison camp is real unity. A new approach, more honest and more honourable, is needed. If the power of coercion has failed to unite the nation, is there any power that can heal the rifts that have been created?

Kamuzu never apologized

Kamuzu asked for "reconciliation and forgiveness amongst us all", as if anyone had wronged him. He did not specify who had wronged him, nor did he specify who had been wronged by him (sorry, I forgot - none had been wronged by him, only by his subordinates and by impostors acting in his name). In order not to be

---

[89] This parallels the findings of an American author who recently claimed that in almost all cases the worst atrocities of the holocaust and other persecutions were committed by volunteers.

forgotten in a time of rapid change and sometimes short memories, I think, it is good to quote the apology in full:

> During my term of office, I selflessly dedicated myself to the good cause of Mother Malawi in the fight against Poverty, Ignorance and Disease among many other issues; but if within the process, those who worked in my government or through false pretence in my name or indeed unknowingly by me, pain and suffering was caused to anybody in this country in the name of nationhood, I offer my sincere apologies. I also appeal for a spirit of reconciliation and forgiveness amongst us all.[90]

Obviously such general calls for reconciliation and apologies for sins committed *by others* do not heal the nation, because they lack two indispensable elements of all reconciliation: honesty and openness.

Criminal justice

One way to bring about a healing would be to pursue the criminals in the courts. But the already overtaxed and understaffed judicial system of Malawi could hardly hope to cope. If against every Jehovah's Witnesses only one crime was committed, that would produce about 30,000 to 50,000 court cases. Even if "minor crimes" can be considered as no longer open for prosecution due to the statute of limitations, thousands of serious crimes would have to be dealt with. A related possibility would be to pick out a few of the worst crimes and prosecute the culprits. This attempt has so far failed in the Mwanza trial, since it was difficult to prove that the real criminals were not those who had killed the victims, but the highest authorities of the state. This led to the grotesque result that both the actual killers *and* the possible instigators of the crime went away scot free.

> XXX who remained behind was caught, tied like a wheel, then thrown into a borehole and he died there. People in the village saw this happen in broad daylight but could not say a thing because they were afraid. When the police came to investigate the matter, the chairman of the League, Mr Magwira denied any knowledge of such an act. He suggested that XXX might have been sent to Dzaleka and the matter ended there.[91]

If a case like this would be taken up by the courts, it would be easy to argue that Kamuzu did not order this particular crime. And it is most unlikely that he did order it. Therefore his responsibility for it can not be established by means of the legal system. But those who actually killed XXX could be prosecuted, because

---

[90] *Daily Times* 5 January 1996 (front page).
[91] Int Michael Job 10 April 1995 [R.M. Soko].

there should be enough witnesses still available. But would they be willing to testify?

Confession

If criminal justice is not very practical in achieving justice and by that healing, confession would be a way. Such confessions would have to be full, honest, personal and open. Then forgiveness and amnesty could be granted. From the Jehovah's Witnesses side there is a great willingness to forgive, but from the other side I have not become aware of even one attempt to confess and/or to ask for forgiveness. Though neither Kamuzu nor anyone else can apologize by blaming others for his sins, to some extent an apology, if not a confession, on behalf of others is a possibility. I propose that one of the churches should start. The leadership could confess their inactivity, the church could then apologize to the Jehovah's Witnesses for the many acts of cruelty against them committed by some of its members, and to make the apology realistic, a sufficient number of atrocities should be mentioned as examples of what the apology is for.

What would help a church to attain peace, would also help a party. Here all major parties should use the opportunity. The MCP has not said a word of apology to the Jehovah's Witnesses, not even in an indirect way. Other parties can hardly confess or apologize in the same way as the MCP should, but individual apologies and confessions would be in order. How many of present day UDF leaders were responsible MCP leaders at the time from 1967 till 1978, when most of the atrocities were committed? If they had any share in them, a confession could bring forgiveness, and if they had no share in them, or if they tried to reduce the persecution, a full disclosure would be appropriate. The same applies to those who were MPs then and now, even if now they belong to a different party.

The National Compensation Tribunal

This tribunal is obviously a serious attempt to address injustices of the past. Compensation can not undo crimes, but it can achieve recognition of the crime and vindication of the victim, and in some measure it is a kind of apology of the public to the victim. Good as the idea is, it may not be as good for the Jehovah's Witnesses, since compensation can be given on application by the victim (or relatives, if the victim is no longer alive). I fear that many Jehovah's Witnesses will not apply because of their distant attitude to the state and its institutions. My proposal is therefore that, in the issue of compensation, Jehovah's Witnesses should not be treated just as anybody else, but that special efforts should be made by the National Compensation Tribunal to make sure that they will not be left out. If I understand correctly, the Tribunal is geared towards individuals. Though Jehovah's Witnesses suffered as individuals, they were subjected to these sufferings because they belonged to a group. Therefore an attempt should be made to take this into account, deal with the group, and if the Jehovah's Witnesses' organization in Malawi should refuse, a similar approach could be made by proxy.

A public record

At the moment it is difficult to discern any major movement toward either apology or confession. Is it that apology or confession is seen as shameful? If no confession is forthcoming, a public record could help to a certain extent. It would not produce forgiveness, but it can produce awareness. In Germany, major parts of the concentration camps have been preserved, as a memorial to remind every new generation as to what crimes our nation has been able to commit. I propose that a simple monument be constructed as a sign of the admission of national guilt to commemorate and honour the victims of the persecution.[92] A good venue for it would be a place not too far from the Independence Arch in Blantyre, possibly in the direction of the Malawi Museum or not so far from Blantyre Civic Centre. The monument could bear a number of names of Jehovah's Witnesses who were killed because of their faith.

Such a monument can only be symbolic, not informative. Therefore a written and printed record would be needed, too. I do not propose to restrict this to one form, but that various ways of collection and publication should be used. It would be good if the government would do its share in such an endeavour, but I think to *wait* for it to do so would not be good. Malawi is no longer a one-party nation, where all responsibility lies with the government. In the new Malawi, a multiplicity of initiatives are appropriate. Let the government do its share, indeed, but let the lawyers, the researchers, the churches, the students, the victims, the poets (and even the perpetrators) do their share (all in their own different and special ways) to put on public record what happened, how it happened, and what the consequences were.[93]

---

[92] One small section of it should serve to honour those who helped them, often under personal risk.

[93] Cf. K.R. Ross, "Does Malawi (still) Need a Truth Commission?" Faith and Knowledge Seminar No. 46, Chancellor College, 13 June 1996. During discussion of this paper Dr Moira Chimombo argued that the University should take the initiative in such an exercise.

7. Christian Experience in Malawi Prisons

Hilary Mijoga

Introduction

During the one-party era, prisoners were among those most markedly on the receiving end of an exercise of power which was often arbitrary, unjust, and unaccountable. No one was accountable to whatever was happening in our prison facilities. The voices of the prisoners were never heard, hence the outside world could hear or do nothing on the plight of these victims. In a situation like this, the prisoners themselves had to find ways and means by which they could survive this arbitrary, unjust, and unaccountable exercise of power by the regime. One thing that kept some of them going was faith. Faith gave them power to resist, survive, endure, and overcome the overwhelming power of the government which removed their liberty and which threatened their life. In this struggle, the Bible was one of the tools used to sustain that faith. The Bible gave them this power through its stories which were comforting, consoling, and encouraging. Though the prison experience was dehumanizing, to some prisoners it had a positive effect in the sense that it had also an empowering effect on them. While in prison, many prisoners had time to think about the future of the country.[1] Here, people met friends from different backgrounds and people who had been arrested for different offenses. In the course of their encounters, they shared and exchanged ideas which might have shaped their views on the state of the country. Indeed, most of the prisoners came out determined to changed the face of politics in Malawi. This is why most of the people who are involved in politics today were once prisoners.[2]

The overwhelming power of the state over the prisoners is clearly manifest in prison conditions. The Amnesty International report of February 1992 sums up the prison conditions in Malawi.[3] The report states:

> Conditions in Malawian prisons are extremely poor.... In prison, inmates have to sleep sitting up, back-to-back. However, there are a number of aspects of the bad conditions suffered by political detainees which appear to be a result of official policy: for example, the frequent ban on correspondence, the denial of reading or recreational materials, the frequent denial of medical attention and,

---

[1] These were mainly the political prisoners as the survey showed.
[2] Among the respondents there was a cabinet minister and a member of parliament.
[3] *Malawi: Prison Conditions, Cruel Punishment and Detention without Trial*, London: Amnesty International, 1992.

above all, the imposition of cruel, inhuman or degrading punishments.[4]

The report also states that "Prisoners ... are reportedly kept naked and chained to the floor, given minimal food, denied medical care and severely beaten."[5] In addition to these inhumane conditions, the government also exercised its overwhelming power by its act on detention without trial, which was also arbitrary. This arbitrariness is evident in the fact that there was "no independent review of the reasons why an individual is detained."[6] To add salt to the wound, when opening Dzaleka Prison in Dowa in the 1960s, Dr Banda said, "I will keep them (political prisoners) there and they will rot." Indeed, prisoners rotted in Malawi prisons in general and Dzaleka and Nsanje in particular.

The Sample

The research was conducted among released prisoners who had walked in the corridors of and languished in our prisons under the conditions described in the Amnesty International report above. 102 respondents (91% male and 9% female) were interviewed country wide.[7] These respondents were classified into three categories according to what they were charged for or what they were supposed to have been charged for, i.e. political (33.3%), civil (19.6%), and criminal (47,1%). In the political category, there were no Roman Catholics and Anglicans. But 40% in this category belonged to the CCAP and 26% were Jehovah's Witness. For the Jehovah's Witnesses, it is obvious that they were detained because of their opposition to buying Malawi Congress Party (MCP) membership cards and their opposition to other government laws.[8] For the large percentage of the CCAP members, it is difficult to say, except, perhaps to suggest that most might have been involved in politics, hence they were political fallouts.[9] The absence of the

---

[4] *Ibid*, p. 3.

[5] *Ibid*, p. 1.

[6] *Ibid*.

[7] Their presentation locations are: Blantyre, Dowa, Lilongwe, Mangochi, Mulanje, Mzimba, Nkhata Bay, Nkhotakota, Zomba, Machinga, Thyolo, Chiradzulu, and Salima. Their districts of origin are: Blantyre, Chitipa, Dowa, Machinga, Mangochi, Mulanje, Mzimba, Nkhata Bay, Nkhotakota, Ntcheu, Thyolo, Zomba, Mchinji, Mwanza, Dedza, Lilongwe, Mzimba, Nsanje, Chikwawa, Chiradzulu.

[8] Cf. chapter 6.

[9] Cf. "A Statement on the Role of the Church in the Transformation of Malawi in the Context of Justice and Peace." Produced by the Administrators Conference, Blantyre Synod CCAP, 22-23 January 1994, p. 4; as quoted by K.R. Ross, "Where were the Prophets and Martyrs in Banda's Malawi? Four Presbyterian Ministers," Faith and Knowledge Seminar No. 41, Chancellor College, 6 February, 1996, pp. 1-2. See also K.R. Ross, *Gospel Ferment: Theological Essays*, Gweru: Mambo Press, 1995, pp. 12-13.

Roman Catholics in the survey could be explained as mere chance although it is possible that they were not closely associated with politics, perhaps until recently.[10]

Most of the respondents in the political category were detained in the 1970s. Between 1973 and 1977, 41% of the respondents were imprisoned compared to 15% in 1960-67, 26% in 1983-89 and 18% in 1990-94. Historically, the 1970s was the Muwalo era in which many people were detained. Most of those who were detained in the 1970s (who, in 1996, are between 63 and 78 years old) were in their 20s and early 30s, whereas those detained in the 1980s were in the late 30s and early 40s. This means that most of those who were imprisoned in the 1970s were young (20s-40s) and this is the most productive age group. Half of those detained between 1990 and 1994 were arrested on 3rd March, i.e. on Martyrs Day. Actually, one of them indicated that he spent four years in prison without being brought before the court of law (this respondent was arrested for being found drunk on Martyrs Day). In the civil category, about 50% of the respondents indicated that they were farmers. The ages that were given (21-40s) would indicate that most of them were young. 55% of the respondents were imprisoned in the 1992-94 period. This was the political transition period.

In the criminal category, 33% indicated that they belonged to the CCAP, 17% were Roman Catholics, 15% belonged to the Anglican Church, and 6% belonged to the Seventh Day Adventist Church. Obviously, the four are the major denominations here in Malawi. 52% of the respondents were 14-29 years old, 40% were 30-38 years old, and 8% were 56-72 years old. This means that a large proportion of the respondents were in their youthful stage (19-48) and as we have already indicated above, this age group is the most productive. 50% of the respondents in the criminal category were imprisoned in the 1992-95 period (cf. the 55% in 1992-94 in the civil category) and only 31% in the 1973-84 period. This suggests that criminal activities are on the increase in the 1990s, especially beginning from 1992 which marks a different era politically. Perhaps, it should be observed that the 1970s and 1980s were economically stable, but politically unstable, hence the few criminal activities. From 1992, the economic situation of the country has not been good, though politically things have changed for the better and hence the few political detainees, and so the increase in criminal activities. Another observation that can be made concerns the large number of CCAP members imprisoned. From the three categories, 40% of the respondents

---

[10] Cf. the 1992 Catholic Bishops' Lenten Pastoral Letter

indicated that they belonged to the CCAP as compared to the 8% Roman Catholics, 8% Seventh Day Adventists, and 7% Anglicans.[11]

Conduct of the research

A questionnaire was drawn up. Research assistants were recruited to administer the questionnaires. Respondents who could read were given the questionnaires to complete, whereas those who could not read, direct interviews were conducted based on the questions contained in the questionnaire. Research assistants were mainly drawn from the Zomba Theological College students. Since the research was conducted in December, 1995 - January, 1996 the principal researcher took advantage of the students going to their various homes for the Christmas vacation. This strategy ensured a wide coverage in terms of districts. The views gathered would then be a fair representation of views of released prisoners in the country.

The Bible: the Most Important Means of Grace

The research revealed that the Bible is by far the most important "means of grace" (100%). Apart from the Bible, prayers, chaplaincy, hymns and sacraments (in that order) also functioned as means of grace to the respondents. For prayers, it was noted in an earlier study that prayers are important to an African.[12] Prayers are said to thank the Supreme Being, praise him, ask for forgiveness and guidance. When people embark on something very important, they must first of all pray. The present study has also revealed that the respondents prayed to praise and thank God, to ask for forgiveness and guidance. Concerning chaplaincy, it was noted that, apart from explaining the Bible, chaplains have the role of comforting and encouraging people. This role is pertinent to the prison situation. As for the hymns, it was pointed out that these do carry special messages which bring comfort and hope to the singers. Respondents also drew attention to the value of sacraments. Holy Communion enabled them to remember the suffering of Jesus at a time when they themselves were suffering in prison. Confession was an occasion for receiving forgiveness of sins. Baptism assured the respondents that they were full members of the church. Prayer, chaplaincy, hymns and sacraments all played a significant role in enabling the respondents to survive during their prison experience. However, it was undoubtedly the Bible which was most prized as a means of grace.

---

[11] The conduct of the interview could explain the large number of CCAP respondents. This is because most of the research assistants were the Zomba Theological College students. We should, however, acknowledge that other factors could account for that number

[12] H. Mijoga, *Biblical Exegesis in African Independent Churches in Malawi*, Sources for the Study of Religion in Malawi No. 14, Zomba: University of Malawi, 1991, p. 38.

With this overwhelming choice of the Bible, respondents were asked whether the Bible is the book of the oppressed or the oppressor. Their answers were:

a) before imprisonment

Category	Oppressed	Oppressor	both	none
Political	26%		35%	24%
Civil	25%	20%	30%	25%
Criminal	29%	11%	17%	19%
Total	27%	10%	26%	22%

The answers might have been influenced by the respondents' prison experience, although the number for "both" is encouraging as compared to that for the "oppressed." On the one hand, since the Bible contains many stories about the oppressed people, i.e., stories about people suffering and how God rescued them, it is no wonder that it would appeal to the oppressed people in a society. These stories would give them comfort and hope. As such the Bible would be the source of inspiration to the oppressed people of the society. On the other hand, it was noted that there was a consensus on the fact that at one time or another, everyone needs a Bible. Hence the Bible would be relevant to the oppressed as well as the oppressors of the society. In fact, the Bible teaches about love, hence its relevance to both groups.

b) out of prison

Category	Oppressed	Oppressor	Both	None
Political	21%		59%	
Civil	45%	5%	20%	20%
Criminal	9%	5%	4%	4%
Total	19%	3%	44%	6%

There is clear indication here that the Bible is believed to be a means of grace to both the oppressed and oppressors of the society. Some of the reasons that were given for "both" include the fact that: the Bible is the word of God to all; oppressors and the oppressed are found in the Bible; the message contained in it is not peculiar to one group; and the Bible would convert the oppressors.

The foregoing presentation supports the claim that was made earlier that the Bible was one of the tools that was used by the respondents to sustain their faith in their struggle to resist, survive, endure, and overcome the overwhelming power of the government. Respondents were asked what the Bible meant to them before their prison experience. From the three categories, it emerged that it is the word of the God, the Bible is a comforter, guide, and source of inspiration. References to inspiration and comfort would raise the suspicious that these responses were influenced by their prison experience. With hard labour and constant torture, comfort, and inspiration would easily find place in respondents' minds. In light of this, it would appear that indeed the Bible was a tool used to overcome and endure the oppressive power of the state. Respondents were asked if the experience of reading the Bible in prison affected their Christian life in prison. 42% of the respondents indicated that it did. Some of the reasons given were that the Bible comforted them and it gave them hope for release. This hope gave them power to endure and survive hardships they experienced in prison.

Respondents were asked if there was any role for the Bible in the prison experience. 84% of the respondents indicated that there was (political: 94%, civil: 80%, criminal: 79%). These respondents had the following to say in support of their answer: a) political category: the Bible reduces load of worries; it cools a person down (i.e. it comforts); it is a source of inspiration; it is for the suffering. b) civil category: the Bible gives hope; it is the book of inspiration; it comforts lonely people. c) criminal category: Bible comforts, guides, encourages; it inspires; it brings peace and hope. The picture that emerges here is that the Bible comforts, gives hopes, and inspires. When people read stories about Paul's prison experiences, the teaching that if one is to follow Christ one has to suffer, stories of the suffering of the Israelites, experiences of Peter, Daniel etc., they get comfort and hope for their own prison experiences. In other words, this helps them to resist, endure, survive, and overcome the unjust power of the state. It is interesting to note that 54% of the respondents indicated that they had moments from their prison experience in which the Bible made the difference. The Bible made the difference in the following ways: a) political category: when the respondents were being tortured, when they fell ill, when some prisoners were killed. The Bible comforted them in all these occasions. b) civil category: when faced with hardships, when sick, when they were afraid of death. In all these occasions, the Bible consoled them. c) criminal category: when depressed, when beaten without cause. In all the instances given, it was either fear of death or physical pain which was involved. The Bible comforted and gave the respondents power to face those incidents.

Now that they are out of prison, respondents were asked what the Bible meant to them. Their answers were: a) political category: the Bible is the comforter to the oppressed; it is the book of inspiration; it helps in time of difficulties; it is a shield and guide. b) civil category: the Bible is a weapon to defeat problems; it is the comforter and shield. c) criminal category: the Bible is the protector (shield); it is the source of power. What is obvious from the answers is that to the respondents, the Bible is a weapon and comforter. It is a weapon and comforter in the face of the overwhelming power of the state. In other words, the Bible becomes a power to overcome the power of the state. 98% of the respondents said that they could recommend the Bible to anyone. From the reasons given, it is obvious that the respondents would recommend the Bible to others mainly because it comforts. This comfort would enable the people to endure hardships created, in this case, by the state.

Relationship between Prisoners and their Guards

The relationship between prisoners and their guards who share the same faith and the same accountability to God is interesting, especially in the harsh and dehumanizing conditions of several Malawi prisons. A good percentage of the respondents (political: 47%, civil: 70%, criminal: 42%) indicated that they knew that their guards were Christians. Though some of these guards were friendly to the respondents, others were not. Those who were not friendly were such perhaps because: a) political category: they might have thought that the prisoners were there to be tortured; they were only interested in earning money; the respondents were the enemies. b) civil category: the duty of the guards was to punish the respondents; they would be relaxing on their hard labour if they were friendly to the prisoners. c) criminal category: the respondents were always prisoners; the respondents were looked at as animals; they were the enemies. The picture that emerges here is that some of the Christian guards were harsh, rude, torturers, and unconcerned. In this case, they abused their power as guards and in the process the prisoners were at the receiving end of that abuse of power.

From the answers given, therefore, the respondents felt that the prison authorities were there to torture and create hell out their lives. While some authorities would claim that they were following orders or what was happening there was considered to be the *status quo* in the prison setting, one would not forget that most of the guards were Christians and as such had moral and religious obligations to their fellow Christians and to everyone created in the image of God. It would be unfair, unless otherwise stated, to attribute the cruelty of the guards towards their helpless prisoners to prison regulations because, as outsiders, the public does not think that it is stipulated in the government regulations that prisoners must be tortured or denied access to God as part of their punishment. If torture and/or denial of access to God are not within prison regulations, then who is responsible for the tortures and all the inhumane activities that took place in our prisons? The task (power) of prison guards is to guard, as implied by their description, if not to care for, the prisoners and to act within the rules and regulations prescribed in their job descriptions. Perhaps what the prison system portrays is the general decay that permeated the society during the one party rule. No one was accountable to anyone.

The Effect of Imprisonment

46% of the respondents (political: 72%, civil: 40%, criminal: 23%) indicated that the prison community life helped them to come out with a vision of the future of the country. One of the respondents became a cabinet minister, another is a member of parliament, and another one is a human rights activist. What these examples show is the fact that imprisonment can be an empowering experience. This is because one has more time to think and one also meets people with different ideas politically or otherwise. On a different note, some respondents saw their imprisonment as being ordained by God (23% of the respondents). Among other things, the prison experience gave chance to some respondents to preach the word of God to fellow prisoners. Others knew God in prison. On this score, one would claim that imprisonment has an empowering effect in the sense that people have the power to preach and be converted. Although imprisonment had an empowering effect on some respondents, to others it had a negative effect. Because prisoners are constantly beaten, are not free to express themselves, some die in prison, this experience makes some prisoners bitter. As a result of this, 35% of the respondents indicated that they came out bitter. Hence, this percentage came out angry and as such it would be difficult for them to contribute effectively to nation building. In fact, it is even possible that these people may not trust anyone in power.

A "Bird's Eye View" of Christian Experience in Prison

Inside Chichiri prison: prayers to keep hope alive[13]

Remand Cell 4 was remarkably different from Cell 2 in which I was earlier housed during my incarceration at Chichiri remand prison. Evening prayer time, for instance, were a rather a casual affair in Cell 4 to the strict discipline that surrounded the occasion in Cell 2. In Cell 2 which mainly housed middle and aged remandees, some of whom had been held for up to 10 years, mostly on murder charges, all other activities ceased as "leaders" took the floor to conduct the prayers. No other discourse or smoking was allowed. The majority of inmates in Cell 4 were young *kabwerebweres* (habitual offenders). Here, groups of inmates talked animatedly, others went about making fires to cook foodstuffs brought in by visitors or smuggled in during the day while yet others shared *nazi* (Indian hemp) and Virginia tobacco as prayer leaders opened the sermons. There was nonetheless a catch in both cells. It came in form of select prayer time choruses which

---

[13] This is an article quoted from *Malawi News* of February 3-9, 1996, p. 10. No author is indicated.

preceded the preaching and which successfully rallied inmates in prayer, momentarily at least in the case of Cell 4.

The popular chorus in Cell 2 was "When I Finally Trudge the Path to Heaven." The chorus went as follows:

As I walk in this troubled world
I find solace in the realisation
that the troubles will soon be over
When I finally travel
the road to the promised land.
When I travel the road to heaven
The land of peace
Where there are no tears
Where death holds sway.

Inmates would then fall into a trance as they joined in the chorus. Some sang with their eyes transfixed at something invisible in the cell's roof or walls; others with their eyes closed. I felt like judgement day at hand.

In contrast, the climax of the prayers in Cell 2 came with the chorus about the prayers of Paul which shook the very foundation walls of the Philippian jail in which they were being held. The chorus was as follows:

Paul and Silas
Their hand and leg irons snapped
Prison walls were shaken to their foundations.
Paul and Silas prayed
Prison doors flung open
The prison warder filled with fear.

The youthful inmates would break into a kind of passover dance as they echoed the lines of the chorus. They would dance themselves to the exhaustion. Their bodies drenched in sweat, they would, as they settled down, each day survey the barred windows and the heavy door to the cell as if in anticipation of a repeat of the Biblical miracle. Disappointed, they would go back to their chores largely oblivious to the rest of the sermon. One theme ran through each day's preaching. Inmates were to accept that they had fallen short of the glory of God. But, like Isaiah to the Israelites in captivity, there will be a sure end to their suffering. However, their lasting salvation (continued freedom), when it does come will be dependent on their complete renunciation of their old ways in favour of the cross.

Conclusion

As the Amnesty International report has revealed, conditions in Malawi prisons are deplorable. This is not only because the country is poor, but also because of the deliberate policy of the then one-party regime. Prisoners, especially political prisoners, were tortured for not yielding to the power of the regime. The respondents in the research were victims of this exercise of power. Since no one could come to their aid, the Bible came to their rescue, as it should. The Bible gave them comfort when tortured and hope for release despite the odds against them. The comfort and hope kept them going, thus they managed to survive, overcome, and endure the massive and oppressive power of the regime.

8. Even in Church the Exercise of Power is Accountable to God

Klaus Fiedler

State Power - Church Power - Counter Power

The church, its message, its personnel, its institutions constitute a power in the land, a political power indeed, and, depending on the historical constellation, its exercise of power may have far-reaching effects. An example is the fact that the founding of modern Malawi in its present shape was largely due to mission interference in (colonial) politics.[1] But the church is a power not only in relation to the political powers that be, but also a power in relation to the people of the country, be they members, potential members or adherents of a competing faith or denomination. The church can fascinate them, deny them (easy) access, offer opportunities of development (or refuse them for theological or non-theological reasons), discipline them, in general, define much of their lives. This power, though, is not unlimited, because the individuals have power, too: the power to invest love, to withdraw support, to change patterns of involvement. The state and its institutions can - and frequently do - misuse their power. For use and misuse of power the state and its institutions are responsible to God, for their own benefit. And for their own benefit, the churches, too, are responsible to God for their use or misuse of the considerable power they have.

The church and its members

The two Scottish Presbyterian Missions became formidable powers early in their history in Malawi, due to the fact that many Malawians wanted to become Christians, more in fact than the missionaries felt they needed. So around the turn of the century the missionaries, "preferring quality against quantity", made baptism and church membership an achievement not so easy to obtain.[2] Things have changed since then, with Christian pluralism gaining ground being one of the reasons. Today the power of any church to discipline its members is limited by the

---

[1] See: A.C. Ross, *Blantyre Mission and the Making of Modern Malawi*, Blantyre: CLAIM 1996 (Kachere Monograph no. 1), esp. pp. 85-104. Also: B. Pachai, *Malawi: The History of the Nation*, London: Longman, 1973, pp. 70-80.

[2] J. McCracken, *Politics and Christianity in Malawi 1875-1940*, Cambridge University Press 1977, pp. 202ff.

power of the people to chose and to change.[3] Therefore, if all exercise of power is accountable to God, in this case the power of the church is also accountable to the people, or, if not accountable, it is at least being checked by the power of the people. The power of the church over its members is structured through the sacraments: baptism, communion, confirmation, marriage, ordination. These are, in Malawi, highly coveted initiation rites and status symbols of achievement which a church can grant, withhold or put price-tags on. On the other hand, church members can resist the demands, opt out of the system or twist it.

A plurality of churches

The churches are in a power relationship not only towards the state and towards their members, but also among each other. Missionary work in Malawi was started by churches who were convinced that they were able to cater for the religious needs of all the people, if not of the whole land, but of the area allotted to them in comity with other missions of like faith.[4] Today Christian pluralism is a well established fact, wholeheartedly disliked by some church leaders, but obviously fulfilling the wishes of many people. One reason for this appreciation of Christian pluralism is that it empowers those that are religiously powerless or of limited power. Christian pluralism allows them to make choices, reject interference, develop their own individual possibilities.[5] This strong Christian pluralism distinguishes Malawi from surrounding Mozambique, with which it shares much in terms of culture. If one takes statistics to be a proper way of measuring Christian strength, Malawi is far more a Christian country than the surrounding areas of Mozambique.[6]

The issue of power relationships has often been studied in respect to African Instituted Churches which were seen often as "break-away churches". This view of seeing breaking away from the mission churches to be the main characteristic is

---

[3] The issue of conversion in all its meanings is the subject for a University of Malawi PhD thesis: Rendell Day, Baptist Conversion in Malawi. Related research is being done by another PhD candidate, Henry Church, for the Free Methodist Church in Malawi.

[4] On the comity principle and its critique see K. Fiedler, *The Story of Faith Missions*, Oxford: Regnum, 1994, 188-193.

[5] See J.C. Chakanza, "Good Shoppers of Religious Goods: Religion in a Multi-faith Malawian Society", in J.C. Chakanza & K.R. Ross, *Religious Pluralism in Contemporary Malawi*, Sources for the Study of Religion in Malawi No. 15, 1992.

[6] About 1975, Mozambique was 34.9% Christian, Malawi 62%, according to D. Barrett, *World Christian Encyclopedia, A Comparative Survey of Churches and Religions in the Modern World AD 1900-2000*, Nairobi/Oxford/New York, 1982. This seems to be reflected, too, by the many Malawian missionary efforts across the border in Mozambique

quite debatable,[7] but they do offer alternatives and therefore limit the power of the mission churches. In my research I touch only lightly on this, but the African Instituted Churches are not the only alternative. A considerable alternative, ever growing in strength and variety, are new "mission churches", which I call tentatively the "post-classical churches" They are "mission churches" just as much or as little as the mainline churches are, they do not usually profess a special openness for "African" culture as some of the African Instituted Churches do, but they offer a serious alternative to the "big" churches, empowering the people to make choices in spirituality, affiliation, acceptance of church discipline, personal involvement and authority. To these churches, often overlooked or considered to be a nuisance, and to their relationships with the "established" (=classical) churches and among each other, I give special prominence in this chapter.

Religion as power relations

It is possible, and I think necessary, to see the Christian faith as a web of power relations:

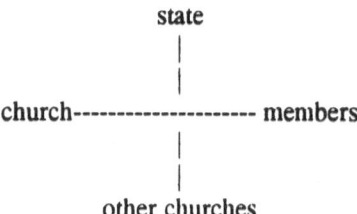

In this web of power relationships there are, to borrow political terms, "one-party" and "multi-party" tendencies, which may be distributed in different patterns. Thus a church may strongly oppose an authoritarian government, but strictly enforce (or at least attempt to enforce) unity, obedience and uniformity among its members. Many church members seem to have a preference for "multi-party" tendencies, but it may also be that a staunch church elder develops these only after his *own* daughter became pregnant before marriage.

Christianity and other religions

Power is not only an issue between the church and the state and within Christianity, but also in relation to other religions. I have not included this issue into my research.[8] But I want to mention three aspects.

J.C. Chakanza, "Sectarianism in Joseph Booth's Mission Foundations 1925 - 1975", *Religion in Malawi*, no. 2, 1988, pp. 6-10 [9].

[8] See chapter 5.

(1) African Traditional Religion is still a power to reckon with, because aspects of its spirituality are a reality to many Christians or a possible alternative to Christians in times of personal crisis,[9] but as *organized* religion it has lost most of its power.[10]

(2) The power relationship between Christianity and Islam is quite stable. Conversions occur both ways, but not in big numbers.[11] There has indeed been an Islamic revival, which shows its power in the strengthening of various Islamic institutions,[12] but not in any major changes in religious allegiance.

(3) During the referendum and general elections campaigns, both the Malawi Congress Party (MCP) as a political and the Charismatics as a religious group tried to capitalize on the threat of impending Islamization, since the leading presidential contender, Bakili Muluzi, was a Muslim. The MCP seems not to have gained votes measurably by these tactics, as Muluzi was heavily supported even in strongly Christian areas.

Theology talked versus theology acted

I understand my research as research into *theology*, but not into learned theology as published in books produced by distinguished authors, but into theology of the people. In my research I distinguish between "theology talked" and "theology acted" The two sometimes coincide, sometimes they conflict. In many churches in Malawi in issues related to power, *theology talked* by the church (as represented by its leaders is very different from theology *acted* (as represented by the same leaders), and in turn the theology *acted* of the leaders may differ from the theology *acted* of the ordinary Christians. In this chapter theology normally means theology *acted*.

Just as much as there is not only one *theology talked*, there is also not just one *theology acted*. Different denominations, social groups or communities act their theology in different ways. In this chapter I will use at certain points the differentiation between the mainline churches (for Malawi these comprise the

---

[9] The new "Mchape" movement of Chisupe is a case in point. See J.C. Chakanza, Mchape. Faith and Knowledge Seminar Chancellor College No. 39, 1995.
[10] I.A. Phiri, "African Traditional Women and Ecofeminism" Faith and Knowledge Seminar, Chancellor College, No. 36, 1995.
[11] William Mumba, "Christianity and the Yao: Empirical Problems of Christian Witness" DiplTh dissertation, Zomba Theological College, 1995.
[12] Alfred Matiki, "Problems of Islamic Education in Malawi" *Religion in Malawi*, 1994, pp. 18-22.

CCAP, the Anglicans and the Catholics) and the (smaller) evangelical churches[13]. Protestant will be distinguished from evangelical, with evangelical being a sub group of Protestant, comprising very different churches which all go back to revivals from the 1830s onwards.[14]

For my analysis I use insights from my previous research, from interaction with my colleagues in the Department (since October 1992) and from interaction with and research done by our students, especially those in the postgraduate programme. I am a Baptist, and especially in the section on the relationship between the smaller and the bigger churches, I find myself often, again using political terminology, on the side of the opposition. My position also shows in the fact that I do not assign to ordination the importance it has in mainline churches as reflected in the Lima Document.[15]

Sacraments are to Organize Power

Power in church can obviously be exercised by church structures and by personalities. But though maybe less obvious, nevertheless it is clear that sacraments are closely related to power, and indeed, much of the power in a church is organized around the sacraments. How is it exercised? Is there accountability? Is the exercise of power through the sacraments in *theology acted* the same as in *theology talked*? How do "ordinary" people perceive the exercise of power in the church through the sacraments?

The various churches differ greatly in their doctrines of the sacraments, but they have one thing in common: Whatever their doctrine is, it is clearly defined. But my observation is that the church members are not so clearly in agreement with the stated sacramental doctrines of their churches, and often it seems to me that even these very churches, which have such clear theologies of the sacraments in *theology talked*, do not always appreciate these same doctrines in *theology acted*.

---

[13] For these churches elsewhere I use the term "post-classical" churches. They go back to missions which were born in revivals from 1830 onwards and/or came to Malawi later than the three big churches.

[14] For a full discussion of the historical typology employed here see: Fiedler, *The Story of Faith Missions*, pp. 13-31; for a brief overview, adapted to Malawi, see: Fiedler "The 'Smaller' Churches and Big Government", in: M.S. Nzunda; K.R. Ross, *Church, Law and Political Transition in Malawi 1992 - 1994*. Gweru: Mambo 1995, pp. 153-170 (Kachere Book no. 1).

[15] This high emphasis on ordination is reflected clearly in the so called Lima Document, where the ordained ministry is seen as the possibly most powerful tool for Christian unity (*Baptism, Eucharist and Ministry*, Faith and Order Paper No. 111, World Council of Churches, Geneva, 1982 [The Lima Document]).

Sacraments in Theology Talked

In *theology talked* the following points in the doctrine of the sacraments seem to me important:

1. The sacraments are "outward signs of inward grace".
2. The denominations differ as to the number of sacraments, but each denomination itself is clear how many there are: Seven for Catholics[16], two for Protestants.
3. The mainline churches all agree that the sacraments are necessary for a healthy Christian life and growth.
4. Several sacraments as means of grace are given at the beginning of a "journey": Baptism, marriage, ordination.
5. All denominations agree that a full Christian life is also a sacramental life. Emphases differ, and expressions vary, but each denomination expects a "full member in good standing" to participate in the sacraments whenever they are offered.

Sacraments in Theology Acted: the churches' side

In the Protestant churches there are only two sacraments, baptism and communion. Their administration is restricted to holders of power, namely the ordained men,[17] a very limited group in terms of numbers. Two "non-sacraments" are equally restricted, namely (clerical) ordination[18] and marriage. Concerning marriage, though for Protestants never defined as a sacrament, the Protestant churches *act* as if it were one: the rite is most solemn, its administration is restricted to the ordained, and in order to receive the "sacrament", the recipients have to qualify, which is not always easy. Though never defined by Protestants as a sacrament either, ordination seems to be the most important "sacrament" to organize the church and to restrict the exercise of power and the access to privileges in it. In all mainline churches (and in many evangelical churches as well) the administration of the sacraments is tied to ordination, and ordination is restricted to few people. Lay Christians are permitted and indeed encouraged to preach, even though they might not have learnt much theology, and even though their theology may be weak or positively flawed. But to administer the sacraments a long training in theology (including Greek, historical criticism, African theology, Islam, church history) is required. But does it really take that long to learn the required liturgies and to

---

[16] In Malawi the Anglicans must be counted as Catholics in some aspects and as Protestants in others.

[17] See chapter 3.

[18] In this chapter ordination means ordination for the clerical ministry. Some churches ordain (in larger numbers) lay elders. They are excluded in this discussion since their ordination does not confer the right to administer the sacraments.

understand the circumstances and conditions for the celebration of communion or the administration of baptism? To me there seems to be a hidden agenda, namely to keep power in the hands of the few. This seems to me obvious also in those churches which have a *clerus major* and a *clerus minor*. The lower clerus is then called "evangelists" or "catechists". Some of them receive a training of several years. Should that not be sufficient to celebrate communion as the common meal of the faithful in anticipation of the coming of the risen Lord? But to restrict ordination to the few establishes hierarchies and restricts power.

The restrictive attitude to ordination seems to explain the reluctance of many Protestant pastors to allow the ordination of women. In the Roman Catholic Church there are to some extent theological reasons against the ordination of women to the priesthood, but in Protestant churches such arguments like: "It is not yet the opportune time" or "Women are too emotional" or "How can they minister in church when they menstruate" or "How can they cook for their husbands when they have to preach on Sundays" etc are quite common.[19] Is not the real question: "Why should we share power with those who are inferior to us [males]?" This restriction of power to the few is clearly visible in the Roman Catholic Church with very few priests, too few according to her own standards. Nice as the constant clamour for more priests sounds, everything is done to keep the numbers of people who join the sacramental ministry low: Marriage is not permitted, though this is not really necessary since in the Eastern Rite Roman Catholic Churches most priests are married. Women also are not permitted to enter the priesthood. Here the fact that Jesus called only men to be apostles is given as a theological reason.[20] Both, historical and theological reasons, achieve the same: Restriction of sacramental (and administrative) power to a few, an élite.

In almost all churches there is a clear and very important distinction between lay and clergy. Ordination does not only assign power over the sacraments, but also administrative power, since most top positions in the church are reserved for the ordained. This shows even in the Presbyterian churches, where the leadership consists of elders (both teaching and ruling elders) and deacons, and where the ordained pastor is just a teaching elder. But in reality he is the ruler of the congregation, since the major events in the congregation cannot take place without him. There are a few churches in Malawi where this strict differentiation between laity and clergy should not apply. A case in point is the Baptist Convention. Baptist theology does not require ordination for the administration of the

---

[19] Cf. Barnabas Salaka, "The Ordination of Women Debate in the Diocese of Southern Malawi", BA(Theol) dissertation, University of Malawi, 1996.
[20] But he did not call Gentiles either Should therefore the sacramental priesthood be restricted to Jews?

sacraments,[21] though this is generally assumed in *theology acted* of the Southern Baptists, the mother church of the Baptist Convention. This assumption was not introduced in Malawi, and communion and baptism are regularly administered by unordained men. The reason, in *theology acted*, seems not to have been the wish to make communion available to church members everywhere easily, but seeing communion not as such an important part of the Christian life.[22] In the African Baptist Assembly (Providence Industrial Mission), the oldest Baptist denomination in Malawi, the situation is very clear: Baptism and communion can only be administered by ordained ministers.[23] This fits in with the generally centralized structure of the denomination.[24]

Sacraments in Theology Acted: the peoples' side

How many sacraments?

For many Protestant Christians there are more sacraments than two. The third is usually marriage. And indeed, is not marriage far more solemn than any other sacrament? Is it not far more difficult to achieve? Could one imagine a wedding conducted by a laymen? Or by a lay woman? In popular perception Protestant marriage is a sacrament, equally indissoluble and soluble as Catholic sacramental marriage, and it is the highest of the sacraments. I have observed this, too, in various parts of East Africa and Zaire,[25] and even Protestant Germany makes no exception.

Burial is no sacrament, wedding is

Is funeral, a major transition rite, also a sacrament? There seems to be a difference in perception between Europe and Africa. In Germany, for example, people can hardly imagine a funeral conducted by a lay person, and even people who never went to church for 20 years are eager to have a minister officiate at their burial. This attitude I have not found in Africa. The funeral is a transition rite just as much as a wedding, but for a funeral no clergy is really needed. Catechists and elders are good enough for that. Why? Because of the urgency the funeral does not lend itself easily to the support of power structures. Communion, baptisms and

---

[21] Baptists prefer to use the term "ordinances" instead of sacraments.

[22] This is definitely not what *theology talked* says, but in the village congregations communion is celebrated infrequently.

[23] Information from Patrick Makondesa, based on research in the Phalombe area, 1995.

[24] Compared to other Baptist denominations, PIM is far more centralized, which is partly due to its American mother church.

[25] See K. Fiedler, "For the Sake of Christian Marriage Abolish Church Weddings", *Religion in Malawi*, 1995, pp. 22-27

weddings can wait till the priest becomes available, and power can be organized around them.

Sacraments are for achievers: baptism

In *theology talked* sacraments stand at the beginning of the journey or accompany the journey from day to day as divine means of grace. This is not necessarily so in popular perception. The sacrament of baptism is nowadays easy to obtain: No baby asks for it and many babies receive it. In the earlier days of Malawian church history this was different. To achieve baptism was hard work. Up to four years of instruction were necessary to be admitted to baptism. The ordained pastors (in those days almost all still missionaries) wielded an immense power related to the sacrament, given the high demand for the sacrament in certain areas of Malawi like Tongaland.[26] Some of this is still true, though denominational pluralism has brought competition and the sacrament of baptism therefore does not lend itself so easily any more to be a means for the stratification of power. If conditions in one church are too harsh, people can opt out and achieve the desired result more easily in another church.

In some churches even infant baptism is not so easy to obtain, because the parents must be church members in good standing, which normally is interpreted that they must be properly married (even though their Christian commitment may not go beyond that). But if baptism is the sacrament of prevenient grace, why should the baby suffer for the parents not being Christian achievers? In churches which teach believers' baptism, baptism is also increasingly easy to attain: It is still administered only on profession of faith, but nowadays even children of as low as six years of age are encouraged to make that confession.[27] In Baptist practice the sacrament of Baptism is easy to obtain, and to quite some extent it seems to have become just a transition rite. Whereas infant baptism is a transition rite accompanying the process of birth, baptism for Baptists has often become an initiation rite into adulthood. This may seem too early for children between six and ten, but the same process of the lowering of the initiation age has happened in

---

[26] McCracken, *Politics and Christianity in Malawi*, pp. 184ff. This situation explains to some extent the phenomenal success of Elliot Kamwana in 1909 who baptized more than 9,000 people in about three months. It also explains why Livingstonia missionaries arranged for his deportation by the political authorities. He had infringed on their sacramental power

[27] I am not sure if this applies in all Malawian churches with believers' baptism. But I saw it myself both in the Baptist Convention and among the Achewa PIM Baptists. In PIM the lowest age is seven or eight (Patrick Makondesa 20 June 1996). I made the same observation in the Baptist type faith mission churches in Kenya and North Eastern Zaire.

traditional initiation and even in Muslim initiation for example among the Yao (*jando*).[28]

The sacrament of communion is more difficult to achieve (and to retain)

For participation in communion a further effort is necessary, called instruction for confirmation. This is quite an effort, but generally accepted as not so difficult since it has become part of the transition rite of initiation into adulthood (and that must not be too easy!). But then it is a great achievement, at least in some churches, to retain the right to participation in communion. The most dramatic case is in the Catholic Church in patrilineal areas of Malawi, where sizable bride price is being paid, and where, as popular *theology acted* demands, a church wedding can only take place after the payment of the full bride price. Here the situation among some Baptist type churches is easier: The Baptist Convention does not demand a church wedding as a prerequisite for communion, nor does the African Baptist Assembly (PIM),[29] nor do the Seventh Day Adventists or the Seventh Day Baptists. But in many congregations of the Baptist convention communion has become rare. Though Baptist theology does not demand the presence of a minister to celebrate communion, popular theology tends that way. This means that many village churches go for months on end without communion. I have not found strong regret about this or attempts to change it, obviously communion is not so important.

The church's option for the rich

Popular custom also demands that the full bride price should *not* be paid before the marriage. Therefore the couple must begin their marriage without a church wedding, which would have been an outward sign of inward grace for the journey of their married life. In many churches the young couple then will be automatically barred from the sacraments which, like communion and reconciliation, were designed to help them on their Christian journey. Finally, after so and so many years, when the family finally has managed to pay the last installment of the bride price, seven, ten or twenty years of married life are crowned by the administration of the highest of the sacraments, the church wedding. Isn't that an achievement? Few make it, but if you make it, you are an achiever.

Popular *theology acted* makes this achievement even a bigger achievement because the administration of the sacrament is indissolubly tied to a big and expensive feast. Not that the church would make the feast a precondition of the sacrament,

---

[28] See A.W.C. Msiska, "The Spread of Islam in Malawi and its Impact on Yao Rites of Passage, 1870-1960", *Society of Malawi Journal*, 1995, pp. 49-86 [73].
[29] Int Patrick Makondesa.

but it concurs with popular theology by providing the sacrament at the appropriate time and by identifying with the achievers in spite of its supposed option for the poor and oppressed. The church wedding is becoming more and more a *civil* event (though conducted partly in church) than a sacrament. It could also be termed a "secular sacrament" of civil religion: The religion of the achievers, of those who have accumulated (or borrowed) enough wealth to be able to afford it.[30] It think that it is highly regrettable that the church actively condones this usurpation of spiritual power by civil religion. In doing this the church identifies with the rich and oppresses the poor, at least in those churches where participation in the sacraments is tied to a church wedding.

One should think that in matrilineal areas of Malawi, with almost no bride price being paid,[31] the incidence of proper church weddings is higher, and that seems to be the case in the Catholic Church. But in spite of the higher number, the *tendency* is similar. The number of church weddings is declining even in solidly matrilineal areas.[32] The problem seems to be the big feast. This is also born out by interviews in the African Baptist Assembly churches. There a church wedding is not really required, but the denomination encourages its members to have their marriages registered. This arrangement accepts that Lomwe marriage is a Christian marriage if entered into by Christians. Registration is not the real marriage, but something that should be attended to after the wedding. The register of all registered marriages is kept at Providence Industrial Mission Mbombwe, not in the local churches (branches) or sections.

This seems to be in some ways a viable alternative to solve the problem of church weddings. But there are three weaknesses at least: First that there is little provision to make the traditional marriage (*chinkhoswe*) *look* like a Christian marriage. It often seems to be just a secular ceremony. The second problem is that there is a tendency in popular *theology acted* to follow the bigger churches and not accept the *chinkhoswe* as the real thing, but only as second best. The third problem is that in popular *theology acted*, again copying other churches, even for the registration ceremony a feast is needed. There is clear evidence in the PIM records that for several years the number of registered marriages has been going down in spite of growing membership. The African Baptist Assembly leadership teaches (as the Presbyterians do), that no feast big or small is needed for a registration/wedding in church, and they are equally unsuccessful. Since this medicine obviously does not

---

[30] I heard of a church wedding of an Anglican priest with more than a thousand guests and costs above 30,000 Kwacha (when the Kwacha was still somewhat higher than today).

[31] I observed recently a marriage (Chewa/Lomwe) where the bride price was 50 Kwacha, just over US$3.

[32] Information from Dr J.C. Chakanza.

work, I propose to stop exhorting, and instead to concentrate on making the *chinkhoswe* wedding the real Christian wedding. In a Baptist setting no clergyman is required for that, and local Baptists can easily do this. They are quite competent in singing, prayers, Christian advice and practical ceremonies. As an important aspect of Lomwe marriage is the appointment of and the advice and help received from the *ankhoswe*, the local church should concentrate on really Christianizing this aspect, which is so central and so much appreciated. Here Baptist women could play an important role, and the already existing office of deaconesses could help make this viable.[33]

Ordination is powerful

In popular theology the *abusa* are seen as men of God, much honour and power is accorded to them, and the clerical collar is valued highly. At the same time pastors are seen as potentially wicked. In nearly all short stories published in Malawi newspapers in which a minister features, his most important characteristics are sexual sins and hypocrisy.[34] But in spite of the fact that ministers are sometimes despised, popular theology neither questions their power nor their necessity, and often, when a minister is involved in sexual unfaithfulness, the blame is not put on him but on the woman, because "she seduced him" (and an otherwise powerful minister must not have the power to resist seduction). In spite of many popular remarks about and accusations against celibate clergy for sexual sins, popular theology in the Catholic Church seems not to be in favour of married clergy.

The highest stage of achievement in ordination is to be a bishop. The bishops are seen as very powerful. Didn't they write the Lenten pastoral letter which after all was stronger than Kamuzu? In non-episcopal churches there are some tendencies to introduce the office of bishop. This has been very clear in Tanzania, where not only all the Lutheran churches opted for the episcopal office, but even churches from traditions opposed to that on principle: The Africa Inland Church opted for bishops, and the Assemblies of God now even have an archbishop. This development has not taken place in Malawi, but the Evangelical Lutheran Church of Malawi has recently opted for episcopacy. The same has happened in many of the so called African Instituted Churches, the Achewa PIM Baptists for example are led by Bishop Ndege.[35] In other churches there is no episcopal office, but

---

[33] Such an office also exists among the Seventh Day Baptists.
[34] Some of such stories are: Murendhle Juwayeni, "Sally and the Reverend", *Malawi News*, 4-10 November 1995; Feston Makaika, "Moral Decay" *Malawi News*, 27 January - 2 February 1996; Evance Moyo, "Nyacharu" *Malawi News*, 9-15 March 1996; Kenneth Phiri, "The Decision", *Malawi News*, 8-14 June 1996.
[35] The Achewa PIM Baptists are a Baptist denomination that separated from the PIM, then led by Dr Malekebu, in 1937 under the leadership of Peter Kamkalamba with Henry Kafulatira with then

episcopal-style leadership. The Providence Industrial Mission,[36] in spite of its congregationalist background, has a strong central leadership. Only the chairman can ordain ministers, the denomination is divided into sections and branches. This episcopal practice dates back to John Chilembwe, who was the only one in the whole denomination who could administer baptism.[37] For many years this was the same with Dr Malekebu, who ordained the first ministers in 1945, 19 years after he had come to Malawi.[38]

The power of non-compliance

The sacraments offer to the churches, to various degrees, means to organize power. However, church members are not powerless. The most powerful means to counteract the church's power is non-compliance. If the church excludes me from the sacraments for not conforming to its marriage laws, so be it. Maybe I can comply later. If the church requires me not to put my sons through the traditional initiation rites, that's a pity, and I won't tell the priest. But in case he should inquire, I am sorry, having my first son put through the rites I can not promise never to do that again because I still have two more sons. But after that the church can make peace with me again.

These attitudes are not infrequent, and I think that they are not taken seriously enough by the churches. Sacraments are means of transmitting divine grace, and that is a great privilege that the church has received to administer. Therefore I think it is not right to tie these precious divine gifts to secondary issues like how a wedding is conducted or if an ordained minister can be found or not. The same would apply to ordination. If ordination is to be set aside for ministry, why are so few people set aside in many churches? And why are those who effectively minister (like catechists or evangelists) denied the divine blessing of ordination?

---

300 members in Traditional Authority Chadzakwenda area, Nathenje, Lilongwe (J.C. Chakanza, *An Annotated List of Independent Churches in Malawi*, Sources for the Study of Religion in Malawi No. 3, Zomba: University of Malawi, 1980). It has now 28 congregations, mainly south of Lilongwe.

[36] This is the oldest Baptist denomination in Malawi. It was started in 1900 by John Chilembwe who had been trained in theology and ordained in the USA. He started PIM as a missionary of the National Baptist Convention, Inc. The official name is now African Baptist Assembly. Chilembwe's successor was Dr Malekebu.

[37] Patrick Makondesa, "The Life and Ministry of Rev and Mrs Muocha" BEd dissertation, University of Malawi, 1996.

[38] *Ibid*.

The power of choice

Another counter-power against the sacramental power of the churches is the power to change denominational allegiance. Early Livingstonia Mission had full control over admission to the sacraments. Since Elliot Kamwana that has never been the same.[39] Presently in a place like Migowi, not far from Phalombe, a person has, within one hour walking distance, a choice between more than 20 different denominations.[40]

Sacramental power is decreasing

Power is an important issue in the churches, and, especially in the mainline churches, the sacraments are often used to organize this power. In this organization of power there is much restrictive tendency, to limit the number of people who have access to this power. In this the churches are still very effective, and accountability to God and man may not always be there. Towards their members the churches have lost power over the decades. This can be regretted, but it also avoids abuses. I think a serious problem is when the churches just do not care that their power structures exclude so many people from the sacraments and, through this, often from effective pastoral care, too.

Christian Pluralism: a Check on Power

One church is enough of a choice

When permanent missionary work began in the country in 1875, the two Presbyterian missions from Scotland divided the country up between themselves, not yet formally, but effectively. The Free Church of Scotland Mission took the northern part (Livingstonia Mission), the Church of Scotland Mission took the southern part (Blantyre Mission, 1876). In 1889 Livingstonia Mission, feeling that its sphere was too big, allotted the area in between the two missions to the Dutch Reformed Church Mission. These three missions understood themselves as being of the same faith, and as being capable of evangelizing the country. There was no real room for any other missions, except maybe at the fringes of the territory allotted. When the Anglican UMCA came back into Malawi from what is now Tanzania in 1881 and finally in 1885, there was no objection to them establishing

---

[39] The Kamwana Movement was among other things a protest against this, and quite a successful one. The Kachere Series expects to publish soon a book on Kamwana and two others: J.C. Chakanza: "Preachers in Protest" For further reference see: H. Langworthy, *"Africa for the African": The Life of Joseph Booth*, (Kachere Monograph 2), Blantyre: CLAIM 1996, esp. pp. 195-248; W.C. Chirwa, "Masokwa Eliot Kenan Kamwana Chirwa: His Religious and Political Activities, and Impact in Nkhata Bay, 1908-1956", *Journal of Social Science* (Zomba) 12 (1985), pp. 21-43.
[40] Research done by Patrick Makondesa, 1995.

their mission on Likoma Island and from there serving the eastern (now Mozambiquan and Tanzanian) shores of the Lake, but as soon as they moved across the Lake to Nkhota Kota and tended to spread from there this was seen as an infringement on mission comity.[41]

This mission comity was often declared to be a means to expedite the spread of the gospel. Duplication of effort and competition between missions was to be avoided so that all forces could be concentrated on the spread of the gospel.[42] This was all true to some extent, but *mission comity was also about delineation of power*. The stated aim of comity was cooperation, but in reality separation of spheres of influence and distribution of power was the theme. "Do not infringe on my territory, and I will not infringe on your territory. And if we all behave nicely, we can perhaps cooperate a bit, too (Bible translation, hymn books, printing)."

Through comity each mission would win a Christian monopoly in its area (and by that, in most cases, and educational monopoly, too). Therefore *mission comity was about limitation of religious liberty*. You can chose your religion (African Traditional Religion, Islam, Christianity), but you have no choice as to what kind of Christianity to choose. If you want a different brand of the Christian faith, you must physically move to that particular brand's territory. Truth became a matter of geography. Not only truth but also education. Since the colonial government was little interested in providing any education to its subjects, leaving this to the missions to provide, and since mission education varied widely according to vision, quality and means, you would have no choice here, either. There was also a racist element in it, since comity limited religious choice for Africans, but not for Europeans, thus *creating a two class system of truth*. The argument advanced was that the "historic divisions of Christianity in Europe meant nothing to the African", so why introduce him (and even less so, her) to them? But how can the struggle for truth mean everything for Europeans (so much that even now the missions and churches cannot unite at all, some not even share in communion) and nothing for Africans? Obviously because truth is not important to them! They are human beings of a different type. This two class system of truth also had the advantage that the missionaries and their churches did not need to grapple with the issue of how to reconcile truth and unity. Comity cemented and therefore secured division.

---

[41] McCracken, *Politics and Christianity in Malawi*, p. 125. The UMCA, on principle, never accepted comity agreements.

[42] William Carey, *An Enquiry into the Obligation of Christians to Use Means for the Conversion of the Heathen*, Leicester 1792, p. 84.

Looking at it from the individual's side, mission comity meant mission control. The missions could set the rules according to their insights. If the mission decided that a 4 year catechumenate was required to achieve baptism (to be *admitted* to it), then it did not matter that in the NT converts were baptized sometimes on the spot on the very day of their conversion.[43] And if "Thou shalt have only one wife" was to be the first of the eleven commandments in Africa, it did not matter a bit that the law of Moses counts only ten. Mission comity is a thing of the past in Malawi,[44] but the ideas and feelings connected to it still have not died. Just as mission comity cemented the status quo so today many churches, usually the older ones, would like their status quo to be safeguarded against infringement. Terminology betrays the attitude: New churches are break away churches, if someone leaves one's own church that sheep was surely stolen,[45] revival movements are separatist, and any dissident is motivated by quest for power or lax morals.[46] Malawi is renowned for its high receptivity to Christianity, but also for its Christian pluralism. A bit of church history may help in understanding.

The Joseph Booth factor

Joseph Booth was a converted atheist of English origin who came from Australia.[47] His training was not theology but business, and since he received his call to missionary work late in life, he did not fit into the (power-)structures. So the various missions he applied to rejected him as being too old. Though in the missions' structures there was no room to accommodate him, his call was still on him.[48] Belonging to an innovative group of Baptists,[49] and being in contact with

---

[43] The argument often advanced by the missions for their policy of slow conversion was that they preferred "quality against quantity", no biblical reason being given. This may be open to theological argument in theory, but in *theology acted* this policy would only apply in Africa, not in Europe. There quantity had the prerogative, and the same rule applied even for the Europeans in Malawi, who were able to obtain the sacraments so easily.

[44] Not so in Zaire where church comity, perpetuating mission comity, is still enforced by the government with the help of the leadership of the Eglise du Christ au Zaire against the wishes of so many Protestant church members.

[45] There is rarely any talk of sheep *running away*.

[46] Assuming that quest for power and lax morals do not occur among leaders of established churches.

[47] For his life see the extensive biography by Booth's great grandson: Langworthy, *The Life of Joseph Booth*.

[48] His wife Mary shared the call, but died of pneumonia 14 days before the intended departure from Australia.

[49] This group can be classified as the "Tabernacle Baptists" They were Baptists in doctrine and practice, but innovative in their concepts. Their churches were to be "for the masses" therefore they were not to look Gothic. The most famous Baptist Tabernacle was the Metropolitan Tabernacle of the famous preacher Charles Haddon Spurgeon in London.

an innovative and alternative missionary movement, the interdenominational faith missions,[50] he turned to one of their innovative concepts, namely that of the "self-supporting industrial mission".[51] Such a mission would be independent of existing power structures. Initial capital would be needed to establish such a mission, but that would be all, and once profitability was gained, its profits could finance further expansion. Thus a chain of self supporting missions could be established easily.[52] In line with general faith mission thinking and practice of his time, he had no intention to compete with the existing missions, intending to start at least 50 miles away from the nearest of them. But economic realities and political circumstances made him establish the first two missions in easy reach of Limbe, the centre of transportation close to Blantyre Mission. For Blantyre Mission Joseph Booth was a direct competitor. He (and the missionaries who soon joined him) did not intend to "steal sheep", and though it happened that people would leave the (Blantyre Mission) Presbyterian Church to join his church, the number was small.[53] More threatening was the competition for *potential* converts, especially as it was easier to *achieve* baptism in the Zambezi Industrial Mission than in Blantyre Mission. But possibly most threatening was the competition for labour, because Booth paid higher wages, thus "spoiling the prices", or, to use the language of power, breaking the cartel established by missions, settlers and government.[54]

Joseph Booth brought confusion into the neatly arranged world of mission comity not only by introducing a new mission or two, but by introducing, with different levels of personal involvement, eight of them, either in the southern or in the central region of Malawi. Here they are under their present names, with names of missions in brackets where applicable:

---

[50] The first faith mission was the China Inland Mission, founded in 1865 by Hudson and Maria Taylor. For Africa the main early faith mission founders were Fanny and Grattan Guinness. For a detailed study of the faith missions in Africa see: Fiedler, *The Story of Faith Missions*.

[51] In Malawi there were two concurrent concepts of Industrial Missions, the Presbyterian type and the Booth type. The Presbyterian type emphasized industrial training, whereas the Booth type emphasized missionary self support as a financial strategy. For Booth's concept, which he based on some of William Carey's ideas, see: Joseph Booth, "The Greatest Work in the World - A Plea for Missionary Enterprise", *Missionary Review of the World* (New York), 5 (Aug. 1892), pp. 573-80.

[52] Though Booth had been a successful business man in New Zealand and in Australia, his profitability calculations for industrial missions were notoriously on the optimistic side (Langworthy, *The Life of Joseph Booth*, p. 33).

[53] That John Chilembwe, his first convert, was rebaptized by him is not true. The John Chilembwe in the baptism register of Blantyre Mission was a different person.

[54] Here is a parallel to mission comity. Truth is decided upon by geography. Here the employers decide alone on what a living wage is or if a living wage is needed at all.

Zambezi Evangelical Church (Zambezi Industrial Mission) 1892
Africa Evangelical Church[55] (Nyassa Industrial Mission) 1893
Churches of Christ (Gowa), (Baptist Industrial Mission of Scotland) 1896
Church of Christ (Namikango) 1906
Seventh Day Baptists 1898/1910
Seventh Day Adventists (Malamulo) 1902
African Baptist Assembly (Providence Industrial Mission) 1900
Jehovah's Witnesses (Elliot Kamwana) 1908[56]

This religious pluralism can be partly ascribed to his character. He was ever the pioneer and had problems working with fellow missionaries. On the other hand there is much more consistency in it than easily meets the eye, if one looks at it not from the classical missions' point of view but from the point of view of his own spiritual background. He was in many ways a religious radical: a convert from atheism, in Auckland (New Zealand) member of a very innovative Tabernacle type Baptist church, a spare time street evangelist in Brisbane, and in touch with the innovative faith mission movement. His political views were radical, too: he was convinced that Africans and Europeans were equal, not only in the eyes of God but also in real life (the church included).[57] It is only natural that a radical will clash with established power structures, which are, by their very nature, middle of the road. Often Booth was unsuccessful, as radicals usually are. But then radicals are needed, if not for success but for vision, and any society needs visions. Through the efforts of Booth and the missions which he brought into the country, any semblance of mission comity was finally destroyed by 1910. This meant that each mission's power was limited by the power of Africans to walk to an alternative mission, which in many areas of the densely populated south was not a long walk.

The Chilembwe Domingo factor

Early unchallenged ecclesiastical power was not only limited by the introduction of new missions,[58] but also through the introduction of "African Independency"

---

[55] Also known as Ntambanyama Synod of the United Evangelical Church which also comprises the Zambezi Evangelical Church (Mitsidi Synod), and the Chididi Synod (Africa Evangelical Fellowship).

[56] He repudiated this allegiance in 1910 and tried to win [with small success] the Jehovah's Witnesses' congregations in Tongaland for the Seventh Day Baptists (Langworthy, *The Life of Joseph Booth*, pp. 243ff.)

[57] This found expression in his book: Joseph Booth, *Africa for the African*, Baltimore 1897; in his petition to Queen Victoria, demanding independence for Malawi before 1920; in his support for the African National Congress in South Africa, etc.

[58] Not all new missions belonged to the post-classical/evangelical type, the most important new missions were the two Roman Catholic Missions (Montfortians and White Fathers) which started

Why, after all, should a mission always be led by a white man? Weren't all human beings equal? In the development of this concept Joseph Booth had a hand, too, but its main exponents in early Malawi were John Chilembwe and Charles Domingo. For both of them "African independency" was neither racist nor exclusive, nor was it in any way syncretistic. But they both vividly questioned the assumptions of those in power: That the white race was somehow better, that churches must be led by white missionaries, that there are established mission spheres. Neither Booth nor Chilembwe were anti-missionary. Chilembwe was an American missionary himself,[59] and Domingo cooperated happily with Joseph Booth residing in Cape Town. Both, as so many of their successors, would have been very happy if they could have received more support from abroad. Though they were neither enemies of white missionaries nor in other ways exclusive, their existence was not always taken kindly. The "native controlled missions", as the then government termed them, were not liked. These missions intruded into spheres which the white missions had reserved for themselves, and they offered venues of advancement which the established missions did not offer: sacraments were available under easier conditions, "native missions" might be in closer reach than the other missions, people with lesser education could still contribute to church leadership, involvement of some who had been disciplined in their previous church was more easily possible.[60] But though all these elements are important, a genuine and personal search for truth must not be left out of the equation.

Since John Chilembwe, Elliot Kamwana, Charles Domingo and Alexander Makwinja, African Instituted Churches have provided a viable alternative to mission instituted churches, giving people full religious freedom, to choose between religions, between denominations and between races. Though they have proven to be a viable alternative, they cannot make exclusive claims nor should exclusive claims be made for them. It is only a minority of Malawians who have opted to join African Instituted Churches. Therefore the exclusive claim that only AICs show what real African Christianity is, is based on ideology. The term AICs is a sociological term, though it is often misused to give or to imply a theological definition of the churches involved. Useful as the term is in analyzing early Malawian church history, I find that the term has lost much of its usefulness for today, and has some dangers. The danger seems to me to be that the term does not take the very different churches seriously by lumping them all together. I propose that they should be taken just as any other church, taking each (even if there are so

---

to claim a share of the potential converts after the Protestants had considered them all to be theirs for 25 years.

[59] Albeit "a foreign missionary in his own land"

[60] For an insightful analysis of the various aspects see Langworthy, *The Life of Joseph Booth*, pp. 219-273.

many!) as an entity of its own, deserving a separate categorization. Naming them according to principles imposed on them seems to be an unwarranted onesided exercise of power. Once each church is taken seriously, differences will become clear, groups of related churches will become visible. This approach requires more effort, but will avoid the undue use of power, even if it is only the power of naming.

New missions after the end of missions

In traditional study of missions it was (and still often is) assumed that the time of the coming of independence to the classical churches in Africa (coupled with political independence) would mean the end of Western missions, at least in the traditional sense of missionaries actually establishing new churches. Reality never matched this assumption, though it is still dear to missiologists and church leaders. In Malawi since 1960 the number of new missions has been considerable.

1960	Southern Baptist Mission
1962	WELS (USA) [61]
1964	Christian Brethren[62]
1973	Free Methodist Church
1977	Church of God of Prophecy
1978	Pentecostal Assembly of Canada
1980	Evangelical Brethren
1985	Brethren in Christ Church (USA)
1990	Liebenzell Mission (Evangelical Baptist Church)
1990	African Bible College

The list, which is not complete, indicates that Christian pluralism has become ever more plural since Malawi became independent and the classical Protestant missions withdrew from direct missionary work in Malawi. Often these "new" missions are ignored or considered just as a nuisance. But this would be to look at them from the point of view of the established churches, who feel endangered by them. Instead it is possible to look at them from the point of view of those who joined them. How then did they come to Malawi?

---

[61] WELS is: Wisconsin Evangelical Lutheran Synod, 3512 West North Ave, **Milwaukee**, Wisconsin 53208.
[62] I found only a few. 20,000 seems to me to be a clear overestimate, also regarding the assumed size of the average congregation.

The [Southern] Baptist Mission came in 1960 on its own accord, feeling that Malawi would be a worthy field to which to extend their endeavours from Zimbabwe. Though its entry into Malawi definitely was a foreign idea, many Malawians welcomed the new mission, so that the Baptist Convention now has something like 80,000 members.[63] Obviously the mission's efforts were not outdated for many Malawians.[64]

The Lutheran Church of Central Africa came to Malawi from Zambia on the request of people who had been in contact with it in Zambia and of those who had read their literature in Malawi or had relatives in Zambia in touch with it. The LCCA is a strongly conservative Lutheran church, which is not in fellowship with most other Lutheran churches, because its conception of truth differs from theirs. By sending missionaries to Malawi the LCCA has introduced a new opportunity to search for the truth.[65]

The Free Methodist missionary work in Malawi was started by a Malawian, Amos Phiri, who had been a migrant worker in Zimbabwe. The Free Methodists are a small church, but growing fast. They also introduced a new variety of theological education, the modular approach.[66] For the Free Methodist Church it is reported that in many places they found a niche at the fringe of the established churches, when people who had been members of these churches, but led in no way a Christian life, experienced a clear conversion and a drastic change of life. I can support this observation: there is indeed a big fringe of church members who lack any real Christian experience, though they may have attended a few classes or even all. And I am convinced that it is better for them to attain salvation in a church like the Free Methodists than not to attain it in a more established church, more respectable and correctly politically engaged though it may be.

The Evangelical Lutheran Church came to Malawi with returning Malawians who had lived for many years in Tanzania and had been active Lutherans there. Why should a return to their motherland mean a change of denomination? Faith, after all, is not a matter of geography but of conviction and experience.

---

[63] The statistics made by the [Southern] Baptist Mission in Malawi give much higher figures, but the system of counting was faulty.
[64] Presently Rendell Day is working for a PhD (University of Malawi) with the topic "Baptist Conversion", analyzing reasons why people became Baptists (or leave them) and what the spiritual content of such conversions is.
[65] This theological separatism does not exclude practical cooperation. An LCCA member, Ernst Wendland, is one of the main consultants for the new Bible translations into both Chewa and Tumbuka.
[66] Church growth and modular theological education are the theme of the PhD Dissertation of Henry Church (University of Malawi).

This list of "newcomers" could be extended considerably. Common to all is that they are in the country not because they wanted to be here but because Malawians want them to be here. Christian pluralism is a living option for many Malawians, not so much for outside missions.

Change is the power of the powerless

Churches are often rigid structures. Though theological pluralism is often welcomed or even proclaimed, organizational pluralism is not. Power in church is usually top-down, with the clergy in the central institutions dominating the structures. The plurality of churches is a check to this power. A young man may have a call to Christian ministry, but his church can't recognize it because his educational achievements are a bit below what is required for entry into the church's college for training pastors. In a different church the entrance qualifications are slightly lower, and he fits in. Assuming that God in his calling is not bound to a minimum educational standard, is it really bad if the young man became a minister of the gospel in a church different from the one he was born into? Many churches, actually most, give women limited opportunities for Christian ministry, at least where either sacramental ministry or leadership is involved. I think it is good that churches exist in Malawi where a woman can be ordained like the Assemblies of God, the Free Methodists or some of the recent charismatic churches. Such a church offers the option of joining it, but even more so its very existence may be a challenge to rethink some theological issues. Change is the option of those left out by the system, and therefore the possibility of a change of affiliation is a wholesome check on excessive ecclesiastical power. If, therefore, Malawians are "good shoppers of religious goods",[67] this should be seen primarily as a possibility for the empowerment of the powerless.

There are so many churches

Christian pluralism is a reality everywhere in Malawi where there are Christians. A map may make this pluralism literally visible. One of the most pluralistic areas is Thyolo   Luchenza   Phalombe. The following map shows the choice of churches anyone has at Migowi, provided she or he is willing to walk up to about one hour. The choice is impressive: There are 28 churches to chose from, belonging to 22 different denominations. The situation in a major town like Nkhata Bay, where building is more costly, is less varied. There are three classical churches in the centre of the city (with two smaller "intruders"), but around the

---

[67] J.C. Chakanza, "Good Shoppers of Religious Goods"

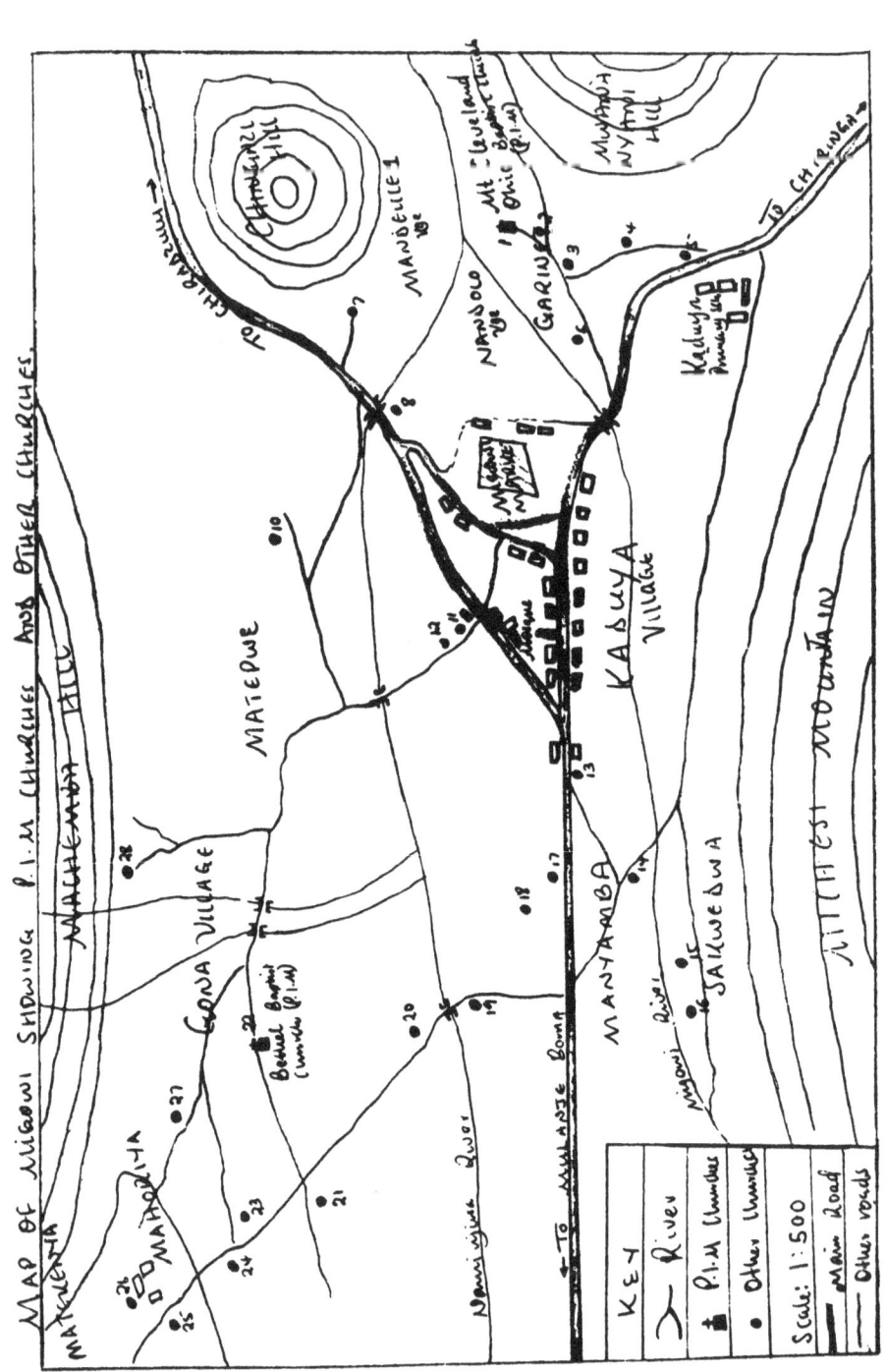

centre there is a group of other churches.[68] The situation in Lunzu Township also shows a lot of diversity. There are 12 churches representing 12 denominations. The biggest church is the Roman Catholic, seating about a 1000, the CCAP seats about 500, the 10 remaining churches can hold about as many attenders as the two classical churches. There are also areas where the original "established" church actually has become a minority option. I am sure that even a casual look at the map of Migowi will convince everyone that religious pluralism is a reality in Malawi, and that is what the people want. This pluralism must be taken as genuinely Malawian, it cannot be explained by outside influences. They could never be strong enough for such a variety, unless the people really wanted it.

The religious landscape in Malawi is changing

Up to now almost all churches in Malawi are growing. This is deceptive, since much of this impressive growth is due to the tremendous population growth, which saw a doubling of Malawi's population under Kamuzu. In addition there was plenty of conversion growth, with the greater part of the non Muslim population becoming Christian. I have no reliable religious statistics for Malawi, and I think they do not exist. But some evidence of developments there is. From some detailed evidence I have come to doubt the conception of an evergrowing share of AICs in the total number of Christians, as seems to be the case in South Africa. A number of AICs seems to be declining while others are growing or being born. The classical churches seem to be still growing, but definitely below the population growth rate. Almost all evangelical churches register growth above the rate of population growth, with a very considerable growth of the Seventh Day Adventists. The fastest growing group of denominations are the charismatic churches.

At this time two major changes take place: The number of people who are neither Christians nor Muslims is converging against zero, and since the conversion rate between Christians and Muslims is close to zero, this means that the reservoir of potential converts for the Christian churches has dried out. The other major change is the declining birth rate. The birth rate is still high, but has been declining over the last decade.[69] And comparative statistics from countries like Indonesia and Kenya show that a further decline can be expected in the immediate future, so that

---

[68] In Zomba the situation is very similar: There is the old CCAP church right at the centre, the Anglican church is a bit further west, and the Catholic Church has a big mission again further west. But south of the main road there is the "area of the new churches"

[69] *Malawi. Demographic and Health Survey 1992*, Zomba 1994, p. 4. At present levels, a woman will give birth to an average of 6,7 children during her lifetime. In Kenya the decline of the birth rate has been very remarkable.

perhaps in 15 or 20 years the growth rate will be close to zero, which would be around 2010, not far away from now.

This projected scenario will mean a tremendous change in the churches' power relations. The early established Protestant churches, both of the classical and the evangelical variety, will seriously decline in numbers. This may endanger their capacity of supporting central structures like training institutions and social institutions like schools and hospitals. On the other hand this may not turn out to be a problem any more than it is now, because due to economic liberalization and declining birth rate economic growth is to be expected that could easily make up for numerical losses. Then the question remains if there will be enough spiritual power, but here predictions are impossible. The evangelical denominations will be then in a stronger position than they are now. They will have to face many issues, which had to be tackled by the classical churches in the 1960s and 1970s, like independence, self support, education. This will demand many additional resources. I have little evidence from which to make any projection for the future of the so called African Instituted Churches. It is easy to predict that quite a number of them will decline or close down, because that is happening anyhow already. But the challenge for them to fulfill the demands of the people will grow with a decline in population growth, which will most probably go along with improved education. The Roman Catholic Church will also start on a membership decline, but more slowly than the major Protestant churches, because usually the Roman Catholic Church loses less members to other churches than the Protestants, and it also rarely gives birth to new churches. Should these projected changes take place, it will mean for the churches that they all must learn to be more careful (or more Christian) in their administration of power.

Revival as Counter Power

No church can be sure of retaining its position and status. Even in times when there was only one legal church, the "territorial church" or the "established church", members could reduce their participation in the life of the church, they could concentrate on worldly matters, or they could even give up their individual faith. They could, and often did indeed, become Christians in name only. Nominal Christianity is a major issue in Malawi today.[70] The church is very much a part of the social structure, its transition ceremonies are much coveted, church attendance is seen as normal. The individual's Christian faith is guided through *makalasi*, and if someone goes through all of them, he or she is surely a Spirit filled Christian.[71]

---

[70] Rev Chienda is preparing for a PhD Dissertation on this subject.

[71] This *theology acted* was clearly formulated in the statement of the Blantyre Synod's Administrators against the *Born Agains* in their membership.

This easy identification of society and church leads to a transfer of position from society to church. As it was put by one contributor:

> Most of them found their way back to church, only to find a generation of the clergy that had not been prepared to handle professional people. For fear of losing them the church gave them positions of leadership to help beef up the collection.[72]

This kind of accommodation of the (established) church to society will help the church for a certain time to keep up its numbers, appearance and social role, but will not prevent an inner erosion from taking place and becoming visible after some time, as has happened in Central Europe over the last decades. Therefore in many churches there is a longing for inner renewal, which would enhance the real involvement of its members not just by structural reform or pious appeal but by an inner change of heart and attitude. This longing is expressed in different terms, one frequently used is *revival*.[73] For a church to remain viable, revival or renewal is needed, and many church leaders implicitly or explicitly wish for it or pray for it. But then they must be aware that revival is not easy to manage when it comes. Revival is power, new spiritual power, people suddenly do things from their own heart which the church leaders had exhorted them in vain to do for so long. But the fact that they do it on their own is a challenge to established church power. Revival is always counterpower. This power may have similar objectives to those of the church leadership, but the source of its power is not in the establishment. A revival creates a lot of spiritual power. The church establishment may welcome this new spiritual power in principle, but will have problems in controlling it.

The Nkhonde Revival

It seems that Malawi shared in the worldwide spiritual decline associated with the events that crystallized into the student revolution of 1968 and a strong longing for flower power and socialism. On the more local level, independence and politics played a role. Though the new government had come to power carried on the shoulders of a nationalist movement which was led by Presbyterians who often had a strong personal Christian commitment, many peoples' energies were absorbed by the feeling for the new era. This era had clearly pseudo religious tendencies, as witnessed by the party usurping a Christmas hymn to make Kamuzu the saviour.[74]

---

[72] Wambali Mkandawire, "Music and Power" (Theology of Life essay).

[73] This word is not to be confused with its secondary American meaning where revival may mean an evangelistic campaign. Though they have sometimes led to a revival, it is wrong to equate anticipated results with the attempt.

[74] Among the many programmes that the radio station had made in praise of the Lion of Malawi, the MBC Band was given a special programme which featured twice Saturday. To show that at this time government was determined to use anything to make Dr Banda the redeemer late

In spite of Kamuzu's religious claims ("church elder of the Church of Scotland", national worship services, the President reading Bible texts at services where he chose to be present, etc.), the party tried to win the people's *first* allegiance, if necessary to the detriment of religion. In some cases Christianity was actually mocked, like in this song from Mlowo in Usisya:

Kubatizika naji gha waka	To be baptized with no reasons
Pakudya chinjwa panji ndi njala	You eat the eucharist you are still hungry
Kweni chokuzilwa mtima	Only to be good in your heart
Wa munthu uwenga atuwa.	To be a good person.

It is always difficult to trace the origins of a revival, and for this one I do not have enough material even to try that.[75] An early appearance of the revival was in the North, adjacent to Tanzania, amongst the northernmost ethnic group in Malawi along the Lake shore, the Nkhonde, who are very similar to the Nyakyusa across the border. The revival, which touched mainly Karonga and Rumphi Districts, was borne on the wings of songs in Nkhonde,[76] which makes it probable that it came across the border from the Nyakyusa area.[77] Its leadership were young people, its name Ukalina implied the same. Its preaching was against sin, but what impressed people first of all was its music. Its musical style was contemporary, and it had similarities with some of the Lake shore types of music. The music was organized around the choirs, which provided almost unlimited room for involvement and also for leadership. Contrary to "established" church music, they added their own body movements, called *mabiti*. This term shows that their musical acculturation was a step of modernization, not an emphasis on traditional values.

Wilson Chirwa made the signature for the recorded programme with a line from a Christian song that was originally from Zambian Presbyterian Christians hymns. It said *chalo chose chilecimba Aleluya Hosana Mau Kamuzu name*. Which means the whole world is singing Alleluya Hosanna the child Kamuzu. The only difference with the original Zambian tune is that Mr Chirwa's version adds the name Kamuzu and leaves out *alitufyaliwe* which appear in the original Zambian version. It means he has been born for us.

[75] It is a pity that so little research has been done on the more recent history of the mainline churches. Most dissertations and monographs deal with the origins and the early years of the three Presbyterian Synods. The dissertation dealing with the most recent period seems to be S.D. Chiphangwi, *Why People Join the Christian Church; Trends in Church Growth in Blantyre Synod of the Church of Central Africa Presbyterian 1960-1975* (PhD Aberdeen, 1978).

[76] Wambali Mkandawire, Music and Power.

[77] For the musical revival in Unyakyusa see K. Fiedler, *Christianity and African Culture Conservative German Protestant Missionaries in Tanzania, 1900-1940*, Leiden: Brill, 1996, p. 141.

The revival gave a voice to the voiceless, the young. It also gave a voice to a minority, by using the local language, not the established church's lingua franca Tumbuka. By providing an alternative power, the revival movement helped many people to regain their allegiance to Christ. In some way the movement was accepted, for example the young people were allowed to preach in church. In other aspects, touching established structures, it was not. The new music (witness of new spiritual power) was permitted as "chorals" besides the "hymns" But the hymns remained the real thing,[78] and this is reflected by the fact that the present Nkhonde hymnbook contains none of them, only real hymns, translated either from the West or from Ngoni hymns which went back to the very first revival in Malawi at the beginning of this century,[79] the Keswick type revival led by Donald Fraser. The question remains: Why were those early revival hymns accepted by the church and not the later ones?[80]

The Revival in Zambia

Information is insufficient still, but it is obvious that a revival within the CCAP Zambia Synod also influenced Malawi. It started among the young people, the youth movement. The elders of the church condemned it as teaching wrong doctrines like the baptism of the Holy Spirit, they preached against it because they dropped the right kind of music and introduced innovations, finally they banned it. The young people then formed themselves into an interdenominational fellowship. When they felt that a fellowship was not enough, they turned it into a church, which was then attached to the CCAP. This happened in the 1980s.[81] Here the ingredients are the same: a revival, led by young people, which forms a counterpower in the established church; and, despite its claim to be the church for all Zambia, the church does not accommodate that which threatens established power. The revival also touched Malawi, but I have no details, only that the small drum and some other local instruments were admitted to churches in Blantyre Synod due to the revival in Zambia.[82]

The 1970s Revival

In tune with spiritual developments worldwide and possibly as a reaction against the religious demands of Kamuzuism, a distinct revival touched Malawi in the

---

[78] This seems to be supported by James Tengatenga's observation that in quite a number of Anglican Churches the youths are permitted to sing choruses, but that the elders jealously guard their privilege of announcing the hymns. See chapter 4.

[79] For a selection of Ngoni hymns with their English translations see K.R. Ross (ed.), *Christianity in Malawi*, Gweru: Mambo, 1996, (Kachere Book No. 3) pp. 49-67

[80] This paragraph is based on: Wambali Mkandawire, Music and Power

[81] Interview with Aaron Longwe, 1995.

[82] Personal communication from an elder of Nkana Congregation near Zomba, late in 1992.

1970s. It was primarily an interdenominational movement, touching most of all educated youths, and as such it had its centres in Blantyre, Lilongwe, Zomba and Mzuzu. The revival's main source were various evangelical para-church organizations like New Life for All or Scripture Union, which took the message to the streets, the schools and the churches. There was also some Pentecostal influence. This evangelical revival was consciously interdenominational, cooperating consciously with almost all Protestant churches, provided that these wanted the cooperation offered. Cooperation was not on a corporate base (parachurch organization - denominational leadership) but on an individual and local base (cooperation with individuals or individual congregations). The revival converted many educated young people, who in many cases moved into positions of leadership not only in society but also in churches and parachurch organizations. Many experienced conversion in this revival and heard the call to the ministry. Some of them, like Emmanuel Chimkwita, Wambali Mkandawire and Akim Chirwa, also influenced more recent political developments. A lasting effect of the revival was to establish the parachurch organizations as a permanent feature of the Christian scene in Malawi, and as such as a permanent source of enrichment and competition for the various denominations. The parachurch movements provide alternative venues for spiritual nurture and for the development of talents of leadership or service. It is telling that the Christian Council of Malawi, the established spiritual authority for Chancellor College,[83] has not been able to appoint a chaplain to Chancellor College since the 1970s, and if one would take away SCOM and Life Ministry and other interdenominational ministries, the situation of Protestant Christianity at Chancellor College would be bleak indeed. But I am convinced that, asked officially, the Christian Council would still claim spiritual responsibility for the Protestants at Chancellor College.

The Charismatic Churches

The next wave of revival to touch Malawi was the Charismatic Revival, which had started in America in the 1960s, and had developed, independently of America, a strong base in Nigeria in the 1970s. Its emphasis on healing, wealth and power clearly shows its deep African roots,[84] though some of its outward trapping came from the West. As in Nigeria and America - and different from the Pentecostal Revival of 1906 - the Charismatic Revival in Malawi was strongly a middle class movement, and as such it could easily pick up pieces from the preceding interdenominational evangelical revival. The combination of middle class income

---

[83] This is documented by the fact that in the early years it contributed a flat for the Chaplain to the campus. The flat has since been taken over by the University, when the Christian Council had no use for it. Cf. p. 116 above.

[84] This is clearly shown in the studies of Matthews Ojo (forthcoming).

and charismatic spiritual fervour made the revival financially viable, sometimes even powerful. Thus the revival could largely finance itself, a thing many established churches could hardly dream of.[85] The fact that it could finance itself made the revival independent. Groups that do not ask for money and are able to finance themselves are possibly the strongest challenge to any established church authority. They do not need to struggle for a slice of the financial cake that the church leadership is administering, they just bake their own cake.[86]

The Charismatic Revival, again in common with America and Nigeria, had no intention at all to form new churches. Their aim was just renewal, their own and that of their churches or (especially in Nigeria) their parachurch organizations.[87] There too many who underwent the renewal experience felt that they found insufficient spiritual nurture in the regular diet offered by their church, so they started to form fellowships. These fellowships would often command their primary spiritual allegiance, but that would not detract their members from being or becoming faithful members of their church, where they are often the mainstay of a congregation and sometimes its main problem, too. All revival fellowship movements have a tendency to develop gradually into churches. With the Holiness Revival in Sweden at the turn of the century it took at least two generations, in the German Holiness revival the stage has not yet been reached, in the Pentecostal Revival it usually took only a few years, because the established churches helped. In the Charismatic Revival a period of 5-10 years seems to be a good estimate for many fellowships to mature into new denominations, but a good number of fellowships seem not to go this way but remain strictly interdenominational or attached to one denomination. This process has led to the establishment of more than 20 charismatic denominations in Blantyre alone. Some have only one congregation and may not intend to branch out, some have several congregations within Blantyre, and others see the whole nation as their field of activity.

In the study of Christianity in Africa often a differentiation is made between "mission" churches and "African Instituted Churches" I do not think that this

---

[85] Here it must not be overlooked, though, that the established churches had more structures like schools and hospitals to sustain.
[86] In ecumenical *theology acted* there is often the idea that there exists a financial cake of fixed (and unfortunately always limited) proportions, which needs to be guarded against too many demands, especially from newcomers (who are they after all to share in it!). It is often overlooked that new spiritual power generates more financial power, so that the cake can grow or new cakes can be produced.
[87] The immense role of the evangelical parachurch organizations in Nigeria for the birth of the Charismatic Movement there is clearly shown by Matthew Ojo. I have not found much evidence for that in Malawi, but in Malawian parachurch movements like SCOM there is a strong tendency to replace evangelical spirituality by Charismatic spirituality.

distinction is really helpful in interpreting the Charismatic churches in Blantyre. The first of them, Blantyre Christian Centre, was established by a Westerner, Rev Barbara Tippett. Others have Western connections. Others again originated in Nigeria or have strong connections that way. So they would be African instituted, but not Malawian instituted. But these differentiations, interesting as they might be for the church historian, seem to major on minors. What the Charismatic churches have in common is their spirituality, their local leadership, their middle class power, their youthfulness, and that they offer a deeply spiritual, deeply African and deeply modern approach to the Christian faith. In this they are a serious challenge to the established churches (and to evangelical churches, coming from a revival closer to the Charismatic Revival, yet different from it). A mere list of the sequence of the birth of new charismatic churches may give some idea of their power in a changing Christian environment:

Name	started	Founder/leader
Blantyre Christian Centre	1980	Rev Barbara Tippet
Agape	February 1982	Pastor Mgala
Faith of God	1984	Pastor Matoga
Living Waters	January 1985	Pastor Ndovi
Glad Tidings	January 1986	Group initiated
All for Jesus	Jan 1993	Pastor Zalimba
Flames of Victory	September 1993	Pastor Katchire
Calvary Family Church	March 1994	Pastor Mbewe
Vineyard	November 1994	Pastor Gama

For nine of these churches the membership was estimated as ranging between 150 and 1000, which, for 20 churches makes an estimate of 4000 seem likely. To that figure the number of children, friends, adherents and enquirers can be added, and a figure of 10-15,000 for the total Christian community of the charismatic churches in Blantyre City alone may not be an overestimate.

Most charismatic churches in Blantyre started as fellowships, a form in which they operated for several years. The next step was to start a church in rented rooms, then the erection of a church building would follow. Three churches at least have entered the next stage of establishing additional institutions. There are three Bible Schools, a bookshop, AIDS counselling and other ministries. Blantyre Christian Centre in 1994 opened its own primary school, not following the pattern of the classical missions' schools, but that of the European/American/South African Christian private (elite middle class) schools, in keeping with its sociological context. Here the financial power of the owners will probably produce a better start for their children, very useful at a time of declining quality in public primary schools. Thus the church answers real and felt needs of its constituent community.[88] From the outside the charismatic church movement looks pretty disunited, and some mainline representatives see it as a chaotic bunch of malcontents. There is a certain amount of disunity and occasional discontent,[89] but why then should Christian unity be necessarily expressed in organizational unity? Charismatics see Christian unity as unity in the Spirit, and that can be obtained even with disunity of organization, and they could easily point out that sometimes in churches with perfect organizational unity the unity of the Spirit is lacking, and maybe sometimes even the Spirit. Organizational diversity includes the possibility of formal cooperation. This found formal expression within the Charismatic community by the foundation of CHAPEL, the Charismatic and Pentecostal Churches association.

The charismatic churches have a strong political involvement, with political claims not commensurate with their small number countrywide, but with the feelings of an elite that knows that numbers do not count when it comes to right or wrong, and equally that divine power is bigger than the power of human numbers. Though it cannot be taken as representing the whole charismatic movement in Malawi, the case of Kamlepo Kalua as a candidate for the first democratic presidency is revealing of an understanding of divine power as unlimited, though adverse powers can temporarily be more powerful. Kalua made his concept very clear a few days before the election when he claimed that, in spite of the fact that his party was tiny and had only managed to field candidates in two constituencies, he was sure that God would give him the victory. The votes he got were as negligible as the size of his party. When I asked him after the election why he hadn't won he told me that he was still convinced that God had given him the victory, but that someone had taken it away. A similar approach to divine power was obvious in other charismatic sections. Before the election there were regular prayer meetings to pray against a Muslim becoming president of Malawi,[90] and I heard that Satan had been bound so that no Muslim could become President of Malawi. I have not heard how or by whom Satan was untied in time for the election. Another report tells that some people were specific, indicating that God had told them in a vision, when they saw a President with Bible in his hand, indicating that a Christian and not a Muslim would rule Malawi. No clear explanation has been forthcoming as to why everything went the other way, except the proposition that "God's promises sometimes take years to be fulfilled"

---

[88] Though this school and also the Bible Schools are clearly identified as charismatic, they are also, in a way, interdenominational, since they accept and welcome applicants from both charismatic and non charismatic churches.

[89] Of the nine churches studied, two were started in disagreement with others.

[90] At least one member of staff was invited to take part in these prayers, but refused.

These two instances may not have been official charismatic theology, but they do belong to charismatic *theology acted*. Official theology was expressed by CHAPEL, when it organized two days' of national prayers on the eve of the general election at Kwacha Conference Centre in Blantyre. Reports differ as to what specific requests were made to God facing the possibility of a Muslim becoming president, but there can be little doubt about a widespread conviction that Malawi, as a Christian country, should be ruled by a Christian.[91] After the defeat, Pastor Taulo Phiri became a kind of court chaplain to Kamuzu, an office which for him included not only the attempt to help the former president spiritually, but also to defend him and some of his claims publicly. What has been reported here most probably does not apply to all charismatics, nor does it form a coherent picture yet, but it does portray aspects of their understanding of power, spiritual and worldly.

The Born Again controversy

Besides the Charismatic denominations there are many Charismatics who remain within the mainline churches, especially within the CCAP, Blantyre Synod. They would attend their Charismatic fellowship meetings, but otherwise be faithful (and often leading) CCAP members. Though not intending to be a threat to established church authority, they were perceived as such, and the church authorities led by the Deputy General Secretary in the absence of the General Secretary, attempted to rid the church of them or to bring them into conformity through a letter which told them either to stop shouting Hallelujah or to get out of the CCAP, where one does no such things.

> Some are bringing some kinds of fellowship which are contrary to the way our fellowships are organised and their teachings are also different. Some of these members have been advised to stop this new teaching but are stubborn and they still hold to it, but they had sworn in the church at their baptism that they will respect the advice of the church elders. For this reason we feel that we cannot hold them hence they should join the church of their choice.[92]

The letter then proceeded to give the right understanding of new birth:

> A person who is born in a Christian family according to the established rules of the CCAP is baptized while still a baby.

---

[91] I have not found any information if any assessment was made of the spiritual value of the Christian confession of Chakufwa Chihana or Kamuzu Banda. This should have been done as in charismatic language Christian is not a sociological term but a spiritual term implying conversion and commitment.

[92] Synod Office, Church of Central Africa Presbyterian, Blantyre Synod - All Congregations, 11 January 1995.

> Having grown he is accepted to be a Christian who receives the sacraments after he finishes to be taught in all the classes of the Holy Book. In this way this person receives the Holy Spirit and becomes a born again.[93]

The letter stated clearly the overriding principle: follow established order, and you will be saved. Do not shout Hallelujah and do not forget to go through all the classes. Then the Holy Spirit will be yours.

The ultimate result of this attempt at cleansing the church from any deviant interpretations of the Gospel cannot yet be assessed. In my understanding the leadership of Blantyre Synod did not take fully into account that the Born Agains had their own effective structures to counteract the attempted expulsions. There is also support for the interpretation that the church leaders thought the Born Agains were just a group of young people, whereas in reality many of them had leading positions in the church. Whatever may have been in the minds of the authors of the letter, the Born Agains refused to be expelled from the church, and they were indeed able to negotiate from a position of strength. Up to now, no actual expulsions have taken place, nor has a split or a major defection occurred.

Revival is power: This is clearly seen in the increased and often sacrificial commitment of those revived. This is power the churches are coveting from their members. But revival is also counterpower, since it has its own theology, its own organizational structures, its own spiritual energies, and last but not least, its own money.

Effective Power to Redeem

Social and political changes, worldwide and local, are bound to influence the church in Malawi. The last 50 years have often been described as the struggle between Communism and the West. Communism did not make it, finding last refuges in countries like Cuba and North Korea. But the last 50 years can also be understood as a worldwide struggle between a liberal approach to life and an authoritarian one, and then not all authoritarianism was in the East and all liberty in the West. Malawi, supposedly a bulwark of the West in its fight against Communism, was on the authoritarian side, but so were and are many structures in Western society, for example government owning "essential" services and industries (and more often than not mismanaging them) or creating and supporting monopolies and reducing or prohibiting competition. Malawi shared to some extent in those things, too.

---

[93] *Ibid.*

Not only in Malawi, the churches share(d) in authoritarian structures. If Kamuzu argued for one Saviour,[94] one nation, one party, no dissidents,[95] and obedience, and discipline, this could be applied to the arguments of quite a number of churches. It's some time ago now that the church burnt witches and heretics at the stake but often even after that churches fought tooth and nail to retain whatever power they had and to make life as difficult as possible for any dissident.[96] Over the last decades the chances of the churches using the state as a tool in their quest for power have reduced themselves, but the attitudes behind this have not disappeared. The political and social change that swept through Malawi starting in 1992 also affected the churches, which in some ways had felt comfortable under an authoritarian government, because they themselves in some ways were one-party structures. If I judge the worldwide social development correctly, in Malawi the changes, dramatic though they were, have only begun. On the more obvious level it is the victory of democracy over totalitarian structures and over many socialist ideologies. On the individual level this means a tremendous increase in freedom to make decisions but also a tremendous increase in responsibility. The authorities that had made the decisions often just disappeared. There is noone any more to tell me not to wear bell bottom trousers, so I have to find out myself if they suit me and if they suit the people around me. To really accept this change takes time for society, more time than it took to gladly accept the demise of the old political regime.

Malawi's economy, and through it the whole population, was deeply steeped in a kind of authoritarian economy in which higher authorities decided which economic gains should profit whom. While the failure of the political system which organized the economy has become obvious (and believable) to most Malawians, few seem to have fully accepted the failure of the authoritarian economical system (which managed to keep the country among the poorest nations in spite of 30 years of peace, foreign assistance, a capitalist economy and development beyond recognition). Few seem to have fully realized that it made the political clique rich,[97] that through it the rural poor subsidized the urban and wage earning population, and though it might have worked well for the profits of PRESS,[98] it

---

[94] Mainly from the stupid Federation.
[95] Except as food for crocodiles.
[96] MacAlpine alerted the colonial authorities in 1909 that Kamwana's activities should be stopped.
[97] As many conversations show me, participation in politics is seen as primarily a means to personal enrichment, and fast for that.
[98] The profitable conglomerate that controlled major sectors of Malawi's economy and was the property of Kamuzu Banda. Important sections of this economic empire were acquired from political dissidents (real or supposed) by means of the forfeiture act. An example is Press Bakeries. (I still have problems in buying bread from PTC [People's Trading Company] shops.)

was altogether an economic system that would eat up most of the profits it generated. Though most have accepted that authoritarian politics are no longer viable (if they ever were), many have not yet accepted the same for the economy. Economic problems are to be solved by appeal to a benevolent state authority (subsidize fertilizer, control prices, organize transport,[99] subsidize housing, subsidize David Whitehead[100] etc) or by identifying the donors; and competition is often still seen as creating unnecessary expense. If the process of liberalization and individualization has started with politics and affected economics only to a limited extent, what about the church? In one way the answer is yes: in the churches people found much more liberty and individuality than the party felt would do them good. But on the other hand there is still a lot of authoritarian behaviour and thinking in the churches, both among the leadership and the members.

Liberalization and the churches

I expect the processes described above as liberalization and individualization to continue in Malawi. Especially in the economic sphere this will be difficult for many people to accept, but I expect that over a period of years many people will come to see the benefits. If this process continues, it will mean a loss of external power for many churches. Were they up to now accepted by many unquestioningly as a necessary part of society, this obvious truth may lose much of its hold over the people. Were, up to now, many decisions of the church leadership accepted unquestioningly (though often not ungrudgingly), more questioning and resistance is to be expected. Many more questions and challenges will come into the open than hitherto. I am convinced that the churches should not regret this coming change. Or, if they regret it, they should accept it as unavoidable and prepare for it and as quickly as possible get rid of all scaffoldings of power to support their structures that are not germane to the gospel. A first and very important step would be to take a hard and long look at the sacramental structures of each church. How far do they mix authoritarian power with the power of the gospel which is a power of redemption, not of control? Another step for the churches would be to stop talking about the option for the poor, and instead take the poor seriously. For many churches this would require a change in the *theology talked* and *acted* of marriage, and for others a change in practice. Another suggestion is to make the financial dealings really transparent, another is to give women a proper share in leadership.

---

[99] I am always amazed when I hear on the radio that the MP for so and so has asked the poor Minister of Transport to bring the Stagecoach buses to an important place in his constituency, as if that could be any of the minister's business.
[100] The only textile factory in Malawi, loss-making.

There is power in the gospel

The loss of authoritarian power must not mean a decline of the churches, since there is an alternative power, the power of the gospel. In changing circumstances emphasis should not be on the defence of (waning) privileges, but on spiritual power. This is the immediate possibility of any church, to seek spiritual power and to make it available to others. There will be a response: spiritual involvement, power of dedication, love and sacrifice. But this will not be achieved by defending waning authoritarian structures, but by challenging an increasingly independent and individualized church membership (and non members, too) with the claims and promises of the gospel. It was a power that withstood the pagan Roman Empire, it was a power that transformed individuals and societies, it was the power that sustained the witnesses and the martyrs, therefore it should be a realistic power for Malawian churches today.

Competition

Things have changed in politics and are changing in economics. Competition is no longer a dirty word, but has been recognized as the key to effectiveness in both politics and economics. What about the church? I am convinced that churches must be as effective as business: Their business is to make eternal salvation and Christian living a reality for as many people as possible in as short a time as possible. Now, if business is made effective by competition and not by authoritarian regulation, why should it be different with the church?[101] Malawi is fortunate in that there is already a lot of Christian competition. But I think that the churches should consciously accept this, not because it can hardly be avoided, but because it is a good thing. Christian competition will make salvation available to more people, will cut out dead wood from church structures, will increase the challenge to spiritual commitment. Isn't that what the church is for? Isn't that what the church wants?

Unity

There have been so many attempts up to now to seek Christian unity in the unity of organization. They have been futile, in spite of some limited results. The medicine does not work, and therefore I think it is best to follow the wisdom of a German *sing'anga* who once told me: If a medicine does not work, I stop administering it. Organizational unity, in spite of contrary claims, was never a Christian virtue. It existed only where it was rigorously enforced by non-spiritual

---

[101] "I share neither your rosy view of economic liberalization nor your thesis that free market economics is *the* model for healthy church life. But it is a voice of opposition to the liberal-ecumenical consensus - so it deserves to be heard." (Comment by Kenneth R. Ross, reading the draft of this chapter).

power. Organizational unity is surely nothing bad, but as soon as exclusive claims are attached to it, it becomes counter-productive and immoral. The unity of the church should not be sought in its structures, but in its aims. If the aim of the Church is to help as many people as possible to receive salvation and to live an effective Christian life of witness and service, then it does not matter if this happens in one church or in 25, and if more people receive the Christian life in 25 churches, then there is a unity in achievement.

Competition is not only a spiritual advantage as competition between churches, but also within churches. Many churches are virtual one party structures, organized from top down. If a member at any point in her or his life misses the right step, he or she is out. Therefore it would be good if within the church there could be also competing structures, where for example leadership talent can be developed even if it is not for the training for the ministry or for election of elders. Parachurch organizations, youth movements, independent women groups etc could do a very good job here. The churches should not fear these organizations and see their main job in controlling them, but further and advance them.

Competition and *cooperation*

Often in economics competition is seen by outsiders as an all out war. It is not. Competition *and* cooperation make for economic success. The same applies in the church and between the churches. Competition is not all out war, it is the other side of cooperation. Both help to achieve effectiveness in Christian ministry and service, and keeping them together is what is needed.

My vision is a united church, organized in a multiplicity of diverse structures, peacefully and creatively competing and cooperating to do its best in the service of Christ, and challenging all its members and non members with the power of the gospel.

9. A Practical Theology of Power for the New Malawi

Kenneth R. Ross

Midwives of Democracy

To the surprise of their friends and critics alike, the Christian churches proved to be highly effective midwives of democracy in Malawi. By common consent it was the Catholic Bishops' Pastoral Letter of Lent 1992 which broke the spell of the Banda dictatorship and awakened Malawians to the need and possibility of radical political reform.[1] Thereafter the Presbyterian-launched Public Affairs Committee became the central engine of political renewal in the period leading up to the National Referendum held in June 1993 which introduced multi-party democracy to Malawi.[2] Probably the churches surprised themselves by playing such an effective role in national politics. Certainly they were operating in uncharted waters. It is now apparent, however, that these developments in Malawi reflect a social and political reality in sub-Saharan Africa, namely that the post-independence era has seen a weakening of the state and a strengthening of the church in terms of public confidence. At independence, throughout Africa, the initiative lay with the nationalist movements which formed the first independent governments. There was considerable uncertainty as to whether the churches would survive the collapse of the Western colonialism with which they had operated hand-in-hand. What has followed is a remarkable reversal. As Terence Ranger has observed: "Even while church leaders kept their heads down, their moral standing had grown indigenous. The churches came to be seen as the only surviving institutions which ordinary people still trusted. Political institutions have lost all credibility, but ecclesiastical institutions have been gaining it."[3] The disillusionment with the one-party state coupled with great confidence in the churches which marked Malawian public life in the early 1990s therefore reflects an important development in modern African history. Whether we like it or not, amidst the demoralisation of the state and the crumbling of state institutions in many parts of Africa, the churches find themselves being expected to take responsibility for the political life of the nation. Already they have proved to have

---

[1] See *Living our Faith*, Pastoral Letter from the Catholic Bishops of Malawi, 8 March 1992; also published as *The Truth Will Set You Free* (Church in the World No. 28), London: CIIR, 1992.
[2] See K.R. Ross, "The Renewal of the State by the Church: the Case of the Public Affairs Committee in Malawi", *Religion in Malawi*, No. 5 (1995), pp. 29-37.
[3] T. Ranger, "Conference Summary and Conclusion", in P. Gifford ed., *The Christian Churches and the Democratisation of Africa*, Leiden: E.J. Brill, 1995, p. 19.

some capacity for this role as witnessed in the movement for democratisation in the early 1990s when churches throughout Africa, as in Malawi, were active "challenging political structures, urging reform, advocating political change, and even presiding over the change itself."[4] Having in many cases led the way in dismantling the dictatorship and ushering in democracy, the churches now carry a burden of expectation that they will have a positive contribution to bring to the ongoing process of democratisation. A searching question for the churches, however, is whether they have a theology of power adequate to the demands of this new situation. In this chapter we shall examine some of the key points at which questions of power and accountability arise in contemporary Malawi with a view to identifying the theological issues at stake.

"Without Remembrance, No Liberation"

It may seem rather perverse at the dawn of a new era to begin by turning attention to the past. There is an instinctive feeling that it is time to "let bygones be bygones" and bend all energies to meeting the challenges of today and tomorrow. However, as Aryeh Neier has written: "There are two crucial reasons for confronting the past. Firstly, as a civilised society we must recognise the worth and dignity of those victimized by abuses of the past. If we fail to confront what happened to them, in a sense we argue that those people do not matter, that only the future is of importance. We also perpetuate, even compound, their victimization. The second reason has to do with establishing and upholding the rule of law. It is important to send a message to the effect that everyone is subject to the law. The rank and office of those who victimized others must not be allowed to immunise or insulate them from society's efforts to confront the past."[5] In the Christian perspective these consideration are powerfully underscored by the evangelical commitment to solidarity with the oppressed and the victimized and the biblical teaching that true peace must be founded on justice. Moreover, basic to Christian experience is the conviction that the guilt of our past must be dealt with before we can enter upon a new life. Indeed the dynamic of being convicted of guilt, making confession, receiving forgiveness and absolution, experiencing cleansing and then living a life of freedom, peace and joy is the very substance of what it is to be a Christian. Hence the churches are particularly well equipped to address a national situation in Malawi which is bedevilled by a guilty past.

---

[4] P Gifford, "Introduction: Democratisation and the Churches", in Gifford ed., *The Christian Churches and the Democratisation of Africa*, p. 3.
[5] Aryeh Neier, Keynote Speech, in A. Boraine, J. Levy & R. Scheffer ed., *Dealing with the Past: Truth and Reconciliation in South Africa*, Cape Town: IDASA, 1994, p. 3.

The fact that thousands upon thousands of Malawians were terrorized, exiled, beaten, maimed, robbed, imprisoned, tortured and murdered under the Banda regime from 1964 to 1993 is one which has to be squarely faced and dealt with before there can be a true foundation on which to rebuild the national life. The extent to which Malawian politics is still preoccupied with this question was very evident in Parliamentary debates in March-April 1996. Whether to maintain or change the national flag, e.g., was a highly contentious issue. Some argued that the flag must be retained as an indication of the continuity of the nation with its beginnings at independence while others found that the flag was so strongly associated with abuses and atrocities of the Banda regime that it ought to be abandoned and replaced.[6] Until Malawians on all sides have come to terms with the guilt and shame of the past, it will be impossible for the nation to be at peace with itself and for the people to face the future with confidence. As Jose Zalaquett has indicated: "A society cannot reconcile itself on the grounds of a divided memory. Since memory is identity, this would result in a divided identity."[7]

This issue was perceived with exceptional clarity by the German philosopher Karl Jaspers when he addressed the situation in his own country at the end of World War II when Germans had to come to terms with the atrocities of the Nazi era.[8] Jaspers understood that there had to be a reckoning with guilt before the nation could rebuild: "the clarification of guilt is at the same time clarification of our new life and its possibilities. From it spring seriousness and hope."[9] He distinguished between four different yet interconnected types of guilt: criminal, political, moral and metaphysical.[10] These distinctions provide a useful grid for analysis of the guilt issue in the Malawi context. Most attention has been concentrated on the question of *criminal* guilt where individuals who have committed criminal acts are identified, brought to trial and duly punished. Amongst all the crimes against humanity perpetrated under the Banda regime the new government chose to concentrate on one particularly notorious incident: the Mwanza "accident" In 1983 four senior politicians suddenly disappeared and were found dead in a saloon vehicle in the remote border district of Mwanza. The official media reported that they had died in car accident while attempting to flee the country. On taking office

---

[6] See *Hansard*, 18-19 March 1996.
[7] J. Zalaquett, "Why Deal with the Past", in Boraine *et al.* ed., *Dealing with the Past*, p. 13.
[8] K. Jaspers, *Die Schuldfrage: Zur Politischen Haftung Deutschland*, Heidelberg: Verlagen Lambert Schneider, 1946; ET *The Question of German Guilt*, New York: The Dial Press, 1947 My reading of this seminal text is much illumined by John de Gruchy's 1993 Karl Jaspers Lecture at Oxford University; see J.W. de Gruchy, "Guilt, Amnesty and National Reconstruction: Karl Jaspers' *Die Schuldfrage* and the South African Debate", *Journal of Theology for Southern Africa*, 83 (June 1993), pp. 3-13.
[9] Jaspers, *The Question of German Guilt*, p. 119.
[10] De Gruchy, "Guilt, Amnesty and National Reconstruction" pp. 8-10.

in May 1994 the new UDF government established a Commission of Inquiry, chaired by Justice Mtegha, which found, as had long been suspected, that "the killing of the four gentlemen was by members of the Police Force. It was premeditated, brutal and diabolic.... Messrs Gadama, Matenje and Chiwanga [and Sangala] were killed by the Police on Dr Banda's orders, because Dr Banda perceived that they were aspiring for his position and that they had rebelled against him."[11] When the Report of the Commission was released early in 1995, former President Kamuzu Banda and his No. 2 John Tembo were arrested[12] and tried in the High Court with four others in a case lasting almost the whole year. Finally they were acquitted on the grounds that there was a lack of legally valid evidence.[13] The state has now appealed to the Supreme Court amid widespread frustration that no one was found responsible or made accountable for this atrocity which had stained the conscience of the nation.

At one time it seemed as if the Mwanza case would be treated as a symbolic act of national cleansing, dealing thoroughly with one of the most shocking of all the atrocities as a means of coming to terms with them all. Later in 1995 the arrests of MCP leaders who had allegedly plotted to kill the bishops at their Emergency Party Convention in 1992 suggested that a wider process of retribution may be underway.[14] Indeed on 4 July 1995 *The Nation* reported that "UDF Southern Region Governor Clement Khembo has said the UDF Government will arrest all those who committed crimes in the past irrespective of their status."[15] This, however, has not occurred and it appears that the Government is content to deal with the issue of criminal guilt by means of a few symbolic cases. So far as the Mwanza case is concerned, it is necessary to consider how far the case has "rebounded" on a nation seeking to come to terms with the atrocities of the past by means of "scapegoating". Jan Kees Van Donge has argued that the failure to pin the murders on specific suspected individuals has the effect of detracting from "the idea of a clear allocation of evil in a few and suggest that MCP rule was much more widely rooted in society. The basic problem to be faced when talking about the wrongdoing of MCP may be that one has to delineate who was not MCP those days in Malawi."[16]

---

[11] [Mtegha] Commission of Inquiry, Mwanza Road Accident Report, p. 82 #12.07, p. 84 #12.17.
[12] *The Nation*, 5 January 1995.
[13] See *Malawi News*, 23-29 December 1995.
[14] *The Nation*, 15 June 1995; the four arrested politicians were Wadson Deleza, Charles Kamphulusa, Hilda Manjamkhosi and Eliam Katola Phiri.
[15] *The Nation*, 4 July 1995.
[16] J.K. Van Donge, "The Mwanza Trial as a Search for a Usable Malawian Political Past", Social Change in Malawi Seminar, Chancellor College, 15-16 March 1996, p. 20.

This leads to the issue of what Jaspers called *political* guilt, based on the understanding that every citizen is responsible for the way he or she is governed. All Malawians, except those who actively struggled against the regime, must accept some responsibility for the atrocities committed by *their* Government. This has been recognised by the establishment of the National Compensation Tribunal through which the state will offer compensation to all who suffered unjustly under the former regime. However, there is need for more vigorous affirmative action by Government on behalf of the dispossessed and the abused if there is to be a clear confession of communal political guilt and due reparation. A good place to start may be with the Jehovah's Witnesses who were hunted, deprived of their property, driven into exile, imprisoned, beaten, sexually assaulted, dismembered and murdered.[17] Of all the groups in Malawi who were victimized under the dictatorship there are none who suffered more comprehensively and more terribly than them. A national initiative of confession and restitution to the Jehovah's Witnesses would be a good place to start in a serious reckoning with political guilt. At a deeper level lies *moral* guilt. Here Jaspers was referring to those "who knew, or could know, yet walked in ways which self-analysis reveals to them as culpable error - whether conveniently closing their eyes to events, or permitting themselves to be intoxicated, seduced or bought with personal advantages, or obeying from fear."[18] When the analysis reaches this level few can exempt themselves from responsibility for the guilty past. Finally, Jaspers invites consideration of *metaphysical* guilt, assuming that there is solidarity between people which makes all responsible for injustice: "We did not go into the streets when our Jewish friends were led away; we did not scream until we too were destroyed."[19] This analysis makes it clear that it will not be adequate to deal with guilt only at the level of those who were *criminally* guilty. There is need for a much deeper national movement of confession, repentance, forgiveness, cleansing and restitution.

If such a movement is to occur in Malawi it must begin with the compilation of a record of all the crimes against humanity which have been committed. Article 19 (the International Centre Against Censorship) made a powerful plea after the referendum of 1993 for the establishment of a "Truth Commission" which would investigate alleged atrocities of the past and make a definitive record.[20] In the event the Commission established by the new UDF Government in June 1994 had

---

[17] See K. Fiedler, *Persecution for Life: the Experience of the Jehovah's Witnesses in Malawi*, Kachere Text, forthcoming.
[18] Jaspers, *The Question of German Guilt*, pp. 63-64.
[19] *Ibid*, p. 72.
[20] *Malawi's Past: The Right to Truth*, Article 19 (International Centre Against Censorship), Issue 29, 17 November 1993.

the remit to investigate only the Mwanza "accident".[21] The idea of a Truth Commission with a much broader remit has been discussed in various fora. In July 1995 even President Muluzi and Second Vice President Chihana indicated that the government was committed to establishing a Truth Commission along the same lines as the South African one. Muluzi was quoted as saying: "When we forgive, we should know what we are forgiving."[22] Yet by mid-1996, two years into the democratic era, no serious action had been taken. Meanwhile, the danger that there might be not only amnesty but also amnesia with regard to past atrocities was highlighted by Kamuzu Banda's "apology" to the nation following his acquittal in the Mwanza trial: "During my term in office, I selflessly dedicated myself to the good cause of Mother Malawi in the fight against Poverty, Ignorance and Disease among many other issues; but if within the process, those who worked in my government or through false pretence in my name or indeed unknowingly by me, pain and suffering was caused to anybody in this country in the name of nationhood, I offer my sincere apologies. I also appeal for a spirit of reconciliation and forgiveness amongst us all."[23] This from the man who not long before had been boasting that his opponents would be "meat for the crocodiles"! No wonder the *Saturday Nation* leader column commented: "Former President Kamuzu Banda's New Year's message adds insult to injury to a nation which has long asked for an apology from the man whose rule caused untold misery to countless souls. What has been passed to the Malawian people as an apology is no such thing. The former president does not accept that he did any wrong himself, to begin with, nor does he hold an unshaken conviction that pain and suffering were indeed inflicted on innocent citizens in his name."[24] Banda's statement is a good example of how *not* to repent! It attempts *both* to play down the wrong which was inflicted *and* to deny responsibility for it. As the *Saturday Nation* concluded: "As a nation we must indeed forgive, but we must fully understand what it is we are forgiving and that is only possible if we know exactly what happened and why."[25]

Without such a process of investigation and acknowledgment there will be no convincing answer to the question of whether such things might happen again in Malawi. As John de Gruchy has warned, there is a "need to avoid confessing guilt too soon before the full enormity of the crime has been exposed, for all that does is to reduce a confession of guilt to vague generalities. A general amnesty which prevents any public exposure of the truth is a more blatant way of achieving the same end. By preventing victims from exercising forgiveness, and by glossing

---

[21] *The Nation*, 13 June 1994.
[22] *The Nation*, 24 July 1995.
[23] *Malawi News*, 6-12 January 1996.
[24] *Saturday Nation*, 6-12 January 1996.
[25] *Ibid*.

over the need for the guilty to make reparation, however, humanity cannot be regained and national reconstruction is impeded."[26] When CCAP church leaders met at Chongoni for a human rights workshop in November 1995, this was a primary concern. The proposed Truth Commission was seen as a highly important institution. Members called for it to be independent and to have authority to go "from A to Z, covering all years and all people" It was not conceived as a vindictive exercise since members were willing to allow for immunity from prosecution for those found to have done wrong. What they felt to be needed was "an honest history" without which they could not move into the future with confidence.[27] There seems to be an instinctive understanding among the Malawian people of the axiom expressed by Wolfgang Huber: "Without remembrance, no liberation."[28]

Such remembrance could perhaps be effected without the formal mechanism of a Truth Commission if other ways of recovering history were deployed. Important symbolic beginnings were made in May 1996 when the main highways in Blantyre and Mzuzu were renamed after two great national leaders who were persecuted and (either directly or indirectly) killed by the Banda regime, respectively Masauko Chipembere and Orton Chirwa.[29] President Muluzi has also appointed a "Heroes Committee" charged with responsibility to identify a Heroes Acre and arrange for the state reburial of leaders assassinated under the dictatorship such as Attati Mpakati and Mkwapatira Mhango.[30] Such initiatives play a constructive role in the formation of a true and unified national memory. However, the symbolic function of street names and a Heroes' Acre must be supported by an authoritative literature.

Little progress, however, has been made. Amnesty International and Africa Watch produced important reports when the abuses were at their height but they were hampered by the fact that it was extremely difficult to get reliable information.[31] Richard Carver, who was the researcher on Malawi at Amnesty International in the 1980s, has admitted that: "The possibilities for a free flow of information out of

---

[26] De Gruchy, "Guilt, Amnesty and National Reconstruction", p. 10.
[27] CCAP General Synod Human Rights Workshop, Chongoni, 6-10 November 1995; personal observation.
[28] Cit. D. Smit, "The Truth and Reconciliation Commission - Tentative Religious and Theological Perspectives", *Journal of Theology for Southern Africa*, 90 (March 1995), p. 3.
[29] See, e.g., *Malawi News*, 25-31 May 1996.
[30] See, e.g., *The Nation*, 25 April 1996.
[31] See *Malawi: Human Rights Violations 25 Years After Independence*, London: Amnesty International, 1989; *Where Silence Rules: The Suppression of Dissent in Malawi*, Washington and London: Africa Watch, 1990; *Malawi: Prison Conditions, Cruel Punishment and Detention Without Trial*, London: Amnesty International, 1992.

the country were extremely limited.... From the early 1980s we focussed on the case of Orton and Vera Chirwa, and then later on in the decade, on the case of Jack Mapanje. These were well-known people at the international level about whom we could campaign, using them as a way of drawing attention to broader abuses of human rights in Malawi of which we had very little detailed evidence. It was not until from about 1988 onwards that we began to gather more extensive and reliable information about political detention for example."[32] Exiled medical doctor John Lwanda in 1993 published his dossier of the abuses and atrocities of the Banda regime but this record was compiled in Glasgow and supplies very limited detail.[33] The free press which emerged in the 1993-94 period contained many personal testimonies to suffering inflicted by the state and reports of cases where the courts awarded damages to plaintiffs who complained of unwarranted injury. The ephemeral nature of the newspapers, however, limits what they can offer in terms of a comprehensive stock-taking of abuses inflicted on the innocent. There is no sign of the emergence of a "Malawian Elie Wiesel" able to muster the determination and the resources necessary to chronicle the human rights abuses perpetrated by the Banda regime.

The implementation of the constitutional provision for a National Compensation Tribunal has been the most important state initiative to address the problem of the sufferings inflicted by the Banda regime. Any citizens who believe they were unjustly subjected to suffering or deprivation may make their case before the Compensation Tribunal which has powers to award financial recompense, to be effected by the state. The Tribunal will sit in every district in the country so that it is readily accessible to all potential complainants. This is clearly an initiative of major importance. It gives to victims of oppression the opportunity to "clear their names", to receive an official recognition that they did nothing wrong and that indeed it was the state which was in the wrong in taking action against them. The Tribunal has the great strength that it is specifically mandated to make reparation to those who suffered unjustly. Though the amounts which are paid may often fail to match the scale of the suffering inflicted, yet so long as they have some substantial value they will have both symbolic and practical importance. The repentance of the nation concerning the guilt of the past would not be serious without an earnests endeavour to make reparation to those who suffered. At this point the National Compensation Tribunal is well placed to play a critical role. At the same time, it is subject to certain limitations. It will hear the cases only of

---

[32] Richard Carver in J. Lewis, P Owens & L. Pirouet eds., *Human Rights and the Making of Constitutions: Malawi, Kenya, Uganda*, University of Cambridge African Studies Centre, 1995, p. 106.
[33] J.L. Lwanda, *Kamuzu Banda of Malawi: A Study in Promise, Power and Paralysis*, Glasgow: Dudu Nsomba Publications, 1993.

those who apply to be heard. It will hear the cases only of those who are alive (though there is provision for dependents of deceased persons to make claims). Its restriction to a compensatory function will limit how far it will go in uncovering the truth about the recent past. Its greatest weakness is that it may amount to a "privatising" of the problem. The matter is reduced to a number of injured persons who may individually be compensated at the discretion of the Tribunal. This tends to evade the communal or national dimensions of the problem. There is more than a line of individuals deserving compensation. There is a nation, a people, requiring to come to terms with itself and its past. A public Commission with official powers remains the most likely means of resolving this issue but doubts remain as to whether too many government ministers with skeletons in the cupboard would resist the appointment of such a Commission.

A remaining possibility is that the churches, together with other religious communities, could be given responsibility for the exercise. Churches would have the advantage of being non-partisan and, since they are in the business of forgiveness, they would not be so readily open to the suspicion of witchhunting. Churches and religious communities, furthermore, would have the institutional capacity to hold hearings in every village and every community. Just as the churches were highly effective in mobilising the population for the Referendum and General Election, so they could use their organisation and influence to make a success of a nationwide Truth Commission. Having chronicled the story of guilt "from A to Z", churches and religious communities would then be well-placed to lead the nation in a concrete act of repentance. The church would repent, first, not on behalf of others but on its own account, recognising, as Misanjo Kansilanga has done, that "the silence of the church was costly to thousands of Malawians who lost their lives and spent their time in prison."[34] At the same time, the church's own contrition could be the vehicle for the repentance of the nation as a whole. This could be done not only at the level of a "National Service of Worship" but at services in every village where those who suffered, those who sinned against them and those who were guiltily silent could come together to confess, repent, forgive, be reconciled and move forward into the future. Such an exercise is important not only for the guilty who need to confess and repent but also for the victims of past repression who are still wounded and grieving and who need to forgive and be reconciled.

Such an exercise will be painful and it is not surprising that many seek to avoid it. The church, however, is called to bear witness to the reality that without the pain of "death" to the old self there is no newness of life. The church stands under an

---

[34] Rev M.E. Kansilanga, address on "Church and Politics in Malawi Today" at CCAP General Synod Human Rights Training Workshop, Chongoni, 8 November 1995.

evangelical obligation to call for and enable the public telling of truth which makes possible an authentic confession of guilt, a true offer of forgiveness and a genuine reconciliation. Furthermore, the church as an "expert in repentance" has the capacity to call for a serious movement of reparation and restitution. The gospel story of Zaccheus tells us very vividly that no repentance is complete without restitution. The wrongs committed have to be put right, as far as possible. Where property has been stolen, it must be returned. Where injury has been inflicted, there must be compensation. Where a good name has been slandered, there must be apology. The nation may pay dearly if communal repentance is neglected. As John de Gruchy has written: "to repress the demons of the past inevitably means the bedevilment of the future."[35] If democracy in Malawi is to succeed it must be built on a foundation where the problems of the past have been faced and dealt with. Without such an exercise there will be no cleansing of power, people will remain suspicious of power and it will be just as liable to be abused in the future as it has been in the past. In the Christian perspective there is no transformation without repentance. Whatever the institutional arrangements, the churches have a theological obligation to bring this perspective vigorously to bear on Malawian public life at the dawn of a democratic era.

Confronting the Spectre of Regionalism

From colonial times Malawi has been divided administratively into Northern, Central and Southern Regions, each with its own cultural, ethnic, linguistic, religious and political identity. These divisions had been transcended in the formation of the nationalist movement in the 1940s and 1950s which, finally organised as the Malawi Congress Party, succeeded in achieving independence in 1964.[36] Almost immediately, however, this national unity was fragmented as Prime Minister Banda, with his own authority under threat, opted to play the tribal-regional card and to attempt to maintain his highly authoritarian rule by means of a hegemony of his own Chewa-speaking people of the Central Region.[37] While the substantial issue in the Cabinet crisis was the nature of government, it could not escape notice that the ousted ministers came either from the north: Chirwa, Chisiza and Chiume; or from the south: Bwanausi, Chipembere and Chokani. Nor that "the repression which followed the break-up of the cabinet was

---

[35] De Gruchy, *Christianity and Democracy*, p. 217
[36] See A.C. Ross, "Some Reflections on the Malawi 'Cabinet Crisis', 1964-65", unpublished paper, p. 13.
[37] See K.R. Ross, "Christian Faith and National Identity: the Malawi Experience", *Journal of Theology for Southern Africa*, No. 93 (December 1995), pp. 55-57; also C.W. Chirwa, "The Politics of Ethnicity and Regionalism in Contemporary Malawi", *African Rural and Urban Studies*, Vol. 1 No. 2 (1994), pp. 100-108.

clearly directed by region. Chiefs from both the Northern and Southern Regions were dismissed but none from the Central Region. Likewise a majority of regional councils in both the Northern and Southern Regions were dissolved - but again none from the Central Region."[38] This set the scene for a political dispensation in which the ruling party continued to employ the language and symbols of the nationalist movement while attempting to establish a hegemony of the Chewa-speaking people of the Central Region.[39]

This took effect not only politically but also culturally, as everyone was compelled to accept Banda's Chewa-oriented version of Malawian tradition. The imposition of "Chichewa" as the national language in 1968 has brought, according to the recent assessment of Pascal Kishindo, "brutalization and humiliation of their language" to the various ethno-linguistic groups which do not have Chinyanja/ Chichewa as their mother tongue.[40] Paul Zeleza has noted the effect which this powerful hegemony had on culture and creativity:

> Banda's regime waged an endless war against plurality, against voices that told different stories or sang different songs, stories or songs that did not glorify the everlasting king's infinite wisdom, ululate the miraculous development the country was supposed to be undergoing, and wonder at its stability, its enviable peace and calm, law and order in a region wrecked by revolutions, wars, poverty and decay.... He had united the people, so that there were no more Chewas, Tumbukas, Lomwes, Yaos, no regionalism, no poor and no rich, just Malawians, one big homogeneous family, under the guidance of the eternal patriarch. An undifferentiated people needed undifferentiated stories. What they wrote, sang, read, thought and dreamt had to be placed under constant surveillance. Censorship was for the public good. It was a protective mantle for a young nation, a juvenile people.[41]

There could be no maturity for the nation, however, so long as differences were denied and submerged in the interests of a political and cultural hegemony serving the interests of a small, select ruling elite. Indeed, for all its apparent dominance, Banda's regime was sowing the seeds of its own destruction by its cultural and

---

[38] *Where Silence Rules*, An Africa Watch Report, p. 57.
[39] This has been convincingly documented and demonstrated in L. Vail and L. White, "Tribalism in the Political History of Malawi", in L. Vail ed., *The Creation of Tribalism in Southern Africa*, London: James Currey and Los Angeles: University of California Press, 1989, pp. 151-192.
[40] P. Kishindo, "The Impact of a National Language on Minority Languages: The Case of Malawi", *Journal of Contemporary African Studies*, Vol. 12 No. 2 (1994), p. 141.
[41] P.T. Zeleza, "Totalitarian Power and Censorship in Malawi" *Southern Africa Political and Economic Monthly*, Vol. 8 No. 11 (August 1995), p. 33.

political marginalization of wide sections of the people of Malawi. The time would come when they would reassert themselves.

In crude regionalistic terms the multi-party movement of 1992-94 can be interpreted as the North and the South striking back against the Centre! Moreover, while the two powerful opposition parties sought to be national movements it soon became apparent that Aford was predominantly a northern party while the UDF was predominantly southern. This was borne out in the results of the 1994 General Election when each of the three regions gave overwhelming support to the party with which it identified. In the presidential election, Chakufwa Chihana of Aford took 85% of votes in the Northern Region against his 8% in the Centre and 7% in the South; Kamuzu Banda of the MCP got nearly 70% of the votes in the Central Region against his 16% in the South and 9% in the North; Bakili Muluzi of UDF got 75% of votes in the Southern Region against his 23% in the Centre and 7% in the North.[42] It could be argued that UDF won the election simply because the Southern Region is the most populous! The problem of national unity now came into the open as an urgent political issue.[43] So much so that Aford and the MCP, sworn enemies hitherto, were able to justify their sudden and short-lived alliance on the grounds of the need to secure national unity.[44] It was the same concern which convinced President Muluzi that he must have a Vice-President from each of the other regions and led to the controversial creation of the office of 2nd Vice President for Chakufwa Chihana. There was a real danger that politicians would regard their accountability in regional terms. National political life in the post-election period often appeared to be no more than a contest between competing regional power blocks. There is no sign of the emergence of a truly national political party. It remains to be seen whether the exercise of power can be conditioned by a sense of national identity and national accountability.

The churches, through PAC, had earlier provided a rallying point for a united national movement. However, the churches themselves were seriously compromised by regionalism. This was most apparent in the Presbyterian Church where the Nkhoma Synod of the Central Region took a line which suggested that its political loyalty came before its ecclesiastical unity with the other Synods.[45] In 1992, when the other church leaders were making their risky and costly prophetic

---

[42] *Daily Times*, 20 May 1994.

[43] See, e.g., *Daily Times*, 19 May 1994; *The Enquirer*, 21-24 May 1994.

[44] See, e.g., *The Monitor*, 29 June 1994; *The New Express*, 30 June 1994.

[45] The Nkhoma Synod grew out of a mission established in 1889 by the South African Dutch Reformed Church. There have always been tensions between Nkhoma and the Synods of Scottish Presbyterian origin - Blantyre in the south and Livingstonia in the north - but they have been ecclesiastically united in the Church of Central Africa Presbyterian since 1926.

social witness, the Nkhoma Synod acted in solidarity with the MCP government. The other churches felt betrayed that Nkhoma appeared to be lining up against them in the struggle for justice and truth in Malawi. This led to the Nkhoma Synod being suspended from membership of the Christian Council of Malawi in November 1992.[46] This did not deter the Synod from working hand in hand with the MCP to resist the advance of the forces of political change. During worship services the pastors often admonished the people to vote against any sort of political change and pronounced the Banda regime to be ordained of God.[47] In Dowa anyone who was suspected of sympathising with the multi-party movement was excommunicated from the membership of the church.[48] Clearly the churches had not been immune from the regional fragmentation which was the legacy of the Banda years. Nevertheless, however imperfectly, the churches had also been able to act as the custodians of national unity. It was notable that the Pastoral Letter of 1992 drew its power in part from the fact that the Bishops were able to appeal to the need to "guarantee the progress of *the nation.*"[49] Likewise PAC was concerned to explain to the government that it was concerned with "*national* issues affecting all aspects of the lives of the citizens of this country."[50] The churches had the capacity to affirm a sense of national identity and to establish a sense of national accountability. In the aftermath of the General Election this was strongly expressed by the popular musician Paul Banda in his song *Tiime Pamodzi* (Let us stand together). Here the fragmentation is understood as the work of the devil while the Christian faith is presented as a resource for fostering national unity.[51] A sense of accountability to God can serve to relativize regional loyalties and thus orient the exercise of power to national responsibility.

The extent of the churches' ability to contribute to the resolution of this problem may well be determined by the success or failure of their own struggle for unity among themselves in the Gospel. One important crucible in which the attempt to move beyond regionalism will be made is the General Synod of the CCAP. It is more than coincidence that the Blantyre, Nkhoma and Livingstonia Synods are identified with the regional power-blocs which have brought a dangerous political fragmentation to Malawian national life. For reasons of mission history the southern Blantyre Synod is ethnically composed of predominantly Yao and Mang'anja, the central Nkhoma Synod is composed of predominantly Chewa, and the northern Livingstonia Synod is composed of predominantly Ngoni and

---

[46] *Daily Times*, 6 November 1992.
[47] G. Chigona, Research Notes on interviews conducted at Madisi, 29-30 November 1994.
[48] *Ibid.*
[49] *Living our Faith*, p. 8, my italics.
[50] Rev M.E. Kansilanga to Hon B. Bisani, 12 October 1992, my italics.
[51] Paul Banda, *Zikomo Ambuye*, (cassette tape), I Y Productions, 1994.

Tumbuka. Presbyterian Christians have to face the question of how far these tribal and geographical divisions inhibit the development of a real centre of ecclesiastical unity in the General Synod, which is widely considered to be "very ineffective".[52] It may be that the CCAP can give a lead to the nation by implementing the recent recommendation of the visiting team from the World Alliance of Reformed Churches: "The process of closer cooperation and unity among the Synods calls for the writing of a constitution for the General Synod which will make it effective and empowering it in the life and mission of the CCAP."[53] It is regrettable to observe, however, that CCAP leaders have become adept at talking about the need for greater unity as a substitute for doing anything about it! By settling for a federalism which is based on inter-regional suspicion the CCAP actively contributes to the division of the country.

While the CCAP has remained one church, this has too often been achieved by settling for "cheap unity" as opposed to "costly unity". A recent World Council of Churches Report explains the difference: "Cheap unity avoids morally contested issues because they would disturb the unity of the church. Costly unity is discovering the churches' unity as a gift of pursuing justice and peace.... Costly unity is precisely to transcend loyalty to blood and soil, nation and ethnic or class heritage in the name of the God who is one and whose creation is one.... Its enemy is cheap unity - forgiveness without repentance, baptism without discipleship, life without daily dying and rising in a household of faith that is to be the visible sign of God's desire for the whole inhabited earth."[54] The evangelical challenge this brings to the ecclesiastical polity is that it must find means of demonstrating that regional differences are dissolved in the waters of baptism. This does not mean that our distinctive origins and identity are destroyed. Deep in all of our hearts is a sense of belonging in a particular area and among a particular people. This is a gift of God for which we give thanks! God did not make us to be rootless drifters - it is good to belong! But the question is: how do we regard those who belong to another family, another tribe, another region? Are they a threat to be countered? Or can we rejoice in the differences that distinguish us from other people? Can we reach out to join hands with them to celebrate the marvellous diversity of the nation God has given us? The struggle within the CCAP at this point may prove to be the make-or-break of Malawi's endeavour to sustain a viable sense of national identity and unity.

---

[52] See, e.g., comments of Synod representatives to WARC representatives, July 1995, Report of Pastoral Team Visit to the Church of Central Africa Presbyterian (CCAP), Malawi, 30 June-3 July 1995, Geneva: World Alliance of Reformed Churches, 1995, p. 3.
[53] Ibid, p. 5.
[54] T.F. Best and W. Granberg-Michaelson ed., *Costly Unity: Koinonia and Justice. Peace and Creation*, Geneva: WCC, 1993, pp. 9-10.

The extent to which the church is a site of struggle on this issue was demonstrated in the Synod of Blantyre during 1995. The issue of women's rights brought out the worst in the Synod when the Report of the Commission of Inquiry into the women's march recommended *inter alia* that "Dr Isabel Phiri should be told not to interfere with the affairs of Blantyre Synod and if she has got some knowledge should go and propagate that gospel in Nkhoma Synod where she is hailing from."[55] This was addressed to a person who was baptised in the Synod of Blantyre and was a practising member of a Synod of Blantyre congregation![56] Such a comment revealed how close to the surface lies a sense of alienation from people of different ethnic and regional origin. Yet the very same Synod which experienced that moment of shame, later in 1995 offered to the nation a very bright sign of hope in the struggle against regionalism. This was the remarkable outcome of the election of a new General Secretary for the Synod.[57] The successful candidate, Rev Misanjo Kansilanga, was distinguished by the fact that he comes originally from Lilongwe District in the Central Region. Yet the Synod placed him at its helm, something that would evidently be unthinkable in any of the main political parties! This election gave a prophetic lead to the nation, demonstrating that there is a unity and mutual confidence which reaches deeper than regional differences. The Synod did not reach that position without a struggle but it showed that, while regionalism is a powerful threat to unity in church and nation, it is not invincible.

The church must also draw deeply on its theological resources to address the issue of regionalism. The heart of the church's faith is the mutual relationality within the life of God which it describes as the Trinity. This profound reality came to be described in Christian thought as *perichoresis* the mutual indwelling and interpenetration of Father, Son and Holy Spirit in the glorious triune life of God. This dynamism of mutual constitutiveness, furthermore, is not only characteristic of God but also of the world which God has made! God's creating and redeeming love gives to the world what Colin Gunton has described as "a perichoretic reality which in different ways reflects within the structures of the temporal and spatial the *perichoresis* which is God in eternity."[58] One of the temporal and spatial structures which is called to such *perichoresis* is the nation. It means that the

---

[55] Report of Commission of Inquiry on Women's Demonstration, Blantyre Synod, February 1995, p. 8.
[56] Isabel Apawo Phiri, An Appeal Against the Commission of Inquiry, 21 April 1995, p. 1.
[57] Meeting of Blantyre Synod, Chilema Lay Training Centre, 22 August 1995, personal observation.
[58] C.E. Gunton, *The One, the Three and the Many: God, Creation and the Culture of Modernity*, Cambridge: Cambridge University Press, 1993, p. 179.

identity of the nation is secured not by the hegemony of a unitary centre of control. Rather, it is found within the *perichoresis* which enables each constituent part to be what it truly is. The fact that the nation contains those who are different from "us" is not a threat to be countered. On the contrary it is a call to find our being in reciprocal relatedness with our neighbour. It is fallacious to suppose that tribal and ethnic identity is necessarily antithetical to national identity.[59] The very awareness of diversity has the potential to become the sense of reciprocal relatedness in which true humanity is to be found. Of course, it *can be* developed in another direction which *is* subversive of national identity   as was well-illustrated by Dr Banda's attempts from 1964 to 1992 to manipulate nationalist ideology so as to entrench structures of domination favourable to the Chewa at the expense of others. The fact that a viable sense of nationhood survived that experience is indicative of the fact that there remains hope of something better. At the dawn of a new era perhaps that may be found in an understanding that ethnic and regional identities are not subversive of but rather *constitutive of* the identity of the nation.[60] From the perspective of Christian faith we are able to hold forth a vision of an enabling nationhood where each constituent part becomes what it distinctively is through its reciprocal relatedness to the others. Diverse identities within the national life are not then a threat to be crushed by the sledgehammer of homogenization. Rather they are the means through which the nation may bring to fruition the fullness of its rich multicultural potential.[61] The challenge to the church is how far it reflects in its own life and witness this profound reality at the heart of its trinitarian faith which is urgently needed to counter the scourge of regionalism and secure the unity and viability of the nation.

A Re-definition of Politics

There can be no disputing the fact that there has been a vast increase in the accountability of those in power in Malawi between 1992 and 1994. The Life President has been replaced by a State President elected to serve for five years with a maximum of two terms. The executive authority of the Presidency is balanced by a careful separation of powers in which serious attempts have been made to secure

---

[59] The possibility of "multiple choices of identity" in the Malawian context has been discussed recently in W.C. Chirwa, "Regionalism, Ethnicity and the National Question in Malawi," *Southern Africa Political and Economic Monthly (SAPEM)*, Vol. 8 Nos. 3-4 (December 1994/January 1995), pp. 59-62.

[60] Pascal Kishindo has argued along these lines in relation to the language question: "There is a need to adopt language policies that can take into account multicultural and ethnolinguistic groupings which make up the state in order to create a truly national unit that can effectively contribute to the overall development of the country." Kishindo, "The Impact of a National Language on Minority Languages" p. 142.

[61] See further Ross, "Christian Faith and National Identity: the Malawi Experience" pp. 61-62.

the integrity of the legislature and the judiciary. All officers must operate within the constraints of the constitution which was provisionally implemented after the 1994 General Election and was ratified by Parliament, with minor amendments, in May 1995. There is a parliamentary opposition which offers vociferous criticism of the government. There is a free press and, while some newspapers remain highly partisan, others are achieving an impressive level of independence and impartiality. All political detainees have been freed and all exiles are permitted to return. Academic freedom is assured to the University. There are active "watchdog" organisations, such as the Civil Liberties Commission and the Foundation for Justice, Peace and the Integrity of Creation, which publicize alleged abuses of human rights and any failure to meet the requirements of the constitution. An Ombudsman has been appointed to whom appeal can be made by citizens who believe that their rights have not been duly respected. The activity of the churches in the public arena has sustained that sense of political life being accountable to the standards of the kingdom of God which was introduced so dramatically with the issue of the 1992 Pastoral Letter.[62] It was striking that when Bakili Muluzi accepted the office of President he immediately invited the churches to offer correction to his government whenever it might stray from the path.[63] Compare this with the situation of two years earlier when one individual enjoyed absolute power, Parliament was a rubber stamp, the law courts were politically manipulated, the press was government controlled and used as an organ for propaganda, any suspected dissident was detained or assassinated, and the witness of the churches was silenced. A transformation indeed!

Nevertheless, democratisation in Malawi is far from complete. A serious question remains as to how far politics has been returned to the people, as opposed to being the domain of a chosen elite who are supposed to have a monopoly of all wisdom. Popular participation in political life remains very limited. As John Minnis has commented: "The party tends to be seen as *the* site of politics, the source of political truth and wisdom; the people, on the other hand, are viewed as being politically immature and in need of 'education' Is this not fundamentally a trait of the colonial legacy? People are seen as incapable of correct and responsible thought; there is no positive need for the parties to find out what the people are actually thinking because they know what is best for the people. The people, of course, are expected to think as the parties tell them."[64] There has been little

---

[62] It was striking to read a front-page headline in *The Nation* of 14 February 1995: "Church Quiet on Mwanza Saga." When it is front-page news that the church is quiet there can be little doubt that its role has dramatically changed!

[63] *The Nation*, 23 May 1994.

[64] J.R. Minnis, "Can Civil Society be a Force for Political Change in Malawi?" Paper presented at Conference on Social Change in Malawi, Chancellor College, 30 June 1995, p. 12.

recognition that a multi-party state may not be the complete answer to the popular cry for democracy. Perhaps a more testing question is that of how far Malawi has gone in the direction of developing "civil society"? Only small beginnings have been made in the formation of civil associations through which people may take the initiative in shaping public policy. Minnis suggests that "There is a vicious circle at work here: a genuine democratic transition requires the mobilization of a demanding civil society, yet how can the poor and the illiterate organize and participate in such a mobilization when they are ignorant of their political rights?"[65]

Here it is of note that the UDF government, while allowing impressive freedom of the press has kept the national radio on a tight rein and has used it to broadcast propaganda not totally unlike that of the old regime! When Johan Fritz of the International Press Institute conducted a survey of Africa in July 1995 he concluded that only four countries possessed a truly free press - South Africa, Namibia, Botswana and (remarkably!) Malawi. This assessment was qualified, however, by the observation that: "In countries such as Uganda, Tanzania, Malawi and Zimbabwe where governments tolerate an independent press while maintaining a tight control over the electronic media, the rural population which has no access to newspapers - is deprived of responsible and reliable information."[66] The development of a healthy democracy in Malawi will depend on the national broadcasting corporation being liberalized sufficiently to become an agent which will stimulate the emergence of the institutions of civil society and promote popular political participation. This can only be achieved, however, through a redefinition of politics which breaks the "top-down" thinking inherited from the colonial era and promotes a "bottom-up" mobilization of the whole community to take responsibility for its social and economic destiny.

Such a re-definition is urgently needed in order to address a related problem which was well described on the eve of the General Election by Felix Mnthali, an exiled Malawian who is Professor of English at the University of Botswana:

> What some of us find patently disheartening in our present game of politics is the ease with which important issues on which the forthcoming election might have been fought are relegated to the sidelines. There is no discussion of the direction which our woefully small economy should be taking. There has never been any debate about how our once breath-taking environment might be restored to something at least close to its pristine glory. Our population growth is surprised only by our fecundity and neither has it been the subject

---

[65] *Ibid*, p. 13.
[66] *Mail and Guardian* (South Africa), 4-10 August 1995.

> of any serious political debate even in the face of a shrinking economy unable to keep up with this ever rising population. The pressure on our precious and scarce little land is becoming unbearable. Our natural forests are gone and with them have gone those good rains on which our much vaunted agricultural success depended. We watch no debates about the efforts needed towards the expansion of our present minuscule industrial base. There have been no debates about the improvements needed by our educational system to enable it to cope with any degree of serious industrialization or indeed with any type of leap into the twenty-first century. These and many other problems would appear to be infinitely more rewarding, more fascinating and more exciting to your average voter that those personality contests with their attendant muckraking on which our politicians and our newspapers seem to be lavishing their time and their resources these days.[67]

Two years after the General Election Malawian politics has not yet risen to the challenge issued by Mnthali. Political debate still appears too often to be concerned with petty point-scoring rather than attempting to grapple with the very serious issues facing the country.

As far as the political structures needed for effective democracy are concerned, fears remain that still too much power is invested in the office of the President. This has been reflected even in the President's conduct of his office. While he has adopted a much more realistic and down-to-earth style than his predecessor, he has also displayed a tendency to imagine that he can rule simply by decree. This was evident as early as the day he assumed office when he announced to a packed stadium that a number of prisons were to be closed and that the New State House in Lilongwe was to be converted into a Parliament building.[68] The latter pronouncement was made without Parliament itself being consulted and proved to be quite impractical. Another Presidential decision which aroused serious concern was his appointment of Chakufwa Chihana as 2nd Vice-President at a time when there was no constitutional provision for such a position.[69] He evidently imagined he had authority to act in this way and was challenged only by a small group of concerned citizens who decided to take him to court for breach of the constitution.[70] Another key issue arose when MCP leaders were arrested on murder charges following the release of the Mwanza Commission's Report. There were fears that the independence of the judiciary was being compromised by government interference in the case. This even went to the extent of a ministerial

---

[67] Felix Mnthali, "The Secret of our Apathy" *The Nation*, 18 April 1994.
[68] *The Nation*, 23 May 1994.
[69] *Daily Times*, 29 September 1995.
[70] *The Nation*, 14 November 1994.

team travelling to the UK to hire prosecution lawyers - something they should have known was not permitted under the new constitution.[71] The idea of the separation of powers was taking root only slowly and tendencies to authoritarianism and unaccountability in government have by no means been eradicated. It is striking to notice that the 50 resolutions passed at the National Constitutional Conference held in Lilongwe from 20 to 24 February 1995 were mostly concerned to limit the powers of the President and to strengthen the Legislature. Yet this popular concern was brushed aside in Parliament which took no heed of the Conference's rejection of the office of 2nd Vice President and its call for a Senate or Upper House of Parliament to be established.[72]

The distance between government and people at this point was evident again in April 1996 when newly designed banknotes were released bearing President Muluzi's portrait and were received with almost universal disgust.[73] While one may appreciate the concern of those in government to have a strong and effective centralised leadership structure, this may lead once again to a Presidency and a government which lack accountability to the people. A particular disappointment is that, rather than opting for the simplicity and austerity which would have signalled a contrasting approach to the use of political power, President Muluzi took over the palaces, the private plane and much of the pomp and circumstance of the Banda regime. Much popular concern has been focused on the conspicuous consumption and suspected corruption of government ministers and others entrusted with high office. Democratization has evidently done little to challenge the "gravy train" mentality inherited from the colonial and one-party periods in which access to resources was centrally controlled and political involvement a matter of bettering oneself through the patronage of the powerful. The most common complaint against the Muluzi government is that its members are using the resources of the state to enrich themselves. Why have the champions of democracy been so lacking in commitment to transformation at this point?

An underlying problem is the tradition of political messianism bequeathed by the Banda era. Ascribing messianic qualities to Banda was at first no more than a calculated tactic to unite and inspire the people in the struggle for national independence. However, it allowed Banda to develop the highly autocratic leadership style and the egotistical brand of oratory which was to be the hallmark of government in Malawi for thirty years. In religious terms Dr Banda was under-

---

[71] *The Nation*, 24 January 1995. The government defended its action by arguing that it merely sought legal advice from British sources.

[72] See Jande Banda, "Aspects of Current Constitutional Change Debate in Malawi" Paper presented at Social Change in Malawi Conference, Chancellor College, 1 July 1995, pp. 12-13.

[73] Personal observation, April 1996.

stood to be the man sent by God to lead the nation. It was a religious duty to give thanks to God for his leadership and to pray for the long life of the *Ngwazi*. Even during the referendum campaign the Nkhoma Synod pastors often applied to Banda the text in Mark 9:7 where God says: "This is my son whom I love; listen to him!" Their message was that people who feared God were bound to support the divinely anointed leader who was identified as Dr Banda.[74] A major question is whether the reform movement can succeed in changing the political idiom or whether it will simply have substituted one political messiah for another. An analysis of the popular songs which promoted political change in Ntaja suggests that the messianic character which had earlier been ascribed to Dr Banda was transferred to Mr Muluzi.[75] *Abale kodi mwamva*, e.g., is a song which emphasizes that it is God who has chosen Mr Muluzi to rule Malawi and that all godly people are obliged to vote for him.[76] Another composition entitled *Kongeresi ife avi* suggests that since God is punishing the Malawi Congress Party no God-fearing person will want to be associated with that party.[77] Another song takes the Christological text "The stone which the builders rejected has become the cornerstone" and uses it to interpret the political career of Bakili Muluzi.[78] It can be observed that here the messiah has changed but the messianic political idiom has remained intact. Looking to the north of the country there is again a different messiah but the same idiom. When Chakufwa Chihana was released from prison at the time of the national referendum he was addressed in these terms by the General Secretary of the Synod of Livingstonia: "We believe that you, like Gideon of old, have been called to deliver us and lead us into a new and just way of living.... We are delighted that you are out of prison, for your own sake and that of your family, but also for the sake of AFORD which has been 'rudderless' in your absence. For many of us, our patience with AFORD has been wearing thin, but we have stayed with it because of the trust and confidence we have in you as a leader."[79]

On all sides it seemed that the solution to all political problems was the great leader! It was understandable that readers of *The Nation* chose Bakili Muluzi as "Man of the Year" for 1994 but to choose him again for 1995 suggests that somehow people are still in thrall to the "great man."[80] It has proved to be a

---

[74] G. Chigona, Research Notes on interviews conducted at Madisi, 29-30 November 1994.

[75] G. Chigona, Research Notes on interviews conducted at Ntaja, 23 November 1994.

[76] *Ibid*.

[77] *Ibid*.

[78] G. Chigona, Research Notes on interviews conducted at Ntaja, 24 November 1994; cf. I Peter 2:7

[79] Rev Dr O.P Mazunda to Mr Chakufwa Chihana, 23 June 1993.

[80] See *The Nation*, 2 January 1996.

harder task than was first supposed to emerge from the decades of dictatorship and to move towards a more mature political life. In fact, a major disappointment of the democratic era has been the extent to which "personality politics" still prevails, albeit in a more open and freely contested public arena. As John Minnis has recently commented: "Political discourse, as evident in newspaper accounts and public utterances of various kinds is narrow in focus, sensationalist, and largely preoccupied with the day-to-day machinations and exploits of particular politicians.... Political leaders spend an inordinate amount of time jockeying for position in ways which promote their personal ambitions. Changing party allegiance is commonplace in the quest for self-aggrandizement. Thus the major parties appear to be monopolizing not only the political space, but are defining the very parameters of political discourse in sectarian terms when they should be doing just the opposite."[81] The redefinition of politics required in Malawi must address the problem of the political messianism and the concomitant personality politics which inhibit popular participation and the emergence of authentic democracy.

Such an exercise will be concerned not only to come to terms with the legacy of colonialism but also to re-examine the understanding of politics and power derived from the African tradition. One of the devices used by the Banda regime to entrench its power was to create a mystique around the person of the leader. This drew heavily on the African tradition where there is an identification between the chief and the ancestors through which the ruler derives legitimacy and authority. Indeed the entire prevailing political structure is given formidable ideological support and legitimation. As Kwame Bediako explains: the "crucial role of ancestors in traditional political organization means that beyond sacralizing the office of the ruler, it is the whole realm of politics as of society itself which is sacralized, since the traditional world view makes no sharp dichotomy between 'secular' and 'sacred' realms of existence, while in the traditional perspective too, the concept of the state is inclusive of the living and the ancestors. Consequently, the institutions of political and social organisation themselves acquire a sacral character, through their association with ancestors."[82] Kamuzu Banda sought to capitalize on this tradition, blending the executive authority of the President of a modern state with the traditional conception of the ancestor-founder of the nation. Central to the rhetoric of the MCP regime was the claim that Banda was "father and founder" of the nation. He was the *Ngwazi* the epic Conqueror, the *Mpulumutsi* the Saviour from whom came all good things, the President *Wamuyaya* - the one who would rule forever. Such language drew heavily on the identification between the ruler and the ancestors and invested Banda's Presidency with a sacral character. The problem was that the one-party state failed to provide

---

[81] Minnis, "Can Civil Society be a Force for Political Change in Malawi?", p. 12.

[82] Bediako, "De-sacralization and Democratization", p. 8.

the kind of checks and balances which would have limited the abuse of power in the traditional context. As Harri Englund has noted:

> From at least the sixteenth century onwards, the Maravi chieftaincies, which were to give the name to the Malawi nation, evinced many obstacles to centralisation. The matrilineal succession of subordinate headmen endowed villages with some autonomy and made loyalty to the Paramount Chief a matter of constant negotiation. Moreover, the all-male secret society *nyau* and the territorial rain shrines had officials of their own, who also represented, usually, a power base distinct from the Paramount Chief.[83]

Likewise Jacob Kumwenda has observed that among the Nkhonde there was a careful balance of power between *Kyungu* (the chief) and his councillors which included their responsibility to kill him when he became too old or sick or confused.[84]

An important role was also played by the "praise poet" who was licensed to offer, in poetry and song, criticism of the leadership.[85] While Banda adopted the tradition of the praise song, Jack Mapanje was quick to notice that "what the new praise song lacks is an element of constructive criticism of either the leadership or the society."[86] Mapanje's poetry may be read as his attempt to fulfil the wish he expressed in 1974 that "what we would like to see is a critical praise-poem to bring about sanity where it is rare to find."[87] Mapanje's imprisonment in 1987

---

[83] H. Englund, "Between God and Kamuzu: The Transition to Multi-Party Politics in Central Malawi", unpublished paper, 1995, p. 3. See also J.M. Schoffeleers, *River of Blood: the Genesis of a Martyr Cult in Southern Malawi, c. A.D. 1600*, Madison: University of Wisconsin Press, 1992, pp. 44-48.

[84] J.K. Kumwenda, "Livingstonia Mission: Challenges for Change. Welfare and Development in the Northern Region of Malawi", M.Th., University of Edinburgh, 1995, p. 60. Similarly, Christo Lombard observes that Shona tradition "knew figures such as the *muzukuru* who could ridicule the leader in public, as well as the ritual killing of inefficient old kings." J. Hunter & C. Lombard eds., *Multi-Party Democracy, Civil Society and Economic Transformation in Southern Africa*, Windhoek, SAUSSC, 1992, p. 7.

[85] See L. Vail & L. White, *Power and the Praise Poem: Southern African Voices in History*, Charlottesville: University Press of Virginia; London: James Currey, 1991, esp. ch. 8 "Of Chameleons and Clowns: the Case of Jack Mapanje"

[86] J.A.C. Mapanje, "The Use of Traditional Literary Forms in Modern Malawian Writing in English", M. Phil., University of London, 1974, p. 32, cit. Vail & White, *Power and the Praise Poem*, p. 286.

[87] *Ibid.*, p. 33. See also "The Release: Who Are You, *Imbongi*", J. Mapanje, *The Chattering Wagtails of Mikuyu Prison*, London: Heinemann, 1993, pp. 71-72. Vail and White notice the "illusion of orality" which characterizes Mapanje's poetry and comment that: "It is the stance of the

was indicative of the regime's failure to allow space for the constructive criticism on which a healthy political order depends. It was lack of the traditional balance of power and accountability which led to the loss of sanity and all the excesses and abuses of power of the one-party era. The outstanding problem in Malawi is that, despite the safeguards of the new constitution, an underlying understanding of the sacral character of the political structures remains very strong. This affects those who find themselves entrusted with political office so that they become preoccupied with their own status and show little concern for accountability. Chakufwa Chihana's extraordinarily *un*democratic leadership style in the Alliance *for* Democracy is a prominent example of this trend.[88] It was with some prescience that Paul Zeleza, in *Smouldering Charcoal*, had Ndatero commenting: "You see, that's where radical movements go wrong. They concentrate all their energies on capturing the state machine. And when they do the state swallows them up and they become reincarnations of the ousted regimes."[89] Equally, an understanding of the sacral character of the political leadership structures inhibits popular participation. Ordinary people hold back from taking responsibility for political affairs because these are understood to have been entrusted to those in high office. Hence the political messianism which we have found to be such an enduring feature of public life in Malawi.

Effective democracy will require new conceptions of political authority and power and here the Christian perspective may be of service. The prophetic religion of the Old Testament is a force which de-sacralized kingship. The Hebrew prophets were continually reminding their rulers of their mortality and accountability - cutting them down to size! Jesus himself stood firmly in this tradition when he told Pontius Pilate: "You would have no power over me if it were not given to you from above."[90] By stressing the derivative character of political authority, Jesus challenged its arbitrary exercise and invested it with moral accountability. Bediako has indicated the significance of this biblical teaching to the African understanding of political authority: "Authority belongs to and derives from the transcendent realm. At this point Christian teaching affirms an important dimension of the African tradition: authority, political power, does not reside with human beings, not even with the sacral ruler, for is not the sacral king merely the one who sits on the stool of the ancestors? But Christianity would take the argument further. For if

---

praise poet, telling the chief what no one else will say and licensed by the medium of which he is master." *Power and the Praise Poem*, p. 299.

[88] After the 1994 General Election Chihana allied AFORD first with the MCP opposition and then with the UDF government without even consulting his Executive Committee, much less the party membership!

[89] T. Zeleza, *Smouldering Charcoal*, London: Heinemann, 1992, p. 151.

[90] John 19:11.

authority does not reside with the merely human, then why should it be located in the realm of the essentially *human* spirits of the ancestors? So, in the perspective of Christian ideas, ancestors too become de-sacralized. Authority truly belongs only to God."[91] To ascribe ultimate messianic qualities or unquestionable ancestral authority to contemporary political leaders is a theological error which the church is responsible to expose. "By doing this," Eberhard Jungel has written, "it protects the state from a religious or quasi-religious self-misunderstanding and thereby serves it in the best possible way."[92]

Dedza villagers voted for multi-party in 1993 primarily in order to reject Banda's religious mystification of the state and of his own leadership. Though they were mostly MCP supporters, their Christian faith prompted them to seek a restoration of the state on to its proper basis and a redefinition of politics.[93] The task of the church is to build on this to develop an understanding of politics in which politicians are understood as servants of the community which, through the engagement of all its members, is charged to fulfil the purpose of God. It is when politics and political power are relativized in this way that they are set free to fulfil their calling. So long as they strive for ultimacy and an absolute status they are destined to be corrupted by the all-pervasive force of human sinfulness. As Bediako concludes: "The recognition that power truly belongs to God, rooted in the Christian theology of power as non-dominating, liberates politicians and rulers to be humans among fellow-humans, and ennobles politics and the business of government into the business of God and the service of God in the service of fellow-humans."[94] Without such a thinking through and working out of the nature of political authority at the underlying religious level, it is doubtful if the institutions of democracy will be viable in Malawi.

The Drive for Popular Participation

Democracy, to be true to its name, must return power to the people. However "politically correct" may be the structures and mechanisms of representative government, there will be no democracy if the popular imagination is not captured by the democratic vision and if the people do not sense that the system genuinely gives them power to have a say in their own destiny. In Malawi there was a tremendous sense of empowerment among the rural people when they were able to

---

[91] Bediako, "De-sacralization and Democratisation", p. 9.

[92] E. Jungel, *Christ, Justice and Peace: Toward a Theology of the State*, Edinburgh: T. & T. Clark, 1992, p. 62.

[93] See H. Englund, "Between God and Kamuzu: The Transition to Multi-Party Politics in Central Malawi", pp. 23-37

[94] Bediako, "De-sacralization and Democratisation", p. 10.

exercise their vote to elect a President and MP of their own choice.[95] Soon, however, the suspicion grew in the popular mind that the political change had failed to bring significant reform to the basic structural injustices in Malawian society and that it had amounted to little more than a game of "musical chairs" amongst the small dominant elite. The historical background is that the small educated elite which took over the apparatus of the colonial government in 1964 was able to use its position to enrich itself at the expense of the rural masses, essentially continuing the colonial system but with a new set of beneficiaries. Today the suspicion is that the rhetoric of democracy is just a smokescreen to conceal what has been, in effect, a palace revolution amongst this small dominant elite which has no intention of disturbing the fundamental social structures from which it benefits. Many Malawians today would sympathise with Jean-Jacques Rousseau's cynical definition of representative government as the freedom of a people once every few years to decide who is going to oppress them![96] Although everyone benefits from the democratic freedoms which so recently were unimaginable, disillusionment has set in because so much more was expected. This creates an unstable situation for the young democracy. As Adam Przeworski has observed in Eastern Europe, it is when "paradise turns into everyday life, disenchantment sets in" and that is when the temptation to revert to authoritarian rule is at its strongest.[97] While most Malawians celebrate the freedom from fear which once was an unreachable paradise, their welcome to democracy is tempered by the fact that "the system" still seems to be an alien reality which works in interests other than their own. Democracy in Malawi has yet to be appropriated by the people. It must face the challenge of becoming *participatory* democracy.

In understanding democratization it is helpful to distinguish between democratic procedures and institutions on the one hand, and democratic norms and values on the other. The former can be constructed through writing constitutions, passing laws and holding elections - matters which can be settled by a dominant elite. The latter cannot be achieved without the participation of the people as a whole. "Democracy," writes John de Gruchy, "is an 'ongoing moral quest' whose success is contingent upon the development of people able to participate fully in the body politic, and therefore of institutions which allow and foster such participation."[98]

---

[95] This could be witnessed at the polling booths in even the most remote areas as long queues of people waited for hours under the hot sun in good order and good humour to cast their votes.

[96] J. Rousseau, *The Social Contract*, London: J.M. Dent, 1963, p. 78.

[97] A. Przeworski, *Democracy and the Market: Political and Economic Reforms in Eastern Europe and Latin America*, Cambridge University Press, 1992, p. 94; cit. de Gruchy, *Christianity and Democracy*, p. 36.

[98] J.W. de Gruchy, "Theological Reflections on the Task of the Church in the Democratisation of Africa", in Gifford ed., *The Christian Churches and the Democratisation of Africa*, p. 51.

It is here that there is a notable gap in the democratisation process in Malawi. Kevin Bampton, who was secretary to the Constitutional Committee of the transitional National Consultative Council in 1993-94, has lamented the lack of public engagement with the process of composing the new Constitution: "Fundamentally, somewhere between the referendum and the election and the adoption of the constitution in its provisional form, there was a skills gap. What I mean is a gap shared by all the players in terms of understanding the timing, the significance, the basic necessity of education of the public, the involvement of the public in order to create a legitimate form of democracy.... This is the major lesson I would like to draw out of the experience in Malawi - that you need to have education for the general public."[99] Democratic government in Malawi has largely been constructed "over the heads" of the ordinary people which explains why there seems to be such a gap between the rhetoric of democracy and the reality. The weakness of the constitution is that, however well constructed it may be, it has not been sufficiently internalized by the people and can easily be disregarded or manipulated by those holding political power. As F.F. Kanyongolo has pointed out: "The constitution articulates values whose validity in the context of Malawi has never been tested by popular referendum or any other means. In the end violations or opportunistic amendments of the constitution do not have a degree of moral blameworthiness sufficient to act as a deterrence or basis for mass political action."[100]

The democratic procedures and institutions are in place but they will remain alien, elitist and very fragile so long as they are not founded upon norms and values which are cherished and nurtured among the people at large. A distinctive challenge here for the church is whether it can deploy the Christian doctrine of "vocation", the belief that every believer has a calling from God, to offer the popular energy and motivation which Malawi's young democracy desperately needs. In the past, as I have written elsewhere, this sense of divine vocation has given ordinary folk the confidence that "*they*, the people, might be the agents of significant political change. This is a dynamic powerful to sweep away the passivity and 'victim mentality' which can obstruct democratic participation.... The liberty promised by Christ acts as a theological imperative in the promotion of maximum participation of all people in political and economic structures of power. Indeed it is doubtful whether participatory democracy can thrive without such a

---

[99] Kevin Bampton in J. Lewis, P Owens & L. Pirouet eds., *Human Rights and the Making of Constitutions: Malawi, Kenya, Uganda*, University of Cambridge African Studies Centre, 1995, p. 60.
[100] F.F Kanyongolo, "State and Constitutionalism in Malawi", unpublished paper, 1996, p. 16.

moral and spiritual drive and dynamic."[101] Such an awareness places the obligation on the churches to fulfil their evangelical task of imparting to their members a full sense of their calling in Christ!

The churches in Malawi also have the significant advantage that they have mobilised massive participation on the part of the ordinary people. Limited though this may be by the hierarchical character of most of the churches, nevertheless it does constitute something which the churches have to offer to democratisation. Just as it was the experience of church life which fostered the formation of the "native associations" which were the seedbeds of the nationalist movement,[102] so today a church life which is authentically participatory may have a powerful "knock-on" effect in the formation and flourishing of the institutions of civil society on which the functioning of true democracy depends. This brings a considerable challenge to the polity and practice of church life - is it, in fact, generating the resources which will foster democratisation in society? Terence Ranger has drawn attention to the "whole rural religious field" which has often been swiftly dismissed as backward and irrational but which has qualities greatly needed in the task of democratic reconstruction: "It offered many openings to female abilities, it enabled local agency in the reconstruction of community, and offered idioms in which to make a powerful critique of the state and the market."[103] Such resources cry out today to be utilized in the struggle for democracy in Malawi.

Where churches and other religious institutions may have a particularly critical contribution is in the "indigenization" of democracy. The democratic system will have limited impact so long as it is confined to language and structures imported from elsewhere. There is need to make connections with the vernacular understanding, to find for the new democratic institutions points of resonance with the African tradition. Otherwise democracy, paradoxically, becomes the mechanism by which the educated elite entrench their supremacy and alienate the rural majority. The need for a reappropriation of the African tradition is heightened by the way in which "culture" was manipulated by Kamuzu Banda as a source of legitimation for his regime.[104] Peter Forster has observed that whereas

---

[101] K.R. Ross, *Presbyterian Theology and Participatory Democracy*, Edinburgh: St Andrew Press, 1993, pp. 15-16.
[102] See J. McCracken, *Politics and Christianity in Malawi 1875-1940*, Cambridge: Cambridge University Press, 1977.
[103] Ranger, "Conference Summary and Conclusions", in Gifford ed., *The Christian Churches and the Democratisation of Africa*, p. 30.
[104] See P.G. Forster, "Culture, Nationalism, and the Invention of Tradition in Malawi", *The Journal of Modern African Studies* Vol. 32 No. 3 (1994), pp. 477-497.

Banda focused on the authoritarian elements in African tradition, the "rebel" ministers who split with him in the "Cabinet crisis" "were prepared to some extent to take pride in traditions, but where they saw virtue in the past, it was in terms of egalitarianism rather than hierarchical authority."[105] Now is the time to recover these very powerful currents in traditional Malawian life on which a democratic ethos and consciousness may be developed.[106] David Clement Scott, one of the early Scottish missionaries at Blantyre made the observation in 1881 that: "The African if he is anything is constitutional no change or step of importance is taken without first open *mlandu* in which *the opinion of all is fully sought and expressed.*"[107] Having identified this strongly democratic tradition among the people of Malawi, Scott moved quickly to incorporate it into the life of the church. In 1894 he ordained seven deacons from among the early converts and these formed the effective governing council of the young church. Scott had no hesitation about their capacity to fulfil this responsibility by drawing on the resources of their own tradition: "One could wish for no weightier justice than that of native *mlandu*-power Christianized into a Church Court."[108] An important question for the church is how far the indigenous democratic traditions which it incorporated in its own life from this early period have survived sufficiently to be reappropriated by the state at a time when it is emerging from a period of despotism and striving to find solid foundations on which to build a democratic order.

Countering Polarization in Society

The process of democratization in society has thrown into relief deep divisions in Malawian society. Prominent in popular consciousness in 1995-96 was the realization that the radical political reforms which have taken place since 1992 have scarcely disturbed the profound economic inequalities which were bequeathed to Malawi by the colonial system and further entrenched under the Banda regime. Both the 1992 Pastoral Letter and the WARC/CCAP Letter of that year had called for the disparity in living conditions between the rich and the poor to be

---

[105] *Ibid*, p. 489.
[106] In framing a proposal for an MA programme in Human Rights Studies at the University of Malawi it has been argued that: "If human rights are to be secured and protected in Malawi over the long term, it will be necessary to develop an indigenous human rights discourse, rather than depending entirely on concepts and language which has been developed elsewhere. Hence there is need for research aimed at promoting an understanding of human rights that is earthed in the Malawian situation." F.F Kanyongolo, P Kishindo & K.R. Ross, "Proposed Programme: MA in Human Rights Studies", unpublished working paper, University of Malawi, 1996.
[107] *Life and Work in British Central Africa* (Blantyre Mission newspaper), November 1891, my italics.
[108] *Ibid*, November 1894.

addressed. It was this part of their critique which was most neglected. The advent of multi-party democracy brought little tangible change. Indeed, the new constitution was marked by the conspicuous absence of any provisions which might allow for affirmative action in favour of those who were dispossessed by the colonialism and neo-colonialism of the past. As F.F. Kanyongolo has argued: "The constitution does not articulate any principles to guide the solution of major social and economic *problems of inequalities* resulting from culture and tradition, internal government policies and the adverse positioning of Malawi in the international political economy. The significance of the constitution is therefore diminished in the eyes of a society which finds that it does not clearly address their concerns on matters such as equitable distribution of wealth, the transformation of the relationship between labor and capital, and the balance of power among the various cultures."[109]

Scepticism about the prospects of the new dispensation promoting a more equitable economic order has been heightened by the conduct of the Muluzi administration. Though the UDF government was elected on a ticket of poverty alleviation, it was not long before the popular joke was that it was actually "PPA" - personal poverty alleviation - as government ministers were manifestly using their new positions for personal economic advantage![110] A typical comment on "poverty alleviation" is: "These words have become like a curse to the poor because they have become even poorer. The rich are the ones who see the blessings!"[111] In light of such popular concern it was surprising that in April 1996 government saw fit to award pay rises of 300% to cabinet ministers and 88% to principal secretaries but only 12% to junior workers.[112] Now people are wondering whether their sense of political empowerment is delusory as they see the benefits continuing to flow to the wealthy elite while they remain in deepening poverty. In early 1995 the popular Kwathu Drama Group's play *Tisaiwale* had a bishop telling his people that if you were married to a husband who was constantly beating you and you decided to remarry only to find that you cannot eat or clothe yourself you would think twice if at all the change was worth it.[113] A sense of disillusionment compounds the hopelessness and lack of initiative inherited from the colonial and one-party periods. Until this situation is addressed and there is a genuine empowerment of the rural population, the exercise of power in Malawi is going to be skewed in favour of the small but dominant middle class. Wiseman Chirwa has noted that even the ethnicity and regionalism which appear to be the dominant forces in Malawian

---

[109] Kanyongolo, "State and Constitutionalism in Malawi", p. 12, author's italics.
[110] See, e.g., *The Weekly Chronicle*, 29 August-4 September 1994.
[111] Anonymous correspondent, December 1995.
[112] *The Nation*, 30 April 1996.
[113] *The Nation*, 2 May 1995.

politics are, in fact, ideological tools used by "the country's bourgeoisie and petit bourgeoisie to inherit the state as a class for purposes of accumulating political power and economic resources."[114] Democracy loses credibility with every day that passes without such issues of economic interests being addressed.

Even amongst the relatively well-off, moreover, economic decline is taking its toll to the extent that it threatens the democratisation process. Minnis remarks that "the failing economy has the potential to not only discredit the new democratically elected government's legitimacy, but also may heighten public misgivings about democracy in general."[115] John de Gruchy's observation is a pertinent one for the Malawi situation: "It is not surprising that in situations of grinding poverty there is a growing sense of alienation and anger which is fuelled by the media-projected vision of 'the good life' which only a few enjoy - particularly if those few are known to be advocates of democracy. Massive inequality must undermine democracy. Poverty, and all its attendant problems with regard to health, housing and education, especially in rural areas, breeds political apathy or revolution rather than informed citizens able to participate in the democratic process."[116] Economic regeneration and the redressing of the imbalances in power which entrench poverty amongst the rural majority in Malawi will be central to securing the accountability of those in power and an empowerment of the people. There will be no viable democracy without a much more serious reckoning with the gap between the rich and poor than has been evident until now. The churches, with their "preferential option for the poor", should be in a position to pursue this question with vigour unless their own leadership is too enmeshed in the existing exploitative structures. Furthermore, it is the churches which may be best placed to take up this issue at the global level. For the impoverishment of the majority in Malawi has to be understood in relation to the world economic order and the point has to be made that, ultimately, there will be no authentic democratization without a serious endeavour to address the gap between rich and poor at a global level. The church, with its ecumenical vision, may have to take responsibility for developing a world-wide engagement with this issue.

The new freedom has brought out into the open the extent to which there is serious abuse of power in the relations between women and men. Recent events have impressed upon us how deeply instilled among men is the conviction that they ought to have unquestioned mastery over women. Too often the marriage relationship is that of master and slave rather than a joyous sharing in discovering the image of God which men and women were created to share. It is only now

---

[114] Chirwa, "The Politics of Ethnicity and Regionalism in Contemporary Malawi", p. 94.

[115] Minnis, "Can Civil Society be a Force for Political Change in Malawi?", p. 12.

[116] De Gruchy, *Christianity and Democracy*, p. 36.

TOWN RAT AND COUNTRY RAT

by Orama & Vunde

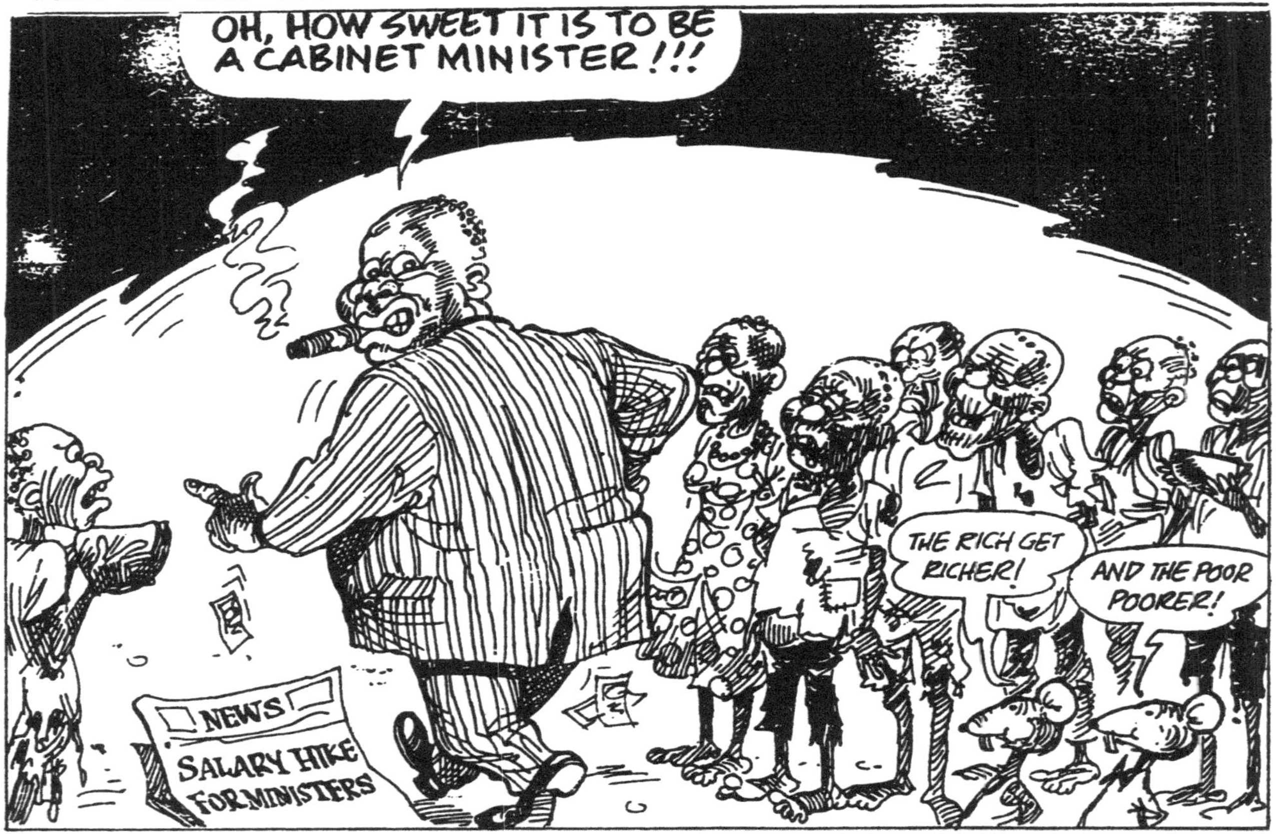

becoming apparent how widespread are rape and other forms of violence against women. In his novel *Smouldering Charcoal* Paul Zeleza pointed up the irony of the domestic behaviour of the men who were most active in the struggle against oppression in Malawi: "They claimed they were fighting for justice, yet they mistreated their wives."[117] Almost all national institutions reflect the fact that men like to monopolise the decision-making power. Even the new Cabinet with over 30 members has hardly any place for women leaders. Almost all of the churches are led exclusively by men. If women raise their voice to question this, they can expect to be quickly punished.[118] Here is an area where repentance has to go very deep. For men are accustomed to having the power and to enjoying the submission of women. Equally, women have been brought up from their earliest years to understand that they are inferior and that their main role is to serve the needs of men. It will mean a revolution when we recognise that women, like men, are made in the image of God and are responsible to reflect that image in all its glory.

Another potentially dangerous gap that can be observed in our society is the gap between the young and the old. Young people can be a tremendous power for good in both church and nation. However, when you ask them if they are given good opportunities to express their talents you will soon meet a sense of exclusion and resentment. Young people feel that they are "used" when their services are convenient to the purposes of older people. They feel that they are excluded from power and responsibility. They are not allowed to participate in decision-making and they feel that those in power do not take account of the needs and hopes of the youth.[119] This can easily lead to an alienation where the youth turn away from adult society and immerse themselves in their own youth culture. Such a divided society would be a weak one. It is therefore shortsighted for older people to cling to power and to want to be in control of the youth. Much better to involve young people in taking responsibility and exercising power; so that young and old together can share in harnessing both the wisdom of age and the energy of youth to build a healthy society.

The Life of the Church and Malawi's Democratisation

The churches, to the surprise of many, have been remarkably effective in the role of midwives of democratic transition in Malawi. History shows, however, that the church's political witness tends to be most effective when it comes to confrontation with manifest injustice. It is less effective when it comes to the task of patient reconstruction after some watershed political change. An immediate challenge in

---

[117] Zeleza, *Smouldering Charcoal*, p. 131.
[118] Cf. Chapter 3 above.
[119] Cf. Chapter 4 above.

Malawi was whether the churches would be able to open up a critical distance from the new government which was composed of people with whom they had worked shoulder-to-shoulder in the struggle for democracy. There have been conscious attempts to adopt a prophetic stance towards the new government, as at the National Service of Worship on 6 July 1995 when Silas Ncozana "made a scathing attack on those in positions of power who only wanted to feel important without contributing to the country's development."[120] A critical question, however, is whether the churches' public witness would be confined to occasional statements of denominational leaders or would there be a mechanism for addressing national issues from a united and consolidated basis? The importance of this question for the integrity of the church itself has been highlighted in recent ecumenical thinking. The WCC Tantur Consultation of November 1994 asked: "Is it enough to say that, if a church is not engaging responsibly with the ethical issues of the day, it is not being fully church? Must we not also say: if the churches are not engaging those ethical issues *together*, then *none of them individually is being fully church*?"[121]

In the Malawi context such a question puts the focus on the Public Affairs Committee which was the vehicle of the churches' united action in the democratic transition. Was it simply an *ad hoc* Committee addressing a particular set of needs at a particular time? Or does it have a permanent place at the interface between religion and politics in Malawi? It is too early to answer this question with any certainty. However, it is notable that in mid-1995, when a number of the new human rights organisations had already lost their credibility, the voice of PAC still carried considerable weight. In May 1995, e.g., PAC was able to bring together leading politicians from all the main parties for a "Round-table" aimed at promoting tolerance and reconciliation. The new PAC Chairman, Bishop Tarsisius Ziyaye, warned the political leaders: "Nobody will come from outside to find solutions to our problems.... Collectively we should endeavour to find solutions instead of pointing fingers at each other."[122] In August 1995 PAC sent an open letter to the President criticising the government for being accountable to international institutions rather than its own people and, in particular, for resisting World Bank recommendations to trim the cabinet while agreeing to remove the subsidies on fertilizers.[123] It is worth noticing the attention which this letter was given in an editorial of the *The Nation*, the country's most respected daily newspaper: "We find this statement significant not only because of its contents but

---

[120] *The Nation*, 7 July 1995.
[121] "Report of the Consultation", in T.F Best & M. Robra ed., *Ecclesiology and Ethics: Costly Commitment*, Geneva: WCC, 1995, p. 64.
[122] *The Nation*, 19 May 1995.
[123] *The Nation*, 24 August 1995.

VERILY I SAY UNTO YOU, SOME PEOPLE ARE VERY IMPORTANT BUT ARE THEY USEFUL?
THIS FELLOW IS RUDE!
WE MUST HAVE HIM ARRESTED!
I WONDER IF HE IS TALKING ABOUT ME.
5TH VEE PEE
4TH VEE PEE
3RD VEE PEE

more because of its source. This is the same body under which the two coalition partners [UDF and AFORD] fought with the MCP to get rid of the one-party dictatorship. This is a body composed of clergy who played a very effective role to transform the country's political system, and whose influence surpasses any other in this country. The statement is reminiscent of the historic Pastoral Letter through which the Catholic bishops unleashed their might behind the suffering of the people of Malawi and helped transform society. We are very hopeful that, coming from the clergy as it does, the concern will be taken seriously by government and that appropriate action will be taken."[124] Such a response to a PAC open letter in the second year of the new political dispensation suggests that the churches may well continue to play an important role in national affairs. At the same time developments in early 1996, notably the appointment of PAC Vice-Chairman and frequent spokesperson Joseph Bvumbwe to the chairmanship of the powerful Press Corporation, led critics to suggest that PAC was now in the pocket of the government and silenced as a critical voice.[125] Powerful are the forces operating to secure PAC's collusion with government and it will not retain its independence without a struggle, especially since government patronage will always hold a strong appeal for impoverished church leaders. Yet the experience of having been compromised and silenced has sharpened the sensitivity of church leaders to the importance of maintaining critical distance in relation to government. The churches are preparing themselves to play the role of watchdog in relation to national political life, exposing any corruption which creeps into the exercise of government and detecting any imbalances in the separation of powers.

To be the watchdog, however, is an essentially negative role concerned with guarding the structures, institutions and mechanisms of democracy so as to ensure that they continue working smoothly. The deeper challenge for the churches is not to stop there but to undertake the positive task of nurturing the spiritual roots of democracy. For democracy to be effective it is not enough to establish a certain legal and constitutional system. There is need for the inner drive and motivation to make the system work. It is when democracy is considered at this deeper level that religious considerations arise, especially in a context where the worldview and behaviour of the people is greatly influenced by religion. To be democratic is to have an orientation and an openness to others, a willingness to accept those who are different and to work together for a more just and peaceful society. "This," as John de Gruchy notes, "is not something which democracy itself can produce; it is a spiritual value of redemptive love which no political system can manufacture."[126] The challenge here to the church is one which cuts much deeper than the

---

[124] *The Nation*, 25 August 1995.
[125] See *Malawi News*, 20-26 April 1996; *The Nation*, 24 April 1996.
[126] De Gruchy, *Christianity and Democracy*, p. 244.

issue of whether it can raise a prophetic voice in relation to the politics of the day. For it reaches to the heart of the church's own life and calls it to be the community whose being is comprised of such outgoing and redemptive love. As we have noted time and again, the deep issues of democratisation which Malawi faces are concentrated in the struggle within the life of the church itself to be true to its calling. The church must take the lead in an exercise of national repentance. The church must be the first to acknowledge its guilty silence to the Jehovah's Witnesses. The church in its own structures must break the spell of regionalism so that, e.g., churches will rejoice to elect a good leader who happens to originate from another region. The church must fulfil its calling to be a church of the poor and the instrument of their economic empowerment. The church must take the lead in protecting the dignity of women and demonstrating its confidence in them by electing them to positions of leadership. The church must be the place where young people feel at home, find respect and a setting where they can exercise their gifts. The church must enable the state to be the state by demolishing its quasi-religious pretensions and awakening the humility and humanity which it needs to fulfil its task. The church must take the lead in generating the organization of people's initiatives which produce a vibrant civil society. The church must be alert to eliminate any traces of corruption and nepotism in its own life - otherwise it will never be able to remove the speck in its brother's eye! It is precisely as the church fights and wins these battles within its own life that it will prove to be an agent of democratisation in Malawi.

Nurturing the spiritual roots of democracy is a matter which must engage the church not primarily in its upper echelons but rather at the grassroots level. In the watchdog function of the church the top leadership is necessarily prominent. Committees, Councils, Conferences, Synods and Assemblies have access to the public arena and top church leaders can address national issues through the mass media. This gives the opportunity to engage with national politics when required. It was through statements issued at this level that the churches were effective as the midwives of democracy. When it comes, however, to the consolidation and deepening of democracy, attention turns to the church at the level of the local congregation or base community. Surveying the African scene as a whole Terence Ranger has observed that: "The opening of the second revolution takes place at the centre and the combined church hierarchy can play a critical role. But sustainability will be won or lost in the regions, the localities and at the grass roots. The mark of the first phase is the making of constitutions; the mark of the second must be the achievement of local autonomy."[127] This indicates the limits of the kind of activity which in Malawi has been channeled through PAC. When

---

[127] T Ranger, "Conference Summary and Conclusion", in P Gifford ed., *The Christian Churches and the Democratisation of Africa*, p. 26.

doing research on Christology among rural people in Northern Malawi I found that quite often respondents would cite PAC as evidence for the connection between faith in Christ and political action.[128] However, it is seen largely as an elite organisation for top church leaders. The question is whether the churches can make the transition needed to be effective in Ranger's "second phase", i.e. to be an organization operating at local level to promote democratic participation and empowerment.

Here the question is whether the church has the kind of *congregations* which can be forces for democratisation. The most exalted vision and the sharpest prophetic witness offered by individual church leaders can very easily be completely undermined by what Peter Walshe has described in another context as "timid local clergy and phlegmatic parishes."[129] The issue of whether Malawi should have a democratic political *system* has been, to a large extent, settled. What remains to be seen is whether Malawi will have the democratic *people* to make democracy happen! Without people committed to democratic participation the system will quickly become discredited and could easily fall apart. The church, when it is true to its calling, is engaged in the formation of people. It is intended to generate people who have a sense of vocation, who are oriented to "the other", who have a vision of a just society inspired by the reality of the kingdom of God. If the life of the church does impart such spiritual values to its members, then it can play a key role in producing the vital ingredient which has been too much missing from Malawi's democracy: informed, committed, dynamic popular participation.

For the church to fulfil such a role will inevitably be disturbing for it will give such a voice to the voiceless and such power to the powerless as will certainly shake the established order. But is this not what democracy is all about? The first institution to be shaken will be the church itself - for a movement of grassroots empowerment will raise questions about ecclesiastical polity. This is something that has already begun to be evident. In the Roman Catholic Church younger priests were ready to point out that the very Bishops who had championed democracy in the political arena operated in their dioceses on a basis of dictatorship![130] It is said that in the new Malawi you can freely criticize the State President but you dare not criticize the Bishop or General Secretary of your church! It was partly the same concern which moved women of Blantyre Synod to march to the Administrators' Conference with their petition on "Justice and Peace

---

[128] See K.R. Ross, "Grassroots Christology in Northern Malawi: A Research Report" University of Malawi (unpublished), January 1996.
[129] P Walshe, *Prophetic Christianity and the Liberation Movement in South Africa*, Pietermaritzburg: Cluster Publications, 1995, p. 143.
[130] Unattributable interviews.

in the Church."[131] Part of the problem is that the exercise of ecclesiastical power is still conditioned by the authoritarianism of the one-party system? Silas Ncozana has acknowledged how powerful this factor was in the past: "The one-party system certainly influenced the way the church exercised its power because when one looks at the Presbyterian system there are so many groups which were being marginalised in decision-making within the church. For instance the voice of lay people has been minimal, even at this time when we have been trying to raise the voices of lay people.... So the church became much more clerical than it ought to have been."[132]

The extent to which this model of church life still prevails was illustrated when the Blantyre Synod Office issued its statement on the "Born Again" issue and defined a Presbyterian Church in these terms:

> This type has a moderator and Senior Clerk as leaders of the General Synod. Moderator and General Secretary in a Synod, Moderator and Presbytery Clerk, Moderator (minister) and clerk of the Kirk Session. *Power* in this type of church is exercised by ministers and members at a General Synod, Synod, Presbytery and Kirk Session. People who are not pleased with the *hierarchy* and *exercise of power* secede to other churches.[133]

Clearly the church has not been immune from the tendency to think of the exercise of power in authoritarian terms and this limits its capacity to be a force for democratization. Similarly, church leadership too often mirrors the corruption and graft prevalent in the wider society rather than offering a challenge to it. Clergy seek power within the church structures in order to gain access to resources (principally money and women!) which they can use to their own personal advantage.[134] The churches have not been able to shake off this colonial legacy which still haunts practically every social and political institution in the country. Through their "theology acted" the churches tend to legitimate a wrong exercise of power rather than offering a fundamental challenge to it. So long as the church understands itself in terms of a power structure there will be limits to its effectiveness as an agent of the transformation of power. There is need for a deep repentance within the life of the church so that it can shake off the tendency to be the church "from above" and be the church "from below." This question of polity reaches deep into the identity of the church and, depending on the kind of answer

---

[131] See *The Independent*, 19-24 January 1995, my italics.
[132] Int. Silas Ncozana, 28 June 1995.
[133] CCAP Blantyre Synod, Statement of Synod Office on "To Be Born Again/Fellowship" 11 January 1995; translated from Chichewa by Rev O. Maliya; my italics.
[134] I am endebted at this point to the research currently being undertaken by Peter van Doepp, a doctoral student from the University of Florida investigating church and politics in Malawi.

it gives, determines the extent to which it can be a significant force in Malawi's democratization.

Church, state and society in Malawi need a deep awareness that all exercise of power is accountable to God. From the Christian perspective this means that all authority must be conditioned by the kind of power which God has revealed in Jesus Christ. It means recognising, with Kwame Bediako, that: "Jesus' way was one of engagement and involvement through a new way of overcoming arising from a unique concept of power the power of forgiveness over retaliation, of suffering over violence, of love over hostility, of humble service over domination. Jesus won his way to pre-eminence and glory, not by exalting himself, but by humbling himself, to the point of dying a shameful death. In other words, his conception of power was that of non-dominating power."[135] What was strikingly original in the life of Jesus, as Edward Schillebeeckx has observed, is that "power goes hand in hand in him with *goodness*."[136] The calling of the church is to discover in its own life an authentic praxis of that wholly different kind of power which was exercised in the life of Jesus. Can it find in its own life a turning to the infinitely demanding but infinitely hopeful kind of power that is found in the kingdom of God? To make the ancient Christian confession that Jesus Christ is Lord, is to know, as Czech theologian Jan Milic Lochman has written, that: "no earthly (or heavenly) ruler, however bristling with power, is the real lord. The true Lord is the serving man from Nazareth. The way he chose, and the way he directs us to take, involves not the love of power but the power of love. Christians and the church itself can convincingly bear witness to and act in the name of Christ's Lordship only by ethically and politically conforming to *this* way, the way of solidarity, for others, the way that leads downward, not by an upward drive for sovereignty and power."[137]

It is only as the church makes this confession of the Lordship of Jesus Christ that it will bring to the exercise of power in Malawi that distinctive quality which it desperately needs. Even the very word used for politics - *ndale* - is a term which suggests intrigue, craftiness and chicanery. It stands, as Augustine Musopole has suggested, for "an anti-human understanding of politics."[138] It is an understanding of politics and power urgently in need of evangelization. It needs to discover, in the words of the Taiwanese theologian C.S. Song, that: "God's politics does not

---

[135] Bediako, "De-sacralization and Democratisation", p. 9.
[136] E. Schillebeeckx, *Jesus: An Experiment in Christology*, London: Collins, 1979, my italics. I am endebted to Rev Jim Wilkie for drawing my attention to this passage.
[137] J.M. Lochman, *The Faith We Confess: An Ecumenical Dogmatics*, Edinburgh: T & T Clark, 1985, pp. 96-97
[138] A.C. Musopole, "A Vision for Theology in Malawi", *Religion in Malawi*, No. 6 (1996).

consist of attempts to seize power. What it aims at is the transformation of power. God's politics has to do with transformation of human politics. It does not seek to rule and dominate but rather to effect a repentance of power."[139] It is only when a transformation of the exercise of power in the direction of the Jesus-style power of the kingdom of God has been effected in church and society that the yearning for democracy in Malawi will begin to be satisfied.

---

[139] C.S. Song, *Third-Eye Theology*, 2nd ed., Maryknoll NY: Orbis, 1990, p. 241.

Select Bibliography

"A Statement on the Role of the Church in the Transformation of Malawi in the Context of Justice and Peace," Produced by the Administrators Conference, Blantyre Synod CCAP, 22-23 January 1994.

Banda, J., "Aspects of Current Constitutional Change Debate in Malawi", Paper presented at Social Change in Malawi Conference, Chancellor College, 1 July 1995.

Bediako, K., "De-sacralization and Democratization: Some Theological Reflections on the role of Christianity in Nation-building in Modern Africa", *Transformation*, Vol. 12 No. 1 (January/March 1995), pp. 5-11.

Boraine, A., Levy, J. & Scheffer ed., *Dealing with the Past: Truth and Reconciliation in South Africa*, Cape Town: IDASA, 1994.

Chakanza, J.C., "The Pro-Democracy Movement in Malawi: The Catholic Church's Contribution", in M.S. Nzunda & K.R. Ross ed., *Church, Law and Political Transition in Malawi 1992-94*, Gweru: Mambo, 1995, pp. 59-74.

Chirwa, C.W., "The Politics of Ethnicity and Regionalism in Contemporary Malawi", *African Rural and Urban Studies*, Vol. 1 No. 2 (1994), pp. 93-118.

Chirwa, W.C., "Regionalism, Ethnicity and the National Question in Malawi," *Southern Africa Political and Economic Monthly (SAPEM)*, Vol. 8 Nos. 3-4 (December 1994/January 1995), pp. 59-62.

"Choosing our Future: Pastoral Letter to the Catholic Faithful on the occasion of the National Referendum 1993", Episcopal Conference of Malawi, 2 February 1993.

Cullen, T., *Malawi: A Turning Point*, Edinburgh: The Pentland Press, 1994.

De Gruchy, J.W., *Christianity and Democracy*, Cambridge: Cambridge University Press, 1995.

Englund, H., "Between God and Kamuzu: The Transition to Multi-Party Politics in Central Malawi", unpublished paper, 1995.

Fiedler, K., *Persecution for Life: The Jehovah's Witnesses' Experience in Malawi 1963-1993*, Blantyre, CLAIM, forthcoming.

Fiedler, K., "The 'Smaller' Churches and Big Government", in M.S. Nzunda & K.R. Ross ed., *Church, Law and Political Transition in Malawi 1992-94*, Gweru: Mambo, 1995, pp. 153-170.

Forster, P.G., "Culture, Nationalism, and the Invention of Tradition in Malawi", *The Journal of Modern African Studies*, Vol. 32 No. 3 (1994), pp. 477-497.

Gifford, P., ed., *The Christian Churches and the Democratisation of Africa*, Leiden: E.J. Brill, 1995.

"Human Rights in Malawi: Report of a Joint Delegation of the Scottish Faculty of Advocates, the Law Society of England and Wales and the General Council of the Bar to Malawi", 17-27 September 1992.

"Justice and Peace in the Church", A Statement by Women Representatives Meeting at Chigodi Women's Centre from 30th November to [date omitted] December 1994.

Kamwambe, G.T.N., *Post-Mortem of 1994 Elections in Malawi*, n.p., 1994.

Kanyongolo, F.F., "State and Constitutionalism in Malawi", unpublished paper, 1996.

Kasambara, R., "Civic Education in Malawi since 1992: an Appraisal", paper presented at Social Change in Malawi Seminar, Chancellor College, University of Malawi, 21-22 June 1996.

Kirche und Gesellschaft in Malawi: Die Krise von 1992 in historischer Perspektive, Hamburg: EMW Informationen No. 98, February 1993.

Kishindo, P., "The Impact of a National Language on Minority Languages: The Case of Malawi", *Journal of Contemporary African Studies*, Vol. 12 No. 2 (1994), pp. 127-50.

Langworthy, H., *"Africa for the African." The Life of Joseph Booth*, Blantyre: CLAIM, 1996.

Lewis, J., Owens, P. & Pirouet, L., eds., *Human Rights and the Making of Constitutions: Malawi, Kenya, Uganda*, University of Cambridge African Studies Centre, 1995

Living our Faith, Pastoral Letter of the Catholic Bishops of Malawi to be Read in Every Catholic Church on 8th March 1992; later published under the title *The Truth Will Set You Free*, Church in the World 28, London: CIIR, 1992.

Lwanda, J.L., *Kamuzu Banda of Malawi: A Study in Promise, Power and Paralysis*, Glasgow: Dudu Nsomba Publications, 1993.

Malawi: A Moment of Truth, London: CIIR, July 1993.

Malawi: Human Rights Violations 25 Years After Independence, London: Amnesty International, 1989.

Malawi: Preserving the One-Party State Human Rights Violations and the Referendum, London: Amnesty International, 1993.

Malawi: Prison Conditions, Cruel Punishment and Detention Without Trial, London: Amnesty International, 1992.

Malawi's Past: The Right to Truth, London: Article 19 (International Centre Against Censorship), Issue 29, 1993.

Mapanje, J., "Orality and the Memory of Justice", *Leeds African Studies Bulletin*, No. 60 (1995), pp. 9-21.

McCracken, J., *Politics and Christianity in Malawi 1875-1940*, Cambridge: Cambridge University Press, 1977.

Mhone, G., *Malawi at the Crossroads*, Harare: Sapes Books, 1992.

Minnis, J.R., "Can Civil Society be a Force for Political Change in Malawi?", Paper presented at Conference on Social Change in Malawi, Chancellor College, 30 June 1995.

Moyo, F.L., "Church and Politics: the Case of Livingstonia Synod", in M.S. Nzunda & K.R. Ross ed., *Church, Law and Political Transition in Malawi 1992-94*, Gweru: Mambo, 1995, pp. 121-133.

Mufuka, K.N., *Missions and Politics in Malawi*, Kingston, Ontario: Limestone Press, 1977.

Ncozana, S.S., "Beginning of the End of a Monolithic Government", unpublished, 1995.

Newell, J., "'A Moment of Truth?' The Church and Political Change in Malawi, 1992", *Journal of Modern African Studies*, Vol. 33 No. 2 (1995), pp. 243-262.

Newell, J., "An African Army Under Pressure: The Politicization of the Malawi Army and 'Operation Bwezani', 1992-93", *Small Wars and Insurgencies*, Vol. 6 No. 2 (Autumn 1995), pp. 159-182

Nzunda, M.S. & Ross, K.R. ed., *Church, Law and Political Transition in Malawi 1992-94*, Gweru: Mambo, 1995.

Pachai, B., *Malawi: The History of the Nation*, London: Longman, 1973.

Phiri, I., Semu, L., Nankhuni, F., and Madise, N., "Violence Against Women in Educational Institutions: The Case of Sexual Harrassment and Rape on Chancellor College Campus", Paper presented to University of Malawi Research Conference, Mangochi, July 1995.

Pryor, F., *The Political Economy of Poverty, Equity and Growth: A World Bank Comparative Study of Malawi and Madagascar*, Oxford: OUP, 1991.

Ross, A.C., *Blantyre Mission and the Making of Modern Malawi*, Blantyre: CLAIM, 1996.

Ross, A.C., "Forty-five Years of Turmoil: Malawi Christian Churches, 1949-1994", *International Bulletin of Missionary Research*, Vol. 18 No. 2 (1994), pp. 53-60.

Ross, K.R., "Christian Faith and National Identity: the Malawi Experience", *Journal of Theology for Southern Africa*, No. 93 (December 1995), pp. 51-62.

Ross, K.R., ed., *Christianity in Malawi: a Sourcebook*, Gweru: Mambo Press, 1996.

Ross, K.R., *Gospel Ferment in Malawi: Theological Essays*, Gweru: Mambo, 1995.

Ross, K.R., "Not Catalyst but Ferment: The Distinctive Contribution of the Churches to Political Reform in Malawi 1992-93", in P. Gifford ed., *The Christian Churches and Africa's Democratisation*, Leiden: E.J. Brill, 1995, pp. 98-107.

Ross, K.R., *Presbyterian Theology and Participatory Democracy*, Edinburgh: St Andrew Press, 1993.

Ross, K.R., "The Renewal of the State by the Church: the Case of the Public Affairs Committee in Malawi", *Religion in Malawi*, No. 5 (1995), pp. 29-37.

Ross, K.R., "Where were the Prophets and Martyrs in Banda's Malawi? Four Presbyterian Ministers", *Missionalia*, Vol. 24 (1996) forthcoming.

Ross, K.R. & Moyo, F.L., *Mazaza Ghose Gha Ulongozgi Ghakufuma kwa Chiuta: Kughanaghanira Vya Boma na Ndyale m'Malawi Wasono*, Zomba: University of Malawi Dept of Theology and Religious Studies, 1995; also published in Chinyanja translation as *Udindo Wonse Wolamulira ndi Wa Mulungu: Kulingalira ndi Kuganizira za Boma ndi Ndale za Malawi Watsopano*.

Shepperson, G., & Price, T., *Independent African*, Edinburgh: University Press, 1958.

Short, P., *Banda*, London & Boston: Routledge & Kegan Paul, 1974.

"The Nation of Malawi in Crisis: the Church's Concern", Geneva: World Alliance of Reformed Churches, 2 June 1992.

The Referendum in Malawi: Free Expression Denied, London: Article 19 (International Centre Against Censorship), Issue 22, 1993.

Vail, L. & White, L., *Power and the Praise Poem: Southern African Voices in History*, Charlottesville: University Press of Virginia; London: James Currey, 1991.

Vail, L. & White, L., "Tribalism in the Political History of Malawi", in L. Vail ed., *The Creation of Tribalism in Southern Africa*, London: James Currey and Los Angeles: University of California Press, 1989, pp. 151-192.

Van Dijk, R.A., "Young Malawian Puritans: Young Preachers in a Present-day African Urban Environment", Ph.D., University of Utrecht, 1992.

Van Donge, J.K., "Kamuzu's Legacy: the Democratization of Malawi. Or Searching for the Rules of the Game in African Politics", *African Affairs*, Vol. 94 (1995), pp. 227-257.

Van Donge, J.K., "The Mwanza Trial as a Search for a Usable Malawian Political Past", paper presented at Social Change in Malawi Seminar, Chancellor College, University of Malawi, 15-16 March 1996.

Weber, H., *Power: Focus for a Biblical Theology*, Geneva: WCC, 1989.

Where Silence Rules: The Suppression of Dissent in Malawi, Washington and London: Africa Watch, 1990.

Williams, T.D., *Malawi: The Politics of Despair*, Ithaca and London: Cornell University Press, 1978.

"Za Kubadwa kwa Tsopano/Fellowship", Letter from the Synod Office to all congregations, CCAP Synod of Blantyre, 11 January 1995.

Zeleza, P.T., "Totalitarian Power and Censorship in Malawi" *Southern Africa Political and Economic Monthly*, Vol. 8 No. 11 (August 1995), pp. 33-37.

Zeleza, T., *Smouldering Charcoal*, London: Heinemann, 1992.

www.ingramcontent.com/pod-product-compliance
Lightning Source LLC
Chambersburg PA
CBHW022227010526
44113CB00033B/583